COLLIER SPYMASTERS SERIES

Consulting Editor: Saul A. Katz,
Founder, 999 Bookshop, New York City

Also by John Lee

Assignation in Algeria
Caught in the Act
Stalag, Texas
The Thirteenth Hour

THE
NINTH
MAN

JOHN LEE

Collier Books
Macmillan Publishing Company
New York

Copyright © 1976 by John Lee

Previously published by Doubleday & Co., Inc.

Collier Books
Macmillan Publishing Company
866 Third Avenue, New York, NY 10022

Library of Congress Cataloging-in-Publication Data
Lee, John, 1931–
     The ninth man/John Lee.—1st Collier Books ed.
       p.   cm.
     ISBN 0-02-040711-4
     1. World War, 1939–1945—Secret service—Germany—Fiction.
   I. Title.
   [PS3562.E3537N56   1989]
   813'.54—dc20   89-9963
                                                                CIP

First Collier Books edition 1989

10 9 8 7 6 5 4 3 2 1

Printed in the United States of America

For my wife, Barbara Moore,
who provides the pear peelings

PROLOGUE

In June of 1942, barely six months after the attack on Pearl Harbor plunged the United States into World War II, two German U-boats headed quietly into American waters and aimed themselves at two isolated beaches, a prelude to one of the most audacious gambits to come out of Nazi Germany during the entire war.

Aboard the two U-boats were eight highly trained German agents, all German-Americans who had lived in the United States before the war and who had trained together through the long spring months of '42 at a hidden sabotage school on Quenz Lake, near Brandenburg, in Germany. Split into two teams of four men each, they had been programed by a small subunit of Abwehr II, the sabotage arm of the German Military Intelligence Corps, to infiltrate the United States on a mission of death and destruction.

One team was billeted on the *U-202*, approaching the Coast of Long Island in New York. The other team of four was aboard the *U-584*, cruising the lower Atlantic toward Florida. They had money enough and explosives enough to last them two years. They had a name chosen with deliberate irony for their mission—Operation Pastorius, after Franz Daniel Pastorius, who led the first group of German immigrants to settle in the United States in the 1600s. They had a profound sense of importance, due to the fact that Hitler himself had demanded action, any action, designed to convince the United States that it was vulnerable to German might.

Unknown to the two teams, the espionage arm of German Military Intelligence, Abwehr I, at the last minute received a piece of intelligence dealing with the planned visit of a very important British person to America. Quickly briefed and provided with several alternative plans of operation, a ninth man had been spirited secretly onto the *U-202* back in Lorient Harbor, dressed as a German naval officer, just hours before the New York team boarded the U-boat. Other than the high command of Abwehr I, only the U-boat captain and his first mate were aware of his presence.

The world now knows, in sketchy detail, what happened to the eight saboteurs from Quenz Lake once they set foot on American soil.

This is the story of the ninth man.

ONE

THE NEW YORK TEAM

THE LANDING

I

The ninth man stood in the conning-tower pit, hands poised lightly
on the wet railing, head cocked as if listening for the telltale sounds
of surf. Beside him in the soft darkness, wrapped in a black slicker,
stood Lieutenant Commander Hoffner, the U-boat captain.

The *U-202* nudged slowly through the fog toward the still-invis-
ible American shore, diesels chugging. Light sea swells rose and fell
along the lumbering flanks of the U-boat, plapping in the darkness
against her bulging ballast tanks. A defective air valve muttered pe-
riodically from a point somewhere on the port side, blowing
flatulent bubbles.

Hoffner cocked his own ears at the sound. He would have to
have that valve repaired when they got home. If they got home. It
was senseless to risk a valuable fighting machine like the *U-202* by
running her into shallow waters this close to American shore batteries, merely to deposit a handful of these cloak-and-dagger people.

He sneaked a glance at the ninth man, the one who called himself
Dietrich, standing there in the fog looking so damnably uninvolved.
A young man, with hard, blank features. Muscular. Dark hair. A
wide, boyish mouth that seldom smiled. The fellow wasn't at all
sociable. He had kept to his quarters throughout the trip, apparently
not wishing to see anyone but Hoffner or the first mate. Hoffner
had tried several times to engage him in conversation, a few friendly
questions, curiosity at why he was masquerading as a U-boat officer
instead of openly identifying himself to the other four passengers.
But the man was civil, and nothing beyond that. Hoffner had never
gotten more than a few words from him, certainly nothing to do
with this mission, whatever it was.

Verdammt seltsam, the man couldn't even speak decent German. Terrible accent. Almost a drawl, like one of the stern American frontier badmen in a Karl May Western. *Der Pfahlmann,* that's what Hoffner's first mate had dubbed him. The Desert-Trail Wrecker. The Man Who Rides Alone.

The other four were different. Good Germans, all of them. Filled with curiosity and pride, they had ranged the boat, asking questions, joking with the crew, explaining many of the odd technical devices in their four crates of explosives. One of the crewmen even reported that they had shown him the money, ninety thousand American dollars, packed in a little leather satchel. They were good men, dedicated men. They would have to be for the German Government to trust them with that much money.

The submarine continued to inch forward in the darkness and Hoffner wiped the sea spray from his neatly bearded face, trying to see. How close were they? How much longer before they reached the sand bars? Damn this fog.

He flicked another uneasy look at the man beside him. A real *Landstreicher,* this. A professional wanderer, like the rootless and jobless craftsmen who roamed the countryside after World War I, looking for work. Hoffner knew the breed, for Hoffner himself had been forced to rattle from city to city during the Depression, seeking a likely spot to earn bread for his family and usually finding trouble instead. But Hoffner had managed to settle down, to become a good Nazi in time for World War II. God only knew what this Dietrich was. There was something vaguely disconcerting about him, something which made those around him uncomfortable. It was as though he was of a different species. A zebra, standing among horses, and the horses knew he didn't belong.

The conning-tower deck suddenly shuddered and Hoffner heard the low moan of the pressure hull scraping against the sandy bottom. He ducked over a speaking tube and said, "Stop engines." The two large diesels burbled to a halt and the submarine settled slightly to starboard.

Hoffner dropped the sea cover over the speaking tube and strained his ears to the distance, listening. Barely discernible over the steady lap-plap, lap-plap of light waves against the motionless U-boat hull, he could hear the first traces of surf, muffled booms that crashed in the distance against an unseen beach. He shrugged nervously and said, "Well, *Herr* Dietrich, does this satisfy you?"

"Where are we?" the ninth man said. His voice was low, and Hoffner had to strain to hear him.

"We should be off East Hampton," Hoffner said. "It's difficult to tell in this fog."

"How far?"

"Three hundred yards," Hoffner estimated. "Perhaps four hundred. It's the best I can do."

A deck hatch swung open forward of the 3.5-inch deck gun and several U-boat crewmen spilled out into the darkness. Hoffner leaned over the rail and watched the shadowy figures form a chain, lifting the four heavy crates of explosives out of the hatch.

"We'll have the boat inflated and ready to go very shortly," Hoffner said. "Perhaps you should return to your quarters and gather your belongings."

The man shook his head. "There's plenty of time. I won't land until the other four are off the beach."

Hoffner hesitated, feeling agitated. "*Herr* Dietrich," he said, "would it not be possible for you to make yourself known to the others and accompany them? My craft is extremely vulnerable in these shallows. I'd like to get you all unloaded in one trip and get out of here."

"I understand your concern," the man said. "But I have my orders."

"Yes, orders," Hoffner said unhappily. "Very well, I will summon the others and get them started. With luck, my men and I can still reach deep water before daybreak."

He spoke quickly into the speaking tube, then returned to the rail to watch the crewmen at work on the deck below. In the shifting gray darkness of the night he could make out the billowy outlines of the rubber boat, filling rapidly with air. A line had been attached to the rear of the boat, so it could be hauled back after the journey to shore. A necessary precaution. In this fog, the two U-boat crewmen would never be able to find their way.

There was a flurry of activity at the hatch when the four members of the New York team scrambled out onto the deck and gathered in a cluster beside the rubber boat. Hoffner looked them over. They were dressed in dark naval work jackets and pants, another landing precaution. If they stumbled into trouble on the beach, they could claim they were submariners and demand prisoner-of-war treatment. If all went well, they would change to civilian clothing and send the work uniforms back on the rubber boat.

Hoffner removed his sea cap and brushed a hand across thinning gray hair. He watched the man beside him in the conning tower for a moment, then said, "Excuse me, *Herr* Dietrich. I must ask. Do you intend to use these four men and the men from the *U-584* for whatever it is that you have been ordered to do?"

Dietrich, if that was truly his name, stared blankly at the U-boat captain. "I may," he said.

Hoffner settled his cap back on his head. "Then permit me another question. A clarification. I have been instructed to rendezvous here with you in three weeks. But nothing was said about these men, nor the ones from the *U-584.* Will they be with you?"

"No. I will be alone."

"Oh," the captain said. He looked down at the four men on the deck with different eyes. "Are they to die, then?"

"Not necessarily," Dietrich said slowly. He suddenly sounded very young. "They may. We all may."

"Then what?" the captain said. "Have they other missions as well?"

"That isn't your province, Captain. You are to put us ashore, then return in three weeks for me. Nothing else concerns you."

Hoffner stiffened. "Very well," he said. "We will, of course, follow our orders." He turned to the rail and drew himself to attention. "I should speak to them before they disembark," he said. "It is my duty as captain. You may wait here."

"No, I'll come with you," Dietrich said.

Hoffner looked back at him in surprise. "You will? Why? I thought you were . . . I thought you preferred to remain unknown to them?"

"I will see them as a U-boat officer," Dietrich said. "I want them to encounter me this one time, so they'll remember me later."

"As you wish," the captain said. He swung over the side and clambered down the conning-tower ladder, with Dietrich following. They strode across the deck to the shivering men.

Hoffner studied the four men carefully in the darkness, trying to put names to dimly seen faces. They looked different to him now, nervous, slightly smaller in stature than he had remembered. He settled on the older one, George John Dasch, the 39-year-old team leader. It was he who had spent the most time in the United States, according to crew scuttlebutt. Some nineteen years, many of them in New York City. His English was said to be near perfect.

The others, clustered about their team leader on the deck of the submarine, were:

—Ernst Peter Burger, 35, a naturalized American citizen who said he had served with the National Guard in both Michigan and Wisconsin. A machinist by trade, he was supposed to be the team expert on fuses and timing devices.

—Richard Quirin, 34. Quirin told crewmen he had lived in the United States for twelve years, working as a maintenance man and house painter during the Depression years. Big and strong, he appeared to be the most dependable.

—Heinrich Harm Heinck, 34. A grim, tough little man with a noticeable German accent when he spoke in English, he had entered the U.S. illegally in 1927, joined the German-American Bund in 1934, and had become a Nazi party member when he returned to Germany in 1939. He handled the high explosives.

Captain Hoffner faced the older one, the leader. "Your crates have been loaded," he said. "Have you the rest of your gear?"

The leader held out a battered leather briefcase. "The money is here," he said. He indicated a navy sea bag held by one of his men. "Our clothing. And we each have a few hundred dollars in case we get separated on the beach."

Hoffner nodded. He gestured at his crewmen to lower the boat. Then he said formally to the four men, "Gentlemen, I do not know the details of your mission, nor do I want to know. But the Fatherland has seen fit to jeopardize two of her valuable U-boats, mine and the U-584, to land you and your compatriots here and in Florida, so I must assume that your mission is vital to the conduct of the war. Whatever it is, do it well. Give the men of the U-202 reason to be proud."

The team leader saluted smartly, but he seemed more interested in watching the two crewmen who had taken up paddles and now dropped into the boat to wait. Dietrich stepped in and touched the team leader on the arm. The man flinched and his eyes flickered around.

"You are aware that you are to remain in New York until you receive instructions?" Dietrich asked him.

"Yes," the man said vaguely. His eyes wavered back to the bobbing boat.

"Look at me," Dietrich said. "Your orders call for you to take a room at the Governor Clinton Hotel under the name George Davis, do they not?"

"Yes," the man said.

"Good. Be sure you keep yourself available. As you know, a man who will identify himself as Richard Goethe is to contact you. He will do so either by telephone or in person, within the next few days. Do you understand?"

"Yes, yes," the team leader said. His head, turning as helplessly as the needle of a compass, swung nervously from the boat to Dietrich and back to the boat again. Dietrich sighed and released his arm.

The man's jumpiness was contagious. Hoffner said, "All right, into the boat. Go now. Quickly. We haven't much time." He glanced at Dietrich, wondering if his voice had betrayed his anxiety, then watched as the four team members slid over the side into the rubber boat.

One of the deck crewmen started playing out the recovery line, and the rubber boat bobbed away from the submarine. The two crewmen in the boat dipped their oars and began to stroke. They were swallowed up by the fog before they had gone twenty feet.

The captain cleared his throat nervously and said, "They are frightened."

"Who wouldn't be?" Dietrich said.

The captain eyed him quickly, searching for similar signs of fear, or at least a natural hesitation. Any man should hesitate before stepping over such a threshold. It would surely be a ticklish journey, infiltrating an enemy country in time of war. But the dark young man looked as neutrally detached as ever.

"I will go below now and collect my equipment," Dietrich said, breaking the silence.

Hoffner shifted uncomfortably. "Yes, good," he said. "I intend to put to sea within the hour, no matter what happens."

2

For George Dasch, the leader of the New York team, the last moments of the landing were a blur of nausea—a sudden seasickness as bad as it had been the whole first week after they sailed from France on the *U-202*. He was nauseated by the pitch of the breakers as the waves crashed from beneath the boat. He was nauseated by the surf booming around them, driving, drenching them. He scrambled out into the surf as soon as they reached shallow water, not so much to help drag the bucking rubber boat forward onto the beach as to get solid land beneath his feet.

The bone-chilling cold of the water shocked him back into control of himself, and at his terse orders the two sailors from the sub quickly unlashed the crates of explosives and hefted them out on the sand. Dasch sent his fellow team members hustling toward the sand dunes with three of the heavy crates, then stripped out of his navy togs and changed to civilian clothing from the sea bag.

One of the sailors had dropped to his knees beside the boat and was fiddling with something in the darkness. "What are you doing?" Dasch snapped.

The sailor looked up and smiled. "This," he said. He held out his cupped hands and showed the contents to Dasch.

"Sand?" Dasch said.

"American sand," the sailor said. "From an American beach." He stuffed the sand into his pockets and reached for more. "I can sell this back on the *U-202*."

A few minutes later, Peter Burger stepped out of the heavy fog and reached for the last of the explosive crates. Dasch tossed the sea bag on top of it and said, "As soon as you and the others have changed, stuff the uniforms in here and bring it back so we can get these submariners off the beach."

Burger was a well-disciplined subordinate. He disappeared immediately into the fog again, following his own tracks in the sand.

Dasch waited by the boat tensely, trying to count the seconds in his mind, wishing Burger would hurry so they could get out of here. He lost count somewhere between three and four minutes, when one of the sailors reached up abruptly and tugged his sleeve. The sailor's eyes were riveted on something up the beach, beyond Dasch.

Dasch craned his neck to see. God in heaven! A flashlight! The muted gleam of a flashlight, bobbing through the fog toward them, not more than thirty or forty feet away.

"Into the water!" Dasch whispered frantically. "Quickly! Shove off before he sees you!"

The two sailors wasted no time. They grabbed the rubber boat and took off on the run for the water's edge. By the time they plunged into the water, they had already begun to gray out in the heavy fog. Dasch turned the other way, intending to make a break up the beach. But he was too late. The flashlight suddenly focused on him, then started coming in his direction.

Damn, damn, damn the fog. If he had seen the light a few seconds earlier, he could have vanished into the dunes with his men. But now he had been spotted. And there was no time to warn the others. There was nothing to do but try and bluff it out.

3

Coast Guardsman Vernon P. Flynn slogged through the sand, flicking the yellow flashlight beam out in front of him, not that it did much good. He couldn't see more than fifteen or twenty feet through this pea soup. Why did they always stick the young guys with beach patrol? But hell, one of the older guys would probably bust a blood vessel, wrestling with this deep sand in the darkness. He'd been walking more than twenty minutes now and he'd barely managed to fight his way a half mile from the Coast Guard station.

He shoved his free hand in his pocket, bored stiff with the silence and the darkness, his legs aching from the strain of plodding, plodding through ankle-deep sand. He marched on, playing the flashlight beam out to the side, toward the water.

That's when he saw the movement. Just a dim flicker through the fog. He stopped. What was it? A man? Two or three men? What were they doing out here at this time of night? Some of the dim figures broke away, carrying some big bulky thing. A boat? And then they were gone, gobbled up in the fog, leaving one lone figure on the beach.

Smugglers? Some of the old-timers back at the Coast Guard station were always yakking about the old days and the rum runners and the way they used to smuggle booze in from Canada. But what could they possibly be smuggling these days? Gasoline? Sugar? Coffee? He'd heard there was a pretty big black market going on in Manhattan. Maybe he'd stumbled onto something. He started walking faster, down toward the single figure at the edge of the beach.

The man just stood there, waiting for him. Flynn ran the flashlight over his face. An older guy, maybe between thirty-five and forty years old, with a long, horsey face and penetrating eyes. He had sandy hair, streaked with gray, and it was brushed straight back from his wide forehead. And wet, as though he had just come out of the water.

"What's going on here?" Flynn demanded. "Who are you?"

The man peered over Flynn's shoulder at the darkness.

"Listen here, fella, who are you?" Flynn said again.

The man blinked in the glare of the flashlight. "I'm a fisherman.

From Southampton. I got lost in this damned fog and ran aground."
He hooked his thumb back at the water.

"A fisherman?" Flynn let a sigh rustle out. That was a relief.
"Where's your boat? You want some help?"

"There is nothing anyone can do at this hour," the man said. "I'll
just wait here on the beach until daylight, then I'll be all right."

"The sun won't be up for another four or five hours," the young
Coast Guardsman said. "Maybe you better come back to the station
with me. You can wait there until sunrise."

"Station?" the man said.

"Yeah, the Coast Guard station," Flynn said. "At Amagansett.
Don't you know where you are?"

"Of course," the man said. "It's just the fog. I lost my bearings. I
thought I was closer to East Hampton."

"No, you're off about three miles," Flynn said. "Come on, I'll
take you back with me. It's only a half mile down the beach."

The man took a few steps with him, then stopped abruptly. "No,
I can't go with you."

Flynn was immediately suspicious again. "Why not?"

"I don't want to stray too far from my boat."

Flynn hesitated. He was unarmed, and if this guy was a smuggler,
he wasn't going to be easy to handle. It might be better if the man
didn't think Flynn was alone. He said, "Look, the rest of my patrol
is waiting for me back up there. They'll think it's funny if I don't
bring you with me. We've been getting a lot of rumors about black
marketeers out here, and some of the boys are kind of suspicious
and trigger-happy. You know what I mean?"

The man regarded the darkness behind Flynn, his horse face
tense. "I really can't go with you," he said with the air of a man
making a confession. "I don't have a fishing permit. Your superiors
might make difficulty for me."

As the man talked, Flynn suddenly became aware of another
figure looming toward them through the fog, coming down from
the dunes. It was a little short guy, moving toward them casually,
dragging some kind of duffel bag in the sand.

"Fishing is my livelihood," the horse-faced man continued, unaware of the approaching figure. "If they catch me operating
without a permit, they might—"

The man with the duffel bag was closer now, and he waved
through the fog at Flynn and the horse-faced man and called out
something in a foreign language. Something guttural, European-

sounding. Flynn's neck muscles stiffened and he sucked in his breath.

The man with the long face and penetrating eyes cringed and whirled around. He shouted, "Shut up, you fool! Go back to the others and wait!" Even in the darkness, Flynn could see the new man's face fold in horror before he jerked back and hurried into the fog, yanking the duffel bag after him.

The man with the horse face grabbed Flynn's arm and said, "Listen boy, do you have a mother?"

"Yes."

"And a father?"

"Yes."

The man nodded. "Then I would hate to have to kill you. But you don't seem to recognize the danger you have stumbled into. You mentioned black marketeers, right? Well, that's what we are. We are black marketeers. And we're desperate. Do you understand?"

"Yes."

The man dug into his pocket and pulled out a wad of bills. He hurriedly counted out several in the darkness and held them out to Flynn. "Here's three hundred dollars," he said. "Forget what you saw here."

"I can't take that."

"Take it," the man insisted. "Take it and have some fun." He stuffed the bills in the pocket of Flynn's blouse, then gestured at the darkness. "Don't mention this to your friends back there. Because if you do, we'll find you. We live in Southampton, remember, and that's not very far from here. If word ever reaches us that you have said something about this to anyone else, we will come to Amagansett and find you. We'll find you and kill you. Do you understand?"

"I understand," Flynn said.

"Well? What's it going to be?"

"I never saw you before in my life," Flynn said.

"That's a good boy. Now go back to your friends and tell them nothing is wrong here."

"Yes, sir," Flynn said. He backed away a few steps, then pivoted and walked up the beach, slowly, carefully, wondering if his nerves would allow him to carry it off. When he had covered about fifty feet and was fairly certain the fog would cover his retreat, he started running.

4

"We should have killed the little *Scheisskerl*," Heinrich Heinck whispered up to Dasch. There were houses somewhere nearby, but in the fog they couldn't be sure how close they might be to some sleeping fisherman, some sunburned vacationer turning restlessly on wrinkled sheets. They had to be quiet, but the fool grunted loudly as he hoisted another shovelful of wet sand out of the shallow hole, and Dasch winced.

"He had companions waiting up on the beach," Dasch whispered back furiously. "I couldn't take the chance."

"You let him bluff you," Heinck whispered. "There were no others. We would have heard them."

Dasch swung around from his lookout position at the top of the dune and glowered at Heinck. "Like you heard him when he stopped me on the beach? He was right under your noses and you didn't even know it."

Peter Burger, resting at the edge of the hole, dropped his head guiltily. "That was my fault," he said. "I saw the two of you on the beach talking, and I just assumed that he was one of the sailors. I deeply regret the error."

"It doesn't matter," Dasch said curtly. "I gave him some money. He'll keep quiet." He looked out toward the swirling fog that was the beach and shivered. "Besides, it's done now."

"It would have been better if we had killed him," Heinck grumbled.

Dasch tried to bully him. "Shut up," he said. "Do exactly wh·t I tell you, and dig. Do you think you're digging a flower gai.
That hole wouldn't even be deep enough to plant a pansy."

Heinck subsided into inaudible mutterings. Grumbling still, and in German, the insubordinate bastard. Heinck knew the orders. They were none of them to speak German. They hadn't been allowed to speak German to anyone for all the months of training, except to two explosives experts who knew no English. Heinck would get them all in trouble. Not that Heinck's English was worth a damn anyway. His accent sounded like he just got off a sauerkraut boat. It was that sort of thing that could get them caught.

Dasch shifted nervously on his perch atop the dune, sweeping his eyes back and forth over the fog. He searched his memory, trying to produce a mental map of Long Island with its 118 miles of beach, wondering just where the hell they were. What was it that Coast Guard boy had said? Amagansett? Three miles from East Hampton? But to which side of East Hampton? He mustn't let the other men know they were lost. Nor that they were practically within shouting distance of a Coast Guard station.

Still, he could get them to safety somehow. No matter where Amagansett was, it was still close to the original landing site. The Montauk road should run parallel to the beach, somewhere to the north of them. All they had to do was walk north when they were finished here, then turn. There was sure to be a train station near the road somewhere. All these little towns had train stations.

Heinck hissed for Dasch's attention. "Isn't this deep enough yet?" he said. "We ought to get off this beach and start moving."

"Dig deeper," Dasch snapped. "Need I remind you of the importance of those crates?"

Even Heinck didn't argue about that. How could he? Four crates packed tight with explosives, detonators, timing devices—enough for two years of assaults on America's industrial might, if one of these bums Kappe had stuck him with didn't get them caught first with their insubordination and bright ideas. Heinck, always sucking up to Kappe, blabbing about some friend on Long Island he wanted to contact for help upon arrival, when it was obvious to any man with a brain in his head they couldn't trust anyone in the United States, even Bundists. "Why you dirty bastard!" Heinck had had the nerve to shout at him. "We in the Bund had to fight people like you." Well, by God, he'd shouted Heinck down: "I'll kill you if you call me a bad German again!" That had shut Heinck up. And he'd meant it, by God. A petty, cowardly little fellow, that Heinck. Dasch knew what had put his nose out of joint this time. Heinck and Quirin had had to settle for quarters with the enlisted men on the sub, while Dasch and Burger had bunks in the noncommissioned officers' quarters.

Was the fog thinning a little? God in heaven, what if they were seen? The heavy fog that had earlier let that Coast Guard kid sneak up on him now seemed like a comforting shield. Were those hazy lights houses off in the distance? That kid *had* seen him, had seen his face. That damned flashlight, shining right in his eyes. The kid had taken a good, long look. Maybe he *should* have killed him. The damned kid wouldn't have a minute's trouble identifying him.

Suddenly overcome with panic, Dasch leaped to his feet. "That's deep enough," he said. "Hurry. You, Burger, Quirin. Give Heinck a hand with the crates."

He scrambled off his dune to help them. They handed the four wooden boxes down to Heinck, who stacked them in two piles in the still-shallow pit. Then Burger handed the sea bag with its treacherous stuffing of German naval uniforms to Heinck and he stuffed those between the crates.

"The shovel, too," Dasch said.

"I know it," Heinck said. "I'm not stupid." He dropped the entrenching tool on top of the crates and boosted himself out. Dasch and the other team members worked quickly, using their hands to shovel loose sand back into the hole.

"Damn it," Heinck said. "It looks darker than the surrounding sand. Someone will see it."

"No, no," Dasch said hurriedly. "That's only wet sand from below the surface. It should dry within an hour or so once the sun rises. Come on, let's get out of here."

He hurried them north, down the landward side of the dunes and into the flats. They trotted furtively in a tight little group. More houses, becoming visible now, loomed around them, and worse, the fog definitely was lifting.

They had been stumbling along for almost fifteen minutes when headlights shimmered out of the fog and rushed past them on a side road some forty feet to their left, sending them diving for cover. Dasch hugged the ground and watched the headlights swish past and dim out in the fog.

"That was a military truck," Heinck whispered. "They've found us out. We're surrounded, boys, we're surrounded."

"Shut up!" Dasch said. "You're crazy." He tried to sound firm, to allay their fears—and his own—but his voice trembled as he added, "Where would a military truck be going at this time of night?"

"Where do you think?" Heinck said. "To the beach. That boy has informed on us. I knew we should have killed him. Now we'll never get out of here."

"Coward!" Dasch said. "We're perfectly safe. We need only keep moving." He pushed to his feet and started jogging forward as fast as he could go, setting an example for them. But as he ran, even with the cold sea breeze pushing him, he was sweating. First the boy, and now military trucks, and they'd barely landed. God in heaven, how could so many things already have gone so terribly, terribly wrong?

5

The ninth man leaned forward in the rubber boat, wondering what
was troubling the two sailors. Neither of them had spoken a word
since setting out from the submarine for the second journey to the
American shore. At first he had thought they were upset only
because they hadn't been warned that they would have to make a
second landing when they thought the danger was behind them. But
now he suspected there was more to it than a simple fear of com-
pounded risk. Something, perhaps, that he hadn't been told.

He had been waiting on deck with his landing gear in another of
the sea bags when the *U-202* crew had hauled the two sailors back
from their first trip. He had seen the two men pop out of the rubber boat and hold a hurried conversation with the U-boat captain,
punctuating their report with nervous gestures. The captain had
given Dietrich a worried look, then consulted his watch and the
steadily thinning fog and had ordered the two men back into the
rubber boat. The two sailors had looked stunned, but did as they
were told.

Now, as they approached the beach, the two men dipped their
oars tentatively, pausing between strokes to peer into the darkness,
listening, waiting, and Dietrich watched them, wondering what it
was all about.

They could see the beach. Not clearly. The fog hadn't thinned
that much. But they could see the hazy outline of sand beyond
the breakers and the diffused puffs of white froth where the waves
crashed on the shore.

As they were about to put their shoulders into the oars again, one
of the two sailors cursed and pointed to the west. A pair of
headlights broke through the wisps of fog and lurched slowly
down the beach, spreading a feeble fan of light across the darkness.

It was a truck in four-wheel drive, bumping and wobbling slowly
across the rippled sand, apparently seeking something. The sailor
who had first seen it whimpered and crouched lower in the boat.
Dietrich grabbed him by the shoulder and pulled him around. "Did
you know about this?" he demanded.

The sailor shook his head, terrified. "Not exactly," he said.

"What do you mean, not exactly?"

"There was trouble earlier. A man. Someone on the beach."

Dietrich stiffened. "Why wasn't I told?"

"I don't know," the sailor said. "That's the captain's duty. Listen, we've got to get out of here. If they catch us, we'll be locked away for the rest of the war. Give the line a yank. Let the boys know we're ready to be pulled back."

"You have to put me ashore first," Dietrich said.

"Put you ashore? How can we? That truck will see us."

"We'll wait until the truck passes," Dietrich said.

But it didn't pass. The headlights swept over something in the sand and the truck jerked to a halt. Someone jumped out of the cab and ran around to the light to peer at the sand. He followed a track of some kind, then pointed up into the darkness. "There," he shouted, and his voice drifted across the restless water to Dietrich and the sailors.

"The fog is lifting," the other sailor said. "Another few minutes and they'll see us for sure."

"Keep your voice down," Dietrich said. He watched the distant truck. There were at least three men out in front of it now, peering at the sand, perhaps more of them in the darkness, outside the periphery of the headlights. Dietrich silently pulled off his navy tunic and dropped it in the bottom of the boat, then stripped off his pants and removed his shoes.

"What are you doing?" the sailor asked.

Tying the shoelaces together, Dietrich looped the shoes around his neck. Then he picked up the sea bag containing his money, clothing, gun and several oilskin packages of identity papers, and looped the drawstring over his shoulder.

"Don't be crazy," one of the sailors said. "Come back with us. No one can blame you for not landing."

"Tell the captain I thank him for his consideration," Dietrich said. "Tell him I will make a point of repaying him when I see him in three weeks." He slipped over the side and lowered himself into the water. It was icy. As icy as December, not June.

The two sailors watched him briefly, then tugged at the towrope to alert the submarine and started paddling back the way they had come.

Dietrich swam easily at first, riding the tops of swells. But as he drew closer to the beach, the peaks and valleys came faster, alternately lifting and dropping him, leaving him at times with arms and legs stroking empty air. Then one of the swells raised him higher than all the others and trembled beneath him and he knew he was into the breakers. He grabbed his shoes with one hand and gripped the loop of the sea bag with the other. The wave burst apart and hurled him headlong into the sea ahead, somersaulting him, driving him down, down, deep into the grinding turbulence. He felt his shoulder scrape along the bottom, his legs churning out of control above his head, then he popped back to the surface and another hefty wave dumped on him, dashing him down again, twisting and rolling him until he lost track of which way was up and which was down. He let his natural buoyancy lift him until his head broke free, but before he could gulp for fresh air, a third wave struck him down again. Just as he thought his lungs would collapse, he found himself standing in five feet of relatively quiet water, between breakers, with his shoes dangling sodden from his upraised hand and the sea bag floating heavily from the crook of his elbow.

The swells built up in the darkness behind him and he moved quickly toward shallower water, slogging through chest-deep waves, trying to get in toward the beach where it was shallow enough for him to stay upright. When he finally felt the sand level rising under his feet, he paused for air and a quick look at the beach. But the angle and the force of the breakers had carried him uncomfortably close to the truck. He crouched in the waves and tried to catch his breath.

A few of the men were still circling around in the front of the truck, poking in the sand. Others had disappeared from the glow of the headlights, possibly up toward the dunes. Dietrich hunched over in the water, breathing hard, fighting the undercurrent, then finally began to move crablike to the side, working his way down the beach away from the truck.

He made slow progress, his hands gripping the shoes and the sea bag, unable to rise out of the water, fighting his way against the inward surge of waves and the hungry outward tug of the undertow. He was almost to a point where he felt it might be safe to creep up on the beach when a sound came drifting across the water and struck a deep chill through his body. It was the two big diesels aboard the *U-202*, cranking up for a withdrawal.

Dietrich jerked his head around and stared seaward, into the last vestiges of the fog. Damn that submarine captain. Surely the two sailors had told him about the truck on the beach. Couldn't he have waited until he was fairly certain Dietrich was clear?

The engines throbbed faintly across the distance as the U-boat backed off the sand bar and made a slow turn toward the sea. The men at the truck heard it, too. Two of them raised their heads, then came down to the water's edge, looking puzzled. They peered out

into the darkness, trying to trace the sound. Dietrich dropped
lower, with just his head above water, worrying that they might see
him.

As the U-boat engines drifted eastward, dimming, dimming, Dietrich was filled by a floating sense of despair. The feeling surprised
him, and he trembled in the cold surge of surf. The sound of the
engines had struck deeply at his senses. It wasn't only that the
sound had endangered him, had drawn the two men from the truck
to the water's edge where they might well have seen him. It was
deeper than that. The submarine, riding quietly out there in the
fog, had represented his umbilical cord to safety, his last contact
with home. Now it was being cut.

The engines moved eastward steadily, growing softer and more
distant until finally they faded altogether and the tumbling sounds
of surf took over. The two men at the water's edge continued to
stand there, searching the gloom, for several minutes. Finally they
appeared to give up and headed back toward the truck.

Dietrich waited until they turned their attention to the sand
again, then rose out of the water and ran across the dark beach, racing toward the dunes. When he reached the first sandy hillock, he
struggled up it and dropped over into the shadows. He flopped
down on his back, exhausted.

He felt drained. But he couldn't dally. He didn't know where the
other men from the truck had got off to, what they were up to. He
sat up and jerked the sea bag open, pulling out his soaked clothing.
He wrung out his pants hurriedly and pulled them on, then
struggled into his wet shirt. It was clammy and cold.

It was too dark to tell whether his oilskin bundles had survived
the soaking without leakage. He would check them more closely
later. The money belt was a problem. He hadn't expected to swim
to shore, so he hadn't bothered to wrap the bills in oilskin. Now
they were probably drenched. He could just see himself later on,
holed up in some hotel room, spreading out the bills, all twenty
thousand dollars' worth, on the bed, the floor, the window sills,
every available surface, trying to dry them out. He shivered in the
cold darkness and strapped the heavy wet belt around his stomach.

He stuffed the oilskin packages containing his papers into his
trouser pockets, then slid the oilskin-wrapped gun under his belt.
He quickly pulled his leather jacket out of the sea bag, then dug a
shallow trench in the sand and stuffed the empty bag in it. As soon

as he had it covered, he popped to his feet and sneaked a look over the top of the dune. The truck was still there.

From the dunes, a hundred yards to the east, he heard drifting voices shouting something at each other. Searching for something? For Dasch and his men? Dietrich dropped low and began to worry harder. Damn it, if only they hadn't been in such a rush to send him. They should have given him time, allowed him to pick his own men. That Quenz Lake group, they had all been selected and trained by some German-American named Walter Kappe. Why entrust an outsider, even with help from professionals like Schulz and Koenig, with the choice of the men? Why hadn't they gone for some of his fellow experts in the Canaris group?

Brisk sea breezes flayed his wet skin and clothing, raising goose flesh across his neck and chest. Dietrich disciplined his runaway thoughts. The questions didn't matter, nor the answers. He had to get out of here before someone stumbled across him. Away from the beach. He would find the railway station and watch. Make sure Dasch's team boarded the train and got away. He picked up his wet shoes and darted inland through the dunes, running at a crouch.

If he had waited three minutes longer, he would have seen a group of men come pouring out of the dunes, a hundred yards down the beach, a spot to which they had been led by following the trail of a carelessly dragged sea bag. He would have seen them rush into the fan of light in front of the truck, bearing the sand-clotted crates of explosives which George Dasch and his men had buried less than forty-five minutes earlier.

THE FIRST DAY

Saturday—June 13, 1942

I

The four members of the New York team clustered nervously in the early-morning shadows of a drooping black willow tree. The Amagansett station, a rectangular yellow and black building with a high peaked roof, was locked. They felt thoroughly out of place. Their clothing was damp and dirty from their groping flight through the countryside before sunrise, hunting the Amagansett depot. Richard Quirin had a welt on his forehead from walking into a clothesline in the darkness. Peter Burger was limping noticeably after turning his ankle in a drainage ditch. Dasch was tired and irritable and frightened, and he, like the others, crouched instinctively as a middle-aged man in shirtsleeves came up the cinder pathway toward the empty building. The man had a newspaper under his arm and he was carrying a brown lunch bag. He climbed up on the station platform and stopped at the door, digging for a set of keys. It was 6:30 A.M.

"It's only the stationmaster," Dasch whispered reassuringly as the man unlocked the door and went inside. They could hear him whistling as he moved around.

"Do we all go?" Heinck asked.

"Someone should check it out first," Dasch said. He waited for a volunteer, but no one spoke. It was typical of them. Just because Kappe had selected him as their leader, they made him do all the dangerous work. He brushed ineffectively at his rumpled clothing and headed for the building.

The stationmaster was behind the ticket counter, shuffling something in a drawer. He stopped whistling as Dasch came in. Dasch paused in front of a bulletin board, trying to look casual, and looked for a train schedule. He could feel the man's eyes on him.

The man spoke, and Dasch jumped. "You're out early this morning." Was there suspicion in the man's voice, or was he just being pleasant?

Dasch cleared his throat. "Yes, we've been fishing," he said. "Didn't have much luck. Has the fishing been this bad all summer?"

The stationmaster went on with his paper-shuffling. "It depends," he said. "I hear they're biting pretty good over to Montauk. Fella the other day said they were biting down to Wyborgs Beach, too."

"Well, my business associates and I are about ready to give up and go home," Dasch said. "What time is the next train to New York?"

"That would be the 6:57 to Jamaica. She'll come through in about twenty minutes. There's another one an hour later, the . . ."

"No, the train to Jamaica is fine," Dasch said. "That's where we live. Jamaica. Can you sell me four one-way tickets?"

"Why not?" the man said. "Being Saturday, she ought to be near to empty. Most folks come *out* on weekends, not the other way around." He reached up to his ticket board. "Four one-way, you say?"

"Yes, that's right," Dasch said. He moved quickly to the ticket counter and waited while the man stamped the tickets. Then he laughed weakly and said, "Isn't that odd? We've been fishing so hard that I must be losing my memory. I can't remember how much the tickets cost."

"Same going in as it was coming out," the man said. "Five dollars and ten cents each."

"Yes, of course," Dasch said. "Now I remember."

He paid the man hurriedly and hustled outside. As he neared the willow tree, his three men stepped cautiously through the branches to meet him.

"Any trouble?" Peter Burger asked anxiously.

Dasch shook his head. "There's a train due in fifteen or twenty minutes. I bought tickets for us all."

The three team members exchanged looks of relief. Dasch passed out the tickets and led them up on the platform by the tracks. They were still the only people waiting when the train rolled in some ten minutes later. Railroad employees were apparently accustomed to weekend fishermen in grubby clothing. To Dasch's relief, the conductor watched them climb aboard with obvious and complete disinterest.

Dasch hurried to a seat and concentrated on looking as unobtrusive as possible. Like a rabbit, sit still. Like a pheasant, hide in cover with mottled, pheasantlike markings. He thought he had handled the matter of the tickets very well, with courage and intelligence, but he still felt frightened. That stationmaster had looked at him. He had seen Dasch's face. That made two.

The others came to pester him for coins that he'd gotten for change from the tickets. They bought newspapers from an untended stack at the front of the car with a cigar box for money sitting on top of them. They began to smile and talk and read each other bits of headlines. Maybe they had something to smile about. *They* couldn't be identified by a Coast Guardsman. *They* couldn't be chosen from a line-up of suspected spies by a stationmaster.

Peter Burger handed him the front section of *The New York Times* and gave him a pointed look. Yes, all right, open it. Try to look like any normal passenger reading the headlines:

JAPANESE MAKE LANDINGS IN ALEUTIAN ISLANDS; ENEMY LOST 15 WARSHIPS IN CORAL SEA BATTLE, U.S. LOST 3, INCLUDING THE CARRIER LEXINGTON

Gaze at a picture of a Japanese aircraft carrier, the *Ryukaku*, burning in the Coral Sea. Glance at a little story in the lower left-hand corner: Long Island authorities clamp down on dimout violators along the Atlantic beach front; remember the Second Corps slogan: "If in doubt, put it out." Dasch grimaced. A lot of good the dimout violators had done the *U-202* last night in that stinking fog.

His eyes moved over the page obediently, but he hardly noticed what he was reading. It was like breakfast, back during training. Reveille at 7:00, calisthenics until 7:30, clean up your quarters from 7:30 to 8:00, breakfast from 8:00 to 9:00, but they wouldn't leave you alone to drink your coffee in peace, you had to read and talk about those *New York Times* and *Chicago Tribune*s and *Life*s and *Collier's* and *Saturday Evening Post*s that never stopped arriving. As if he needed training in American manners and speech. That's what had impressed Kappe so much about him in the very beginning. That, plus his intelligence, was what had made him Kappe's first choice for the teams.

"Hey, what's this?" Heinck said, and Dasch jumped again. Heinck scrambled out of his seat and rushed over to Dasch. "These tickets," he whispered. "They say Jamaica. I thought we were going to New York?"

Dasch looked around to see if the conductor was watching. "Be quiet," he snapped. "Jamaica is a part of New York. It's a place in Queens."

Heinck frowned at his ticket. "Then, why don't they call it New York?"

"Don't worry about it," Dasch said. He glanced toward the rear of the car again, checking the conductor. "Listen, when we get there, I think we'll split up for a while. You and Quirin can go to Manhattan by subway and shop for some new clothing. Burger and I will stay in Jamaica to shop. We'll meet later in the afternoon."

"I don't like it," Heinck said. "Why can't we stay together?"

"We're less likely to attract attention if we split up," Dasch said. "At least until we get some clean clothes."

The train lurched and rumbled and began to move. Heinck looked startled, then smiled jubilantly. He returned to his seat. Dasch leaned back and watched the Amagansett station drift slowly past the window and drop behind. They had made it. They were on their way.

He was tentatively testing the feeling, trying to convince himself that there was no longer any need for tension, when Peter Burger startled him yet again by touching his arm. Dasch jerked nervously, but saw only Burger's round face and receding chin, smiling in wry amusement at the newspaper in his hands.

"There's a new movie in New York that we should go see," Burger said. "It gets a nice review."

"We don't have time for movies."

"We ought to see this one," Burger said, nodding at the newspaper. "It's called *Nazi Agent*."

2

Two hundred miles to the southwest of New York City, at the Maryland home of the late Congressman Prentiss T. Cogswell, about thirty minutes north of downtown Washington, D.C., Captain Andrew Blaszek, U. S. Army, White House Security Liaison, was under severe attack. On two fronts. The first attack was a frontal assault, aimed at him by the tanned Mr. and Mrs. team on the far side of the net. The second attack was more subtle, but far more painful. It came from his tennis partner, Gay Cogswell.

Andy crouched forward, sweating in the early-morning heat, his eyes pinned on the middle-aged man bouncing the ball at the opposite end of the court, prior to service. The man—Gay had introduced her house guests to him as "former neighbors and dear,

dear friends" (whatever that meant)—had quickly spotted Andy's weak backhand and apparently had passed the intelligence along to his wife. For the past ten minutes they had been concentrating on him, aiming lobs and forehands to his left, rubbing his face in it. His own partner, who had taken it upon herself to tutor him in tennis, could hardly play for laughing.

Andy was fairly certain the next service would be another whistler down the center stripe, challenging his backhand, and he cheated a few steps to his left to meet it, dangerously exposing his wide-open right. Even with the cheating, when it came, as he had expected, to his left, he flubbed it. He jerked upright, long arms rigid, and grimaced. It was his third failure in a row to return service.

"Nice try, old buddy," the man called jovially.

Gay Cogswell, Andy's pretty blond tennis partner, raised her eyes to heaven and said, "Lord, baby, when are we going to get the lead out of that backhand of yours?"

"Stop ragging him, Gay," the little woman across the court called. "Howard and I like your young man's game just fine."

"You would, Blanche dear. You're winning." She glanced slyly at Andy and said, "He's usually a much smoother partner. I'll have to spend a little more time this weekend helping him perfect his stroke."

Ridiculously, Andy felt his bony face flushing, and that so embarrassed him that he blushed even deeper. Gay burst into laughter.

"Come on, you two," the middle-aged man yelled. "Blanche and I have you on the run. This is match point." He switched sides and started bouncing the ball.

Gay shook her racket encouragingly at Andy and said, "Stay in there, lover." Then she called, "All right, Howard. Serve, damn you. I could beat you by myself if I wanted to."

Andy crouched and watched Gay Cogswell get ready. He liked looking at her. She was dazzling on a tennis court, her plump, comfortable body coiled and poised for action, a hint of panties and buttocks old-fashioned in their opulence peeping from beneath the short white tennis skirt as she leaned forward, plump tan legs braced for the serve, round tan breasts straining ripely against the V of the skimpy white shirt, threatening to rip out of their moorings at the first flurry of athletic activity. They always threatened, but nothing ever happened. Not out here anyway.

The middle-aged man named Howard zinged his service at her

and she walloped it back, brief skirt flouncing. She charged the net, trying to keep them from Andy's left, but the female dear friend lobbed the return over Gay's head and Andy had to contend. This time, to his relief, his backhand cleared the net. Gay cried, "Well done, Andy," and danced into position. She held them off at the net for three volleys, then Howard got past her and blistered another shot to Andy's weak side and it was all over.

"Game, set and match!" Howard shouted.

Andy wiped the sweat from his dripping forehead and growled to Gay, "So help me, if he jumps the net I'm going to punch him right in the mouth."

She chuckled. "Be patient, baby. They'll only be here the one night."

"How about it, old buddy?" Howard called. "You and Gay want to take another crack at us?"

Gay gave Andy a measuring look and called back, "No, he's had enough for one morning. Let's go have breakfast."

The man helped his wife gather up their towels and racket presses. As they walked back toward the house, he said genially to Andy, "You know, old buddy, you could really make a good tennis player if you'd just keep working at it. You've got the musculature for it. Nice and lean. Good long arms and legs. I'll bet you were good at basketball when you were a kid. You had us sweating a couple of times out there."

Gay laughed. "Sure, when he went to the water cooler. You were afraid he wouldn't come back, and you'd have to face me alone. But give him time, Howard. He'll be a real tiger one of these days. On the courts, I mean."

Blanche, a deceptively frail-looking woman with a wicked forehand, ignored Gay's innuendo politely. She twined her fingers in her husband's and said to Andy, "You just keep practicing like my Howard says, Captain. My Howard knows what he's talking about. He could have been a pro, if he'd wanted to. He used to beat the Congressman regularly. And the Congressman was a fine player."

"So I've heard," Andy murmured, just as politely. Indeed, since the simultaneous arrival of spring and this tennis kick of Gay's, he sometimes thought he heard little else from the successive sets of "The Congressman's Dear Friends" who had been showing up at Gay's invitation to ruin his weekends and strengthen his game. God knew, he tried to be good-natured about it, and being good-natured was one of his compulsive traits. "Like a big friendly puppy dog," Gay teased, "the kind that always knocks over the furniture." Gay, her long blond hair tangled, rumpling his short black hair. Gay, always curious, quick, high-spirited, sometimes tender, always laughing: "My sweet big old long-eared baby puppy dog."

Laughing as usual, and talking tennis as had lately become usual, she led her guests to the west patio and a white-painted wrought-iron table already set with linens and silver. Massive old elm trees shaded her house and it should have been cool, but their glasses of orange juice, once chilled, had been overcome by the growing heat of the morning. Mattie, Gay's black cook, came bustling out with a huge tray, grumbling about the hot food getting cold, and dealt plates across the table like a faro dealer. Lukewarm waffles, lukewarm country sausage and lukewarm shirred eggs. Mattie gave Andy a commiserating glance. She knew it was his favorite breakfast and she knew it had been spoiled by the delay. Andy dug into the lukewarm food with a show of enthusiasm, a wordless way of trying to say thanks.

But Gay and the visiting couple had already had Andy, their mutual pupil, for breakfast, and they exhibited more interest in talk than in food. Between sips of coffee, Howard said, "Gay, when are you going to bring this fellow up to Philadelphia for a visit? We'd be happy to put you up, Captain Blake."

Andy's fork paused in midstroke and he said, "Uh, the name is Blaszek."

"Oh?" Howard cocked his head. "I could have sworn Gay said it was Blake."

Gay nodded, not at all put out. "He's been thinking of changing it. Haven't you, baby?"

"No."

"You ought to," she insisted. "You told me yourself that your mother wanted you to." She turned to the others. "Andy's thinking of going into politics. I'm afraid people won't be able to pronounce his name unless he Anglicizes it. What do you think, Howard? Blaszek or Blake?"

"I don't know," the man said. He repeated the name, as if tasting it along with his coffee. "Blaszek? Blaszek? What is it? Slavic?"

"Hungarian," Gay said, answering for Andy.

"My, how interesting," the visiting wife said. "Is he from Hungary? That would be something of a handicap for going into politics, wouldn't it?"

"No problem," Gay said. "He's from Colorado. Native-born and all that."

"Maybe he ought to stick to Blaszek, then," the woman mused. "He'd get all the Hungarian vote in Colorado that way. Don't you think so, Howard?"

"Now, girls," the man chided, "don't discuss him as if he weren't here. Are there many Hungarians in Colorado, Captain? Maybe I've got my voting blocs mixed up, but I thought Colorado's minorities were mainly Italians and Mexicans."

Andy shook his head. "The state doesn't have many Hungarians, as far as I know. At least not in Trinidad, where I'm from. And I'm not really giving much thought to politics anyway."

Gay shot him a scolding look. "Yes he is," she said. "This damned war isn't going to last forever, and Andy would be perfect for a political career."

"Is your family still in Colorado, Captain?" the woman asked.

"My father, yes. My mother is dead."

"Oh, what a pity. And what does your father do? Is he in business?"

"He's in mining," Gay put in quickly. "Andy's really awfully well connected in the state. A former lieutenant-governor in Andy's home town is practically his second father, and Brigadier General Jeremiah Roach—you remember him? He used to run the Quartermaster Corps or something, but his wife got TB and he moved her to Colorado—well, he's practically, well, Andy's third father, you might say. The general has always been very active on Andy's behalf, and so was Horace Tucker, but he retired from the Army last year, damn him. But then, of course, there's Andy's job at the White House. That gives Andy a really marvelous political base."

"What kind of thing do you do at the White House?" the man asked.

Andy said amiably but firmly, "Damned little. It's a phony job. Impressive title, but no influence."

"Baby!" Gay scolded. She patted his hand and told the others, "Andy is the liaison officer between the executive and the military. It's a euphemism for looking after the President's security. Very hush-hush. He's just being modest about it."

"The heck I am," Andy said. "You should come down sometime and watch everyone ignore me."

"They couldn't ignore you too much," the man said. "Gay tells us you're going up to Hyde Park next week when the President meets with Churchill for the secret war talks."

Andy's face clouded. Even more firmly now, he said, "That wasn't supposed to be talked about, Gay."

The man laughed. "Loose lips sink ships, right? Don't worry, Captain. We're trustworthy."

The woman laughed too and said, "You'll have to forgive us if we sound like prosecuting attorneys, Captain. It's just that Gay is so dear to us. We're very interested in her friends. Gay, wherever did you find this charming young man, anyway?"

"At a bar about six months ago," Gay said promptly. "He picked me up."

"No, really. Don't be such a tease."

"Honest," Gay said. "He was sloshed and sitting on a bar stool. Every time a woman passed him he gave her the old once-over, but he's a picky bastard, so naturally he picked me. What was it you said to me, dear? Oh yes. He said, 'Lady, you're a little fat, but I like my women built for comfort, not speed, so how about it?' Naturally, I was so overwhelmed that I literally threw myself at him."

"My," Blanche said. "How original."

Andy couldn't keep from smiling. "She's lying."

"Oh?" Gay said. "Well, maybe I've got you mixed up with one of my many other admirers."

"It was at a cocktail party," Andy said. "I was sitting on a couch, minding my own business, when you walked up and said, 'Listen, buster, I've been trying to catch your eye all evening and you haven't looked up once. Now are you going to take me home or not?'"

Gay threw her blond head back and roared. "You rat. That's not true, either, and you know it!"

Blanche smiled a little stiffly. "Well, never mind, it's just lovely that you two did meet . . . somehow. Poor Gay has been so alone since the Congressman's untimely death. My, what a pity that was. He and Gay made such a lovely couple."

"Yes, that's what everyone tells me," Andy said.

"And that lovely little daughter, Gaylynn. She's such a lovely little thing. She looks a great deal like the Congressman, don't you think, Captain?"

"I never met the Congressman," Andy said. "I've only been in Washington about a year now." He pushed his chair back and said,

"Gay, I wonder if I could use your telephone? I really ought to call the office and tell them where I am."

"Of course," Gay said. She stood up with Andy. "You two will excuse us a moment, won't you? I want to talk to Mattie a moment about lunch."

Once inside the house, Gay whispered, "What's this bullshit about calling your office? You know damned well they know where to find you if they ever need you."

"I guess I needed a breath of air," Andy said. "And speaking of bullshit . . ."

"Now, lover, there's no harm in gilding the lily a little. Lesson number thirty-seven in politics: impress everyone you run across. You never know when they might be useful."

"That's another thing, this politics business."

She grinned and touched his face. "You're just mad because Howard and Blanche have been giving you the old third degree. They're only trying to protect me, honey babe. You know how it is with us merry widows, all hot and bothered from lack of sex. We're pushovers for unscrupulous young bachelors like you."

Andy had put in too much time with Gay to be able to keep a straight face. For a clock's tock of time they stared at each other silently, then they both began to laugh.

"Me?" Andy said. "I'm the one who needs protection. I'm just a poor innocent little country boy, snared in the clutches of a designing older woman."

She giggled. "You bastard. If you're so damned innocent, stay in your own room tonight. Maybe you should anyway." She fluttered her eyelashes at him. "I wouldn't want my dear old friends to get the wrong idea about you. Howard's got connections all over the place. I want them to like you."

"The hell with that."

"But what if they hear you tippy-toeing through the halls in the dark of night?"

"Gay, honey, they don't have to listen for suspicious sounds. With that charming, sweet, big mouth of yours, you'll tell them all about it at breakfast tomorrow morning anyway."

3

"Hey, you hear about them spies?"

Dietrich raised his head abruptly from the shelf of hardware tools and looked back at the teen-age clerk behind the soda fountain. A radio on the counter yodeled tinny doggerel: *Give me land, lots of land, under starry skies above.* Even in his alarm, Dietrich's mind absorbed words of the song, and quick association rushed in. Yellow-green mesquite trees and dry brown land stretching from blue horizon to blue horizon. He blotted out the image.

A customer took a stool at the soda fountain and said, "What spies?" He had two little boys with him, and he was dressed foolishly. Blue shorts and a brown shirt, left open to exhibit an aging, almost hairless chest. Summer people, probably. New York from the accent, but then all eastern accents sounded harsh to Dietrich's ear.

"About ten or twelve of them," the teen-age clerk yapped. "Just down the beach from here. The Coast Guard spotted them. They come in by sub, that's for sure. One of the Teasdale brothers up at Montauk saw a whole fleet of subs putting out to sea this morning."

"Sure, sure," the customer said. He seemed unperturbed. The little boys ran to the comic-book rack near Dietrich. Dietrich suppressed an urge to leave. Instead, he forced himself to glance at the kids casually, then move to the magazine rack, closer to the soda counter. He chose a copy of *Popular Mechanics* and began leafing through it.

"No, it's real this time," the little clerk said. "The Coast Guard fellows found tracks all over the place. Mr. Kennedy said there might have been as many as twenty of them, landing on different beaches between here and Southampton."

"Yeah, sure," the customer said. "Kennedy went down there and counted them in person, I guess. Give me a block of ice, Al. We've got a bunch of freeloaders coming out this afternoon."

"Well, but Mr. Kennedy says the Coast Guard has called in the FBI," the clerk said, sounding deflated. "A block of ice, Mr. Ross? I'm afraid we're all out of ice this weekend. You might try the gas station."

"Everybody is out of everything these days," the customer said. "Hell, what happens if the war lasts clear into '43? Are we going to have to close down the country?"

"Our soldier boys come first, Mr. Ross. It takes sacrifice to win a war."

"I don't see how a block of ice contributes much to the war effort," the customer said. One of the little boys clamored for a cherry Coke, but his father got up wordlessly and headed out the front door. The two boys followed, whining their disappointment.

Dietrich added the magazine to his small stack of purchases. A bottle of snail poison. A shiny pair of hedge clippers. Sticking out of his jacket pocket was a pair of ragged gardening gloves and a trowel encrusted with dried mud, stolen earlier from a garage left temptingly open to the dawn. The garage had also provided him with an old hoe, which he had leaned in a corner as he entered the store. A few trappings appropriate to an itinerant workman, Dietrich had decided, would help provide camouflage.

"That'll be a dollar sixty-five," the clerk said.

But Dietrich didn't pay right away. He slid onto one of the stools and said, "Give me a cherry Coke." He tried to say it rapidly, without any twang or drawl. When in Rome, blend into the surroundings.

The clerk was sullen. "A fat lot Mr. Ross knows," he said. "Double shot of cherry?"

"Sure, why not," Dietrich said, keeping it casual.

"They'll murder him in his bed one of these nights," the clerk said with relish. "I guess he'll believe me then."

"Maybe he's heard that kind of rumor before," Dietrich said.

"Yeah, but this time it's for real," the clerk assured him. "Boy, I'd like to see Mr. Ross's face when the FBI hits town."

"You think they'll really come?" Dietrich said.

"You bet they will. Are you kidding? With German spies all over the place? Sure they'll come. Maybe they're already here."

Dietrich put his hand in his pocket and fingered one of the sodden twenty-dollar bills he had put there, and drew it out under the counter. It was still wet. Too wet. To distract the young clerk, he nodded at the radio and said, "Funny it hasn't been on the news. Or has it?"

The clerk glanced at the radio. "Nah, those radio people are always worried they'll scare folks. Teasdale, up at Montauk, he spotted at least three subs. For real. But they'll never put that kind of thing on the radio."

Dietrich quickly placed his wet twenty on the counter and reached for the Coke, letting his hand sweep clumsily. The glass toppled and spilled all over the counter, and Dietrich jumped up to avoid the sticky flood. "Damn," he said. "That was clumsy." His magazine was wet. So were the clippers. More importantly, so was the twenty-dollar bill.

The kid mopped up rapidly. "It was your fault," he said.

"I know. Don't worry, I'll pay for it."

"It's a dime for double cherry. I got to charge extra for double cherry."

"That's all right."

Somewhat mollified, the young clerk said, "You want another?"

"No, thanks." Dietrich tried to look disappointed. Watched the kid pick up the now-sticky bill with distaste and mop it with a wet rag, then slide it into the cash register. As the kid made change, Dietrich debated whether or not to tip him. A nickel? A dime? But no, he was a workman, somebody's gardener and handyman. It was bad enough that he'd been given nothing smaller than a twenty before he left Germany, but he was banking on the kid figuring it was his week's wages. He took the change and pocketed all of it. "Sorry about the mess," he said.

The kid watched the change disappear without any apparent consideration of a tip and turned sullen again. "Yeah," he said.

Outside, his hoe over his shoulder, Dietrich looked at the sunny Amagansett street, trying to decide what to do. Probably the kid was talking through his hat, spreading the usual wartime rumors. Only this time there could be some substance to it. Damn that overeager U-boat captain, cranking up the diesels last night while there were still people on the beach. Now there would be officials out here, poking around, asking questions.

What's more, the captain had landed them off target. Amagansett, not East Hampton. Actually, it was rather a remarkable piece of navigation, coming up only three miles from target after three thousand miles of ocean. But it created a problem for later. Where was Dietrich to rendezvous with the submarine at the end of his mission? Here? East Hampton? The captain would surface only long enough to see Dietrich's flashing signal from the beach. But suppose Dietrich was on the wrong beach? Perhaps it wouldn't matter. The captain thought he had dropped the men at East Hampton, so he would return to East Hampton. If the weather was good enough for him to get his bearings. If the weather wasn't good, if it was another foggy night, he wouldn't be able to see Dietrich's signal anyway.

Problems. There were always problems on these hasty missions. At least Dasch and his men had made it. Chopping skunk cabbage and fiddleheads from the lawn of a shuttered house near the Amagansett station, working slowly enough so that, if he was noticeable in any way at all, it was only because workmen didn't always get out so early, Dietrich had watched them board the train that morning, obviously oblivious of the furor and excitement their encounter on the beach last night had created.

Now the problem was how Dietrich was to get out of here. No train, not if there was a chance the FBI might be called in. Better not to steal a car, either, better not to leave a trace. It was near noon, far too late for an alternate mode of transportation that had been suggested to him—hitching a ride with the daily exodus of trucks bearing fish and early vegetables to the city—but somebody somewhere surely would be going into town.

He tucked the sticky new hedge clippers under his arm and squared his shoulders and started walking southwest. Southwest, if he could walk a couple of thousand miles, that's where home was. Had been. Once. It didn't matter now. What mattered was the next step and the next. Somewhere on the edge of town he would stop and put on the frayed gardening gloves, dirty the new clippers. The more thorough the camouflage the better, particularly with the threat of FBI involvement.

4

The Director of the Federal Bureau of Investigation looked at the ring of faces surrounding his desk and said, "Opinions?"

One of the senior agents said, "It appears to be authentic, sir. Three of our agents have examined the confiscated crates. They found an explosive material in brick form, some shaped to look like lumps of coal and painted black, fuse coils, detonators, incendiary devices disguised to look like pen-and-pencil sets. Practically a full arsenal, sir. Our New York office has concluded that the contents are of foreign origin."

"That doesn't necessarily mean German," the Director said.

"There are the uniforms, sir. The Coast Guard dug up a duffel bag which contained four sets of military fatigues. The buttons bear the insignia of the German Navy."

"Perhaps it was only some kind of sortie," another of the agents said. "Perhaps they merely buried the explosives on the beach and went back to the submarine."

"Unlikely," the first agent said. "Why would they discard the uniforms?"

The Director drummed his fingers on the desk. "I don't like it," he said, "but it looks as though we're stuck with it. Get on the tele-type. I want our best New York agents out there on that beach where the explosives were found. Rent a house somewhere in the area. A full twenty-four-hour watch. If anyone comes back for those boxes, I want our people to be there, waiting."

"Yes, sir."

"And a team to question aliens. I want every alien on that island interrogated. Nobody could have landed that smoothly without help."

"Yes, sir. Anything else?"

"That depends. Where are those crates now?"

"They've been transferred to our New York office."

"Good. I want the Coast Guard frozen out of this. If we have to risk taking the blame, then I don't intend to share the credit. Thank them for their co-operation and shut the door in their faces."

"Yes, sir. I'll pass that word along. Discreetly."

The Director waited until the room had cleared, then leaned back and laced his fingers across his belly, his bulging brow knitted in consternation. Amateurs. The world was filled with amateurs. Even the so-called professionals were amateurs. The U. S. Navy, allowing German U-boats to wander at will off the East Coast. Great God. The first U-boats hadn't come until January, more than a month after war was declared, yet they had caught the U. S. Navy totally unprepared. Five miserable U-boats. Only five. But in the first ten days they had sunk twenty-five American merchant ships. It was a shooting gallery, a paradise for German submarines. Ships running fully lit. Lighthouses and navigational buoys blinking away. Cities and resort areas lighting up the horizon. Now, six months later, every beach on the East Coast was dirty with oil from sunken ships and the whole of New England and the Central Atlantic states was strangling in a gasoline shortage.

But for all their rampaging success in coastal waters, this was the first time they had been brazen enough to try a landing. Nazi spies fresh from Germany? Here in the United States? Well, by God, he'd already proved to the German masterminds that they weren't dealing solely with amateurs or inept professionals. When it came to spies, they were up against a top-notch professional organization that wouldn't blow it. They were up against the FBI.

Of course, the FBI's successful roundup of the entire German espionage system in America the previous year had started with a lucky chance, but the Director took full credit for turning that chance to his nation's advantage. It began when a naturalized German-Jew named William Sebold, returning from a trip to Germany, walked in off the street and announced to FBI agents that, coerced by Nazi intelligence men with threats of harm to his family, he had just turned German spy. The Director decided on a cat-and-mouse game. Sebold got an FBI-built shortwave radio station and a mid-Manhattan office fully equipped with hidden mikes, fake mirrors and FBI men behind the mirrors shooting films of every visitor who slipped into Sebold's office to pick up microphotographic instructions brought from Germany and turn over messages on American war production and shipping schedules. When the FBI was sure it had every member of the ring pinpointed, it moved in. By early 1941, even before Pearl Harbor, thirty-three top Nazi agents were convicted on espionage or related charges.

And that was just the beginning. With Pearl Harbor and the requirement that enemy aliens come in to register, the FBI, with a little necessary help from co-operating law-enforcement agencies, started a clean sweep. Japanese. Germans. Italians. A handful of Hungarians and Rumanians and one Bulgarian. It made for a huge workload—2,601 aliens released when they managed to prove their loyalty immediately, another 1,017 released after a hearing, but 4,345 interned, 34 repatriated, 2,804 paroled, some 1,200 cases still awaiting disposition.

Yes, he'd broken the back of the Axis espionage system. It was bizarre, it was insulting, but no wonder they were trying to smuggle new men in.

The Director leaned back in his chair, pondering. Maybe he should have left some relatively harmless remnant of the Sebold group out of last year's trap. He could see, in retrospect, that it might have been profitable just to keep a few men under surveillance to provide a linkage to any new Nazi intelligence efforts. Like this one. After all, he couldn't expect another set of spies just to walk in off the street.

"It was like shooting fish in a barrel," one of his men had proclaimed with happy triumph when they'd picked up the Sebold contacts.

Only now he had no barrel waiting for these men.

Where the hell were they? How do you catch virgin agents once they disappear underground?

5

George Dasch knew New York intimately, with good reason. Since stowing away as a youth on a ship bound from Germany to Philadelphia, he had spent many of the intervening years as a New

York busboy, fry cook and, finally gaining status, as a waiter. Naturally he hadn't told them that back in Germany. Being a waiter was no better than being a servant. Maybe it was worse. The tipping system left his income at the whim of the customer. How he'd hated that, taking tips. Better to become like the men whose manners he had studied, the ones who sat eating the food he was forced to serve. He'd tried again and again to elevate his station in life, but the one time things were looking good—that time he'd moved to St. Louis and started doing pretty well selling sanctuary supplies for a firm servicing Catholic churches—his fool of a boss got himself fired, and the new sales manager brought in his own men, and it was back to New York and the restaurants. So he'd lied and told German officialdom he had been a salesman for an export-import company, it sounded more dignified. Had America not refused him the dignity and pride in work that every man has the right to aspire to, he might never have returned to Germany.

And now the Germans had sent him back. At the moment, it seemed like a cruel joke, and at the busy Long Island Railroad transfer point in Jamaica, Dasch sank into the anonymity of New York like a hunted fox slinking wearily into a familiar burrow. He arranged to meet Heinck and Quirin late that afternoon in an Automat at Eighth Avenue and Thirty-fourth Street in Manhattan, and took Peter Burger away with him to replace their soiled clothing, using funds out of the money satchel.

They had money enough to start a bank, but even that was a worrisome problem to Dasch as he led Burger to a haberdasher near the railroad station. The money was mainly in consecutively numbered fifty-dollar bills that had reached Germany before the war, but who in God's name could know whether the United States had kept track of the numbers and was watching for the bills to show up? Dasch had warned his men over and over that no more than one bill should be spent in any one place. And he'd already saved them from certain execution because of money, although a fat lot the team seemed to appreciate it. Well, maybe it was a member of the Florida team who had first spotted the problem, but had he not pointed out its true significance? There were gold certificates among the bills Kappe had first received from an Abwehr II man in charge of the money matters. God in heaven, gold certificates, which the U.S. had withdrawn from circulation years before! Try to spend one of those, and see what kind of an investigation would start before you could even get out of the store! That was the trouble with this whole operation. That was the kind of care German intelligence took of men being sent on a dangerous mission!

They cautiously bought cheap slacks at one store. No problems with the bills. Dasch began to feel a little better. "Nothing like spending someone else's money, eh?" he told Burger.

Burger grinned a little. "It's our duty," he said obediently. "We must change as many bills as possible, to have a supply of safe money."

And soon they were on a shopping spree. Finding their cheap slacks unsatisfactory, they stopped at another clothier's and chose summer-weight suits; then, while the alterations were being made, they raided a nearby dry-goods store, buying shirts, underwear, socks, ties and handkerchiefs. At a shoe store down the street, Burger bought a pair of two-tone black-and-white shoes with wing tips, and Dasch picked out a brown pair which he thought would go nicely with his suit. Dasch also led them into a jewelry store where he bought an expensive watch. They shopped so intently that they forgot to take time out to eat, so by the time they took a train in to Manhattan and walked into the Automat to wait for Heinck and Quirin, they were good and hungry. Dasch had plowed through two salads and a glass of milk and was eating coconut pie when Heinck and Quirin came in about fifteen minutes later. He'd missed fresh foods on the submarine.

Richard Quirin, his eyes excited and his enormous nose almost twitching, plopped down across from Dasch and blurted, "We saw a parade! On Fifth Avenue. There must have been a hundred thousand soldiers!"

Heinck slid in beside him. "I wish I'd had a machine gun. We could have ended the war right there."

Dasch eyed the clothes they had chosen. Loud checked jackets, cheap trousers, colorful sport shirts open at the collar. Their arms were full of other packages and string-tied parcels. "Where did you buy those clothes?" Dasch said. "You'll attract attention dressed like that. People will look at you."

Heinck frowned. "George, what's wrong with you? Why are you so nervous?"

"Nervous? I'm not nervous."

Heinck looked at Dasch oddly, but he finally shrugged and changed the subject. "Say, did you know they have gas rationing up here?" he said. "You have to get little colored stickers to put on your car. You should see the lines of cars waiting for gas. A man told us it's because of the U-boats, prowling off the East Coast. They're sinking everything in sight." He smiled. "It makes you proud, doesn't it."

"I expected it," Dasch said. But he hadn't. It made him freshly nervous, hearing how things had changed. He said, "We'd better not spend too much time together here. It's too public. Maybe we should check into hotels now. As leader of the team, I am to take a room at the Governor Clinton. Peter will come with me. It's big and busy, so it's just the kind of place we'll need. I'll be registered under the name George John Davis, from St. Louis. Peter will use his own name. If there's an emergency, call on the phone. Don't come by."

"All right," Heinck said. "Where do you want us to stay?"

"Try the Chesterfield. It's near here. Don't forget to buy suitcases before you check in. Hotel clerks notice people without suitcases."

"Stop worrying," Heinck said. "We know all that."

"Just be careful. Also, I think maybe we should stay close to our hotels for a while. Stay off the streets for a week or so until Kerling and the others arrive from Florida. We don't want to make any foolish mistakes."

"What's this?" Heinck said, smiling slyly. "Is our leader frightened?"

"Of course not!" Dasch said. "Only . . . well, don't forget that boy on the beach last night. If he tells anyone about us, they'll start searching. We may as well wait until things cool off a bit."

"Let them search," Heinck said. "How can they find us in a city of so many millions?"

Dasch looked from Heinck to Quirin and Burger. They were all watching him oddly now. He dropped his eyes and said, "I just meant we should be careful. It makes sense to be careful."

"All right, all right," Heinck said, "but hiding in hotel rooms is the quickest way to attract attention. We can at least start looking over the bus stations and railroad depots and the department stores owned by Jews."

"What for?" Dasch said.

"What do you think?" Heinck said. He grinned. "To stick a couple of bombs in their ears. What better way to tell the world we're here?"

Dasch felt a small bubble of . . . what? fear? anger? . . . in his upper abdomen. He would have to do something about this fool, or Heinck would rush out and start planting trivial little bombs and give them all away. Whatever they were here for, it wasn't to waste time on trivial pecks at civilian morale. Kappe had given them a whole list of possible reasons for their training. Halting airplane production and disrupting rail transportation. Blasting New York's bridges and rail supplies. The list of potential targets was endless: aluminum plants in New York, St. Louis and Tennessee. The Ohio River locks near Pittsburgh, the hydroelectric plants at Niagara Falls, some cryolite plant in Philadelphia, and God only knew what else. But above all, nothing at first. Not for at least two weeks. Apparently some priority mission was in the wind. Kappe had warned Dasch and Kerling, as team leaders, almost at the last minute, looking harried, that they might be receiving special instructions at some point early in their sojourn in the United States. He wouldn't elaborate. Just told them that they were to get their men established safely and wait. Dasch hadn't paid much attention. It seemed too unlikely. How could anyone send them fresh orders this late in the game? It would take more than two weeks for a letter even to get out of Germany and through the various decoy addresses in neutral countries before it could be sent to a general delivery address in New York. But wait, hadn't someone mentioned something about that on the submarine? One of the U-boat officers, appearing out of nowhere at the last minute, sticking his two cents in while Dasch was trying so hard to get his men organized? Who was that fool? No, that was ridiculous. What would some rattled kid on his first U-boat tour know about anything? It didn't matter. The important thing was just to follow Kappe's orders, to sink into the safety of obscurity and wait. Only he would have to do something to control Heinck. Otherwise Heinck, with his characteristic impatience, would ruin everything.

"There will be no preliminary bombing," he said to Heinck. "Do you hear? None. Our orders are that we do absolutely nothing until we hear that Kerling and his men are safely in position. What do you want to do? Get them in trouble?"

"We don't have to plant the bombs right away," Heinck said. "Just look around and make some plans."

"No," Dasch said. "Don't even think about it. I'll tell you when we're ready to start." He picked up his packages and gestured at Burger to follow him.

"Wait a minute," Heinck said. "When do we meet next?"

"In a few days," Dasch said.

"I think we ought to meet tomorrow," Heinck said.

Dasch hesitated, but Burger and Quirin were still watching him uneasily. "Okay," he said. "Tomorrow night. We'll meet you at Grant's Tomb. At six-thirty."

Heinck watched as Dasch and Burger left the Automat. He settled back with a sigh and shook his head at Quirin. He said, "You know, Richard, I felt good when we came in here. Now I don't feel so good. Our glorious leader appears to have a case of the nerves. And it's catching."

Quirin nodded somberly. "Yes, I feel nervous too."

"What do you say we find our own hotel?"

"I think that would be a very good idea," Quirin said.

Twenty minutes later, Heinrich Heinck and Richard Quirin checked into the Martinique Hotel at Thirty-second and Broadway, signing the register as Henry Kaynor and Richard Quintas. It cost them $5.50 a day each, an outrageous price. But it gave them peace of mind.

THE SECOND DAY

Sunday—June 14, 1942

1

Dietrich had searched the news columns of the Sunday morning newspapers, checking every page twice, but had found no mention of the rumored submarine landings on Long Island. Perhaps that meant that everything was all right. Perhaps not. The newspaper silence could easily be some kind of police ruse. He hungered to seek out George Dasch before catching the train to Washington, D.C., in order to question him more closely about the confusion on the beach the night of the landing. But his orders were specific, and apparently with good reason. The teams were to be completely settled in and free of suspicion before Dietrich made his presence known to them, for if anything happened to compromise them, it must not happen to him. Either Dasch and his men would manage to survive the difficulties and would appear when he summoned them, or he would have to rely solely on Edward Kerling's team once they made their way north from Florida.

Before he bought his train ticket at Penn Station, he spent some time in the men's room, cleaning and brushing the sand and dirt from his clothing. He then sought the disinfected sanctuary of a pay toilet so he could unwrap one of the oilskin packets of identification cards, selecting a driver's license and a draft registration made out to Frank Daniels of Waxahachie, Texas. He also peeled the oilskin from his gun for a quick look, to make sure the salt water hadn't got to it, then rewrapped it and stuffed it back into his belt, under the leather jacket. It was too hot for the jacket, but until he reached Washington and found a place to stash his gun and the rest of his gear, he would wear it.

On the unfamiliar, unclean streets of New York and in the claustrophobic bowels of Penn Station, Dietrich had little reason to feel conspicuous. He was just one more face in a faceless crowd. But that changed once he climbed aboard the train. The Washington express looked like a troop transport. Every chair car was jammed with uniforms, filling the seats and the aisles, perched on armrests and upturned suitcases, overflowing six deep into the lavatory and vestibule sections. There was an occasional woman with a child on her lap and an older man or two in mufti, but the overwhelming majority of the passengers were khaki-clad. Soldiers on leave, soldiers on the way to new assignments in Washington, soldiers in transit to the south, soldiers with bleary eyes trying to go to sleep on their arms before the train even pulled out of the station, soldiers staring introspectively through the windows at unseen futures, soldiers brooding with homesickness behind open magazines.

Dietrich forced his way through the crowded aisles, looking for a quiet place to disappear, but there were no quiet places. He passed soldiers choking with forced laughter as they tried to impress each other with chatter, got lodged as an unwilling eavesdropper on an argument in the making between two red-faced privates about whether Doolittle's raid on Tokyo came from the Chinese mainland or from a Russian airfield, found a small opening and passed on when a third private moved to join the debate.

The train began to hiss, pant, then roll before he was settled down, and he found himself reaching out for support, jostling the arm of a corporal by the men's lavatory. The corporal gave him an ugly look and turned away. Dietrich spotted a window just outside the lavatory with a smaller than normal crowd and eased up to it, wedging himself in, thankful that the window was open.

The train gathered speed, rumbling through underground tunnels for the next several minutes, then burst into the sunlight on the other side of the Hudson, steaming through northern New Jersey. Dietrich took a deep breath and watched cluttered loading docks, tiny back yards and vigorous stands of acid green weedy growth roll by.

But here and there, among the weeds along the railway bed, grew wild roses, small, delicate, pale-pink blossoms, and Dietrich stared at them eagerly. Despite the filth and the crowding men had created, little wild roses had managed to survive. Survival was all. It was the one personal goal he had set for himself. He would do his masters' bidding, but he would go through his gaits wearing self-chosen blinders to block out all the confusions and strains their chronic in-fighting succeeded in generating. He could not afford distractions. He would follow the orders, and he would survive.

The miles clacked off behind them and the train swayed and picked up speed. The corporal by the lavatory was still watching him. But that was just another distraction. Ignore it. And stop worrying about George Dasch and his men. They were for him to use, he had been instructed, a kit of tools, nothing more, borrowed at the last minute from another Abwehr unit and probably not even told that they were being borrowed. That was the way of the Abwehr, and Dietrich approved of it. There were fewer distractions that way. But he knew things without being told. It didn't take special training to be able to deduce that the rumors around Abwehr I of how Hitler had screamed for action against the United States might be true, not when one considered the precipitate nature of his orders. It hadn't taken Oberstleutnant Grützner's grave emphasis that no single word, no faint hint, of his dual target was to be dropped to a single other Abwehr man, not when one considered the way his superiors looked when they even mentioned the name "Canaris." Hitler and Canaris. He'd never seen either of them, and didn't ever expect to. It would be like expecting to see God and Jesus strolling along a hallway. Or maybe it was God and Judas. The knowledge that his own superiors did not fully trust their titular head had come to him early. Was Admiral Wilhelm Canaris, "High C" as he was called by the admiring faction of his Abwehr subordinates, even aware of the report that the British Prime Minister and the President of the United States were to meet secretly—much less that nine of his men had been commandeered to execute them?

No, Abwehr hummed with secrets that were not secrets to any halfway observant man. Were he the head of Abwehr, instead of Canaris, there would be far stricter internal security. Masks, maybe. Fitted leather masks, issued as standard equipment, to prevent men's features from giving them away.

Dietrich smiled a little at the thought, and looked up to meet a hostile stare from the corporal by the lavatory door. The corporal had been joined by another soldier, and they were nipping from a pint bottle in a brown paper bag. Dietrich stopped smiling and told himself to stop thinking. Better to look at the scenery, what there was of it. Better to watch for wild roses and keep his own mask in place.

But after the first thirty minutes or so, the corporal's mood began

able checks to Colorado. If they were too big, his father decided they were extravagant and refused to cash them. It became a constant guessing game, trying to figure what would be small enough to suit his father, yet large enough to ease his own conscience.

Then he pulled out a sheet of paper and toyed with the idea of writing. But what could he say? Another week like the last. Initialing passes to the War Room. Shuffling the memos and duty rosters Sergeant Huffman handed him. Trying to look busy. It would be nice to write his father about this week's upcoming trip to Hyde Park on the President's train, hobnobbing with all the British security brass who would accompany the Prime Minister, but that was still classified information.

So what was there left to write about? Gay? Blond, sexy, a little plump like Mama, maybe a little managing like Mama, but with money running out of her ears. Papa was no prude. He'd understand about the blond and bedable part, although the sexual life of a son was somehow something that couldn't be casually discussed with a parent, not in this day and time. The money part, that would impress and interest Papa. He had always shared Mama's opinion that if their Andrzej would only eat his beets, keep his room tidy, study harder at long division, play harder on the high school basketball team, be polite and grateful to the local Rotary Club president (and him such a big-shot former state politician) who took such an interest in Andrzej/Andrew, why then Andrew would maybe end up running the mine that his father only worked in, and would surely become rich himself one day. But a high-powered woman like Gay would also make Papa uneasy, and Andy wasn't sure he was altogether easy about her himself.

How in hell had he ended up with a classy, crazy dame like Gay in the first place? It was like living in a harem, with six or seven women, one for each day, each mood. Give her the cue, and she became what you wanted. The playmate, giggling like a little kid, mocking, wisecracking. Sheena of the Jungle, with her crazy wild blond hair floating around her face and her teeth bared, eye-bursting with her lush figure and quick-triggered smile, slashing out of the trees to pin him helplessly to the ground. More rarely, there was the soft and tender woman, Earth goddess, all white silk and welcoming arms, melancholy madness to match his moodier nights. Bedmate, friend, imp, witch, tough, sensitive—the female as a total woman. But there was also her most recent incarnation, one which Andy hadn't yet been able to come to terms with. The mentor with the new/old toy, looking for signs of approval from strange quarters. This was the side of her which Andy had not seen until recently, and he didn't know quite what to make of it.

Of course Andy had never lacked for mentors. He'd been lucky, he guessed, dating back to the day the coach had called him off the basketball court during practice and introduced him to Mr. Allenby. Trumpets! Drums! A handshake and a friendly smile from George T. Allenby, attorney-at-law, Trinidad, Colorado's most notable citizen. "Governor Allenby," some of the townfolk called him, particularly those who weren't too sure exactly what a lieutenant-governor was, the kind who got confused and asked, "How're things up in Washington, Mr. Allenby?" instead of, "How're things up in Denver?" Allenby took a paternal interest in his town and its deserving young men, and after high school good-natured, hard-working young Andy Blaszek went to the Colorado School of Mines instead of the coal pits. Mr. Allenby was even understanding when Andy flunked trig for the second time (damn higher mathematics anyway; he, too, had had trouble with long division). Not everyone needed to be a mining engineer; switch to business administration and end up owning the mine instead of planning tunnels for one.

But there was a little matter of the Depression years lingering on when young Andy finished his degree, and it took all of Mr. Allenby's patient searching of his connections to find something a little more appropriate for his protégé than fighting forest fires and building campsites for the CCC—assistant to the president at retired Brigadier General Jeremiah Roach's cardboard-box manufacturing company.

General Roach took to his new assistant from the very first. The young man was tall and rangy, with the knobby good looks of an habitual outdoorsman, a ready and good-natured smile and a willingness to tackle any job General Roach assigned him with energy and enthusiasm. It was too bad when the company went broke, and nobody's fault but maybe General Roach's for having counted too heavily on his old Army buddies to keep him in contracts, and General Roach looked around for some compatible niche for this fine young fellow. The military? Of course, just the thing. "Peace in our time," what nonsense. The way the Germans were kicking up, anyone could see there would eventually be war. Young Andy would be in on the ground floor. The general still had friends in the right places. He'd keep track of the boy, too. Least he could do.

General Horace Tucker, for whom Andy ended up working, likewise had few initial criticisms of his new personal aide. Young Lieutenant Blaszek needed to be taught how to dress, that was the main thing. Those trousers, their crease wasn't quite, quite straight. Send them back to the cleaner's until they learned how to press them right. Tie the tie just so. Cut the thick black hair shorter. Buff the black shoes to a mirror gloss. In time, under General Tucker's tutelage, Lieutenant Blaszek became Captain Blaszek, and looked damned good in a perfectly tailored (and pressed) uniform with piping on the sleeve and a Good Conduct Medal on his chest. Good enough, in fact, that General Tucker used to lend him out as escort to spare ladies for those cocktail and dinner parties in Washington.

That's how Captain Andrew Blaszek had first met Gay. Gay, the handsome young widow lady whose beloved and influential husband had, while eating *tournedos morateur*, choked to death in her presence (and that of twelve dinner guests) nearly two years ago. Gay, who dropped out of the party swirl for the polite year and went into mourning, content to lavish her presence and her lonely affection on one person only, her six-year-old daughter. Then, as she tentatively emerged from her weeds, Andy's good general decided she should be out in the mainstream once more among the bright people and had lent her his young aide from Colorado as an escort to a formal dinner party at the Mayflower.

They had stayed through soup, feeling something unfathomable and electric rising between them, then Gay begged off on the basis of a headache and they had headed back to Maryland and her six-bedroom house. Andy didn't know how it happened, still couldn't remember all the words that passed between them, stumbling words that ricocheted against each other, but he remembered those bedrooms. Except for the little daughter's room (due to Andy's sense of delicacy, not Gay's), they had made love in every last one of them over the weekend, that first weekend, while General Tucker called around town, getting, as Gay later phrased it, progressively more pissed because he couldn't locate his vanished aide.

That had started it. Andy kept his apartment in town, a place where mail could accumulate and his spare (perfectly pressed) uniforms could hang, but he spent his weekends and his evenings at Gay's house, sometimes in a guest room when the daughter was home, waiting for the mother to come to him in the night, sometimes as lord of Gay's own giant bed, when daughter and domestics were out of pocket.

The general never forgave him (like most men who gazed on Gay's lively face and ripe body, he undoubtedly harbored his own unfulfilled hopes), and took his revenge two months later, on December 10, 1941. With the attack on Pearl Harbor, General Tucker sat back and entertained sober thoughts of what might happen to him if he were lucky enough to draw a combat theater, and decided forthwith to retire to a fish hatchery in Iowa and draw his sizable military pension. But a faint, remembered warmth for lucky, good-natured, well-dressed young Captain Blaszek stayed General Tucker's impulse to recommend him for active service. Instead, he gave Andy a lukewarm rating as command material, then dictated adjectives of high praise to a quartermaster general in Fort Sill, Oklahoma, who was seeking a clean, mannerly young aide. When Andy's reassignment papers came through, they were predictably a one-way ticket to Lawton, Oklahoma. General Tucker thought of Mrs. Gay Cogswell's cleavage and of the dreary Wichita Mountain artillery range, and was content.

But Gay wasn't. The late Congressman had had many good friends, and she quickly scouted around and pulled some political strings and announced to Andy she had gotten him attached to the White House. Andy felt uncomfortable about it. Gold stars were going up in windows, and posters were proclaiming, "Uncle Sam Wants *You*," and Andy had inner doubts that Uncle Sam really wanted him to be nothing but a desk drone. But every time he thought of active duty on a war front in those early months, General Tucker's final rating report rose up to haunt him, and faced with the realistic choice between the Fort Sills of the world and the ample bed of Gay Cogswell, Andy did the rational thing. He accepted the White House and Gay.

The pity was that he had never even been able to introduce her to his father. He'd tried. Leave was easy to arrange when you used White House stationery, and he had asked Gay to come with him to Colorado, to meet his father and see where he had grown up. Somehow, she always had a good excuse for not accompanying him, and he always ended up postponing the leave. There were times lately when he began to suspect that Gay, so casual, so warm, so open, was more than just the tiniest bit of a snob, but he didn't like to think about it.

But hell, that wasn't something he could lay on the old man in a letter. He sighed and jotted a quick note, saying things were popping and he would write more after next week, with something interesting to report. That sounded nice and mysterious. Papa would enjoy pondering what big affairs his Andrzej was mixed up in, and Andy would take care not to disillusion him. He stuffed the note into an envelope with the check and was hunting up a three-cent stamp when the phone rang. He grabbed it and said, "Hello?"

Her voice, a blend of mischief and blatant sex, purred at him. "They're gone, lover. The coast is clear. Come on back."

He frowned at the phone. "Yes, madam? Who is this? I fear you have the wrong number, madam."

"You bastard," she breathed. "Get back on out here. I miss your body."

He grinned. "Gee, I don't know, lady. I'm all booked up this month with a nice widow woman out in Maryland. What did you say your name was?"

"This is Cinderella's wicked stepsister, you asshole. And if you don't get out here quick, I'm going to borrow her glass slipper and plonk you right between the eyebrows."

"Ah," he said, "now I think I place you. Blond hair? Foul tongue? Big mouth? Give me a few minutes, Goldilocks. I've got to drop some uniforms at the dry cleaners for the Hyde Park trip."

She was silent for a moment, then said, "You don't have to go on that trip, Andy. You're just doing it to get even with me."

"That's not true," he said. Then, a little edgily, "Although I will admit that I'm getting a little tired of playing tennis with your house guests."

She let another silence hang for three heartbeats, then said, "No one's coming next weekend. I promise, Andy."

"Don't, Gay," he said quietly. "You knew I'd be up at Hyde Park, so why waste guests?"

"Bastard," she said. Then he could almost feel her begin to smile over the phone. Her voice became friendly. "Okay, Andy. We'll keep it clean. Are you coming?"

"You bet," he said. "Tell Mattie to take the night off and go play bingo. I feel like clattering around in the kitchen."

"That's a lovely idea," she said. "And I'll call Miz Cogswell the elder and ask her to keep Gaylynn one more night. We'll cook nude."

"Maybe *you* will, but I'm wearing an apron. I always get spattered with grease when I cook."

She laughed. "By all means, lover. Wear the apron. Save the machinery for later."

He hung up smiling. His eyes fell on the note he had written to his father. What *would* the old man think to discover his son had fallen for a 32-year-old widow woman (three years his elder, for God's sake), with a six-year-old daughter and everything? What would he really think of his young Andrzej's newest . . . mentor?

He put the thought out of his mind and put the envelope in his pocket, then he picked up the empty suitcase (might as well get some use out of the damned thing) and carried it into his bedroom and tidily packed all the dirty uniforms he ran across so he could have them cleaned and ready in time for the Hyde Park trip.

3

George Dasch paced from the hotel window to the dresser, from the dresser to the window. His teammate, Peter Burger, watched solemnly from the side of the bed, looking progressively more nervous with each circuit of the room.

"You've hardly said a word since breakfast," Burger complained. "What is it? What's troubling you?"

Dasch continued pacing. "I may have to make a very difficult decision," he said.

"What kind of decision?"

Dasch didn't answer.

"George?" Burger insisted. "George, please. At least stop that pacing. You're driving me crazy."

"Then go back to your own room," Dasch said harshly.

"I won't go until you tell me what's troubling you."

Dasch sighed. He walked slowly to the bed and sat down beside his teammate. "I suppose I ought to tell someone," he said. "I may need some advice. The thing is, we really screwed up. That damned Coast Guard kid. That changes everything. If they catch us, they'll kill us, you know."

Burger stared at the rumpled bedspread. "Heinck said they'd never find us in the city."

"What does he know? I tell you, these G-men really know their business. You know what they do to spies in wartime. And we're spies."

"But we're safe now, aren't we?"

Dasch shook his head. "Not as long as there are people who can identify us. Besides, those G-men have other ways to find us. They collect clues. Fingerprints. Little bits of glass and paint. Clothing. They can learn almost anything just by running some tests. You read about it all the time."

"They still wouldn't know where to look for us."

"You think not?" Dasch said. "They only have to catch one of us, you know. That damned Heinck. He's so damned careless. Or Richard. They'd make him tell about the rest of us. Then suddenly, one night when we aren't expecting it, they step out of a dark doorway and grab us by the arm and we've had it. From then on we're dead men."

Burger looked shocked. After a pause, he said, "How do they do it to spies? Do they shoot them, or hang them?"

"Shoot them, I imagine. Hanging is for criminals. Hell, I don't know. Maybe they use the electric chair. What difference does it make? We end up just as dead."

"Maybe we could . . . just disappear. Not do anything."

"They'd still catch us eventually. That Coast Guard kid saw my face. So did the stationmaster. We haven't got a chance."

"What can we do?"

Dasch took a deep breath. "I'm not sure," he said. "I've been thinking about it, but I only get one answer. Give up. Give ourselves up before they catch us. Surrender."

Burger winced as though he had been kicked in the stomach. He rubbed his nose and said, "For the love of God, George. We can't do that. Giving up wouldn't make any difference. They'd kill us anyway. We'd still be spies."

"Not if we gave ourselves up before Heinck does something crazy. We could say we didn't want to be spies. We could say we hate the Nazis and that's why we're giving ourselves up."

"What if they didn't believe us?"

"They'd have to believe us," Dasch said. He glanced at Burger's trembling chin. "I'm sorry, Peter. I can't think of any other way. I've tried. God, I've tried."

"You've already made up your mind?"

"Not yet," Dasch said morosely. "But I have to decide soon. If we wait too long, they might catch up with us and arrest us. Then we lose the advantage. God, if only I knew what was best. What should we do, Peter? What do you think we should do?"

They were still going over the same ground, over and over, as they got off the subway late that afternoon at 116th Street and started up the underground steps on their way to Grant's Tomb. Dasch walked slowly, hands in pockets, but soon, too soon, he could see Richard Quirin and Heinrich Heinck in their loud jackets, sitting on the broad sweep of steps up to the tomb, as if enjoying the waning sunlight.

Burger said, for the twentieth time, "I don't think Heinrich and Richard will go along with it."

"Maybe not," Dasch said. "Well, we won't tell them."

"What about the Florida team?" Burger said. "Would you turn them in, too?"

"How can I turn them in? I don't even know where they are."

"You have the handkerchief, George. With the mail addresses. Haupt's uncle in Chicago and Kerling's friend in New York." He shook his head, chin down, watching the cracks in the sidewalk. "I don't think you should tell them about the handkerchief. It looks just like any ordinary handkerchief. They'd never know, really, George, they'd never know."

"All right, damn it, I won't tell about the handkerchief. To hell with the Florida team. They're on their own." Quirin and Heinck had spotted them by now and had risen to their feet. Dasch said, "Look, Peter, I know this is going to be difficult, but we've got to act as though nothing has happened while we're talking to the boys. Can you do it?"

"I can try," Burger said. "But you've got to promise not to make up your mind yet. Not until we talk more about it. Do you promise, George? Please?"

"All right, all right. Don't worry," Dasch said.

They headed up the steps. Dasch forced a smile as Heinck and Quirin came down to meet them.

"You're almost an hour late," Heinck said. "We were beginning to worry."

"Worry?" Dasch said. "Why? Everything is fine, isn't it?"

"Well, yes, but . . ." Heinck cocked his head. "You seem to be in a good mood. That's a change. You acted funny yesterday."

Dasch laughed, trying to sound cheerful. "Of course I did. I was nervous. We all were. Keyed up and tired. A good night's rest makes all the difference."

Heinck nodded. "Good. That's good. That's better than yesterday."

"Don't worry about me," Dasch said. "I know what I'm doing. Did you and Richard have any trouble getting into a hotel room?"

Heinck and Quirin exchanged quick looks and Heinck said, "No. None at all. We're fine. You?"

"It went smoothly," Dasch said. He fidgeted, then said, "I really don't see any point in our meeting daily like this. I am going to set our next meeting for Tuesday. I don't think Kerling and the boys can get here before then. There's a restaurant on West Fifty-second Street. It's called The Swiss Chalet. Seven o'clock?"

"Do they serve German food?" Heinck asked.

Dasch nodded.

"Good," Heinck said. "Perhaps we can have dinner together."

"Sure," Dasch said. "That's a good idea. We'll see you there." He watched them start down the steps, then, on impulse, said, "Heinrich, wait."

Heinck stopped and looked back. "Yes?"

Dasch opened and closed his mouth, then said, "Nothing. Buy some new clothes, will you?"

"Sure. In a couple of days."

Dasch watched the two men stroll down the steps and strike off toward the subway stop. He continued to stand there, hands fiddling unconsciously at a button on his coat, until Heinck and Quirin were a block and a half away. Then he straightened and said, "Let's go."

Burger, who had waited uneasily for him to speak, said, "Where?"

"A phone booth," Dasch said. He started down the steps.

Burger caught up quickly, looking frightened. "Who are you going to call?"

"The FBI," Dasch said.

"You can't! You promised. You said we could talk about it."

"This isn't to turn us in," Dasch said. "This is just a call for the record. So if they catch us before we're ready, we can say we already tried."

"It's too soon," Burger said. "We don't have to do it this soon."

"I won't tell them much," Dasch said. "I won't even use my right name. I'll use the code name for the operation. I'll say I'm Franz Pastorius. That way I can prove later that it was us."

Burger brushed his hand across his face, rubbing sweat from his forehead. He drew a heavy breath and said, "George, did you ever dream of falling? You know, when everything drops out from under you and you fall and fall and keep on falling?"

Dasch looked at him sympathetically and nodded. "Yes. I've dreamed that. But I always wake up before I hit."

4

Special Agent Fred Shea hung up his telephone fifteen minutes later and shook his head. Boy, that one was a lulu. He rolled a sheet of paper into his typewriter and poised his fingers over the keys. What did the man say his name was? *Pastorius? Postorius?* It probably didn't matter. It seemed every nut in New York had been on the phone to the FBI office in the six months since Pearl Harbor. Still, you could never tell. Someday one of these nut calls might pay off. He began to type:

Re: F. D. Postorius, Memorandum for the file.

Please be advised that at 7:51 p.m. on this date, Frank Daniel Postorius called this office by telephone, and advised the writer that he had made the call for the purpose of having a record of it, in this office. Postorius advised that he had arrived in New York City two days ago from Germany. He would not reveal his present address in the city, and remained uncommunicative concerning any information that he might be able to furnish this office. He refused to come to this office and report his information, but he wanted this office to make a record of his call. This memo is being prepared only for the purpose of recording the call made by Postorius.

He pulled the memo from the typewriter and read it over for spelling errors, then signed it and laid it in his out box.

Because the New York office of the FBI was so large and handled so many different affairs, word of the discovery at Amagansett and the ongoing hunt on Long Island had not yet filtered down to Shea's cubicle.

So he couldn't be blamed when his mind turned to other things and the memo was forgotten.

THE THIRD DAY

Monday—June 15, 1942

I

She was a stout little woman with friendly eyes and small, helpless-looking hands. Her aging face peered cheerfully through the screen door at him. She popped a morsel of cheese and crackers into her mouth and said, between ladylike chews, "Can I help you?" There were cracker crumbs on her upper lip, clinging to a faint gray mustache.

"I've come about the room," Dietrich said quietly.

She brushed her fingers on her blue-and-white print dress and said, "Of course. Come in." She unlatched the screen and swung it open. "I'm Mrs. Fikinney."

"Daniels," Dietrich said. "Frank Daniels."

"How do you do," she said. "The room is on the second floor. Thirty dollars a week. You have to clean it yourself, I'm afraid. My girl went off home to Shreveport three months ago, and I'm beginning to think she's never going to make it back. But you get icebox privileges. All my tenants get icebox privileges."

"Thirty a week?" Dietrich said. "That's a little high."

Mrs. Fikinney smiled at him, an almost flirtatious little smile that told him suddenly that she must have been very pretty in her youth. "It *is* high, isn't it? I'm sorry, but it's the standard rate. Housing is at a premium these days."

Dietrich smiled back. "Yes, I'm finding that out," he said. "I've been looking for a place most of the morning. Most of them are rented by the time I get there."

"My room would be too," she said, "but I didn't like the looks of the people who came by to see it. Married, they said, but I didn't see any wedding ring. Would you like to inspect the room?"

Dietrich glanced around the airy foyer in which they stood. The

white paint was mold-spotted near the ceiling and the soft crimson
rug underfoot was old, but the big, rambling house must have been
imposing enough in its day, a graceful surrounding for a graceful
young Mrs. Fikinney who flirted automatically when she smiled.
"I'm sure I'll like it," he said. "If it's available, I'll take it."

The young smile appeared again briefly on faded lips. "I'll get
you a key. Just come with me back to the kitchen. You'll be sure to
lock up carefully if you come in late at night, won't you, Mr.
Daniels? My mother-in-law and I are all alone here now, except for
Jim. And the tenants, of course. It gives me the spooks. If you hear
anyone scream in the night, don't worry. It's just me, having
another nightmare. Better yet, *do* worry. What if it were an in-
truder? I hope you'd come to my rescue."

She laughed and led him down a hallway booby-trapped at regular intervals with heavy old mahogany chairs. A bell—silver, from
its tone—tinkled sporadically from somewhere to the right, but
Mrs. Fikinney ignored it. The mother-in-law? No matter. At the
back of the house, Dietrich followed the woman into a linoleum-
floored kitchen and watched patiently as she rummaged through a
drawer by the sink. The room was hot, partially because of the
summer weather and partially because of an iron propped upright
on an ironing board next to a table. He'd apparently interrupted her
in the middle of housekeeping chores. There was a glass of milk and
a small plate of cheese-and-cracker sandwiches on the table, next to
a huge pile of linens.

She produced a key and said, "How long will you be staying, Mr.
Daniels?"

"I'm not certain yet. A couple of weeks, probably."

"You have someone in the hospital?"

Dietrich raised an eyebrow. "I beg your pardon?"

"The University Hospital," she said. "Most of my roomers stay
here so they can be close to relatives while they're mending. You've
got someone there?"

"No. I'm here on business."

"Oh? What kind of business? If you don't mind my asking, that
is."

"Not at all," Dietrich said. "I'm in the oil business, in a very
minor way. Wildcatting, down near San Antonio. But we've been
having a considerable problem getting enough pipe, so I've come up
to see what can be done about our priority rating. The country
needs oil nowadays, you know."

"Oh, my, doesn't it ever. I wish I was in the oil business. Maybe I could get enough gasoline to keep my old Packard running. Well, that'll be thirty dollars in advance, Mr. Daniels. Unless you want to pay for the whole two weeks. I'm afraid I can't guarantee the room past what you pay."

"I'll pay for two weeks," he said. He counted out three wrinkled twenties and handed them to her.

"Good heavens, what's wrong with this money?" she asked, inspecting it curiously.

He smiled and said, "I ran into a rainstorm in Fort Worth. I got soaked to the skin before I could get back to my hotel."

"Poor boy," she said understandingly. "That's the icebox," she said, gesturing at a bulky white Frigidaire with coils on top. "You just feel free to store your snacks in it. Nobody will bother them. You can take ice cubes out, too, if you want iced tea or cold water. But try not to take more than four cubes a day, all right? My mother-in-law practically *lives* with an ice pack on her brow in the summertime."

"I'll be careful," he said.

"Your room is at the top of the stairs. Second door on the left. The convenience is at the end of the hall. Oh, and I hope you aren't addicted to alcohol. My mother-in-law hates drinking in the house."

"No, I don't drink much," Dietrich said.

"That's fine," she said. "Well, I hope you enjoy your stay with us, Mr. Daniels." She turned to her ironing board and unrolled a sprinkled bedsheet with a sigh. "I just hate ironing," she confided, "but I can't bring myself to give my tenants wrinkled linen. That's one thing you'll have in my house, Mr. Daniels—nice, unwrinkled linens, once a week."

Dietrich thanked her and backed out of the kitchen. A nice woman, he thought. Friendly. Hard-working, although she quite obviously was not accustomed to work. A widow, no doubt, come down to renting rooms in her pleasant old home just to make ends meet. Americans were hard on widows. No, not hard. Indifferent. His mother had learned that. Hard work and hard drinking had killed his father, but as his Aunt Silke always said, it was indifference that killed his mother. Indifference and hard-faced, sun-burned neighbors who couldn't see beyond their own heat-baked pastures.

He reached the top of the stairs and let himself into his new room. It was a hot, dark square with a high ceiling and a single window facing a narrow side yard. There was a double bed and a wobbly table and a richly carved but mirrorless dresser and two fat overstuffed chairs with the kind of slick upholstery that caused the resting posterior always to slide slowly toward the floor. He tried the light switch, but it didn't work. That left the small silk-shaded lamp by the bed. No matter. Light would make the room seem even hotter and more oppressive.

The room smelled musty. Mrs. Fikinney's previous tenant must not have been much of a housecleaner. He peeled off his leather jacket and opened the solitary window to a faint huff of hot air, like fevered breath. Down below was an overgrown side yard, flat, burning itself to brown under the summer sun. An ancient black man crept out of the basement and stood staring at a lawnmower that was probably twenty years old, but still fifty years younger than himself. Was that Jim?

The old fellow would never get through that tall, dry grass with such a mower. Dry. Dusty. Sun-stunned earth, shimmering in heat haze. Dietrich didn't need a mirror on the dresser. There was his mirror down below, dry and brown, parched, dirty. His whole life seemed to revolve around thirsty land, yawning hotly beneath a coffin-lidded sky. A chinaberry tree hanging limp in the Texas afternoon, and the zinnias Aunt Silke planted every March drooping on the stalks by every June. Dirt streets where they lived on the edge of town and a boxy new frame house painted blue, not one of the strong old *fachwerk* houses with its gallery and peaked dormers, and a big shed out back where his veterinarian father used to keep sick cows and hunting dogs that were brought in only after all folk remedies had failed and they were on the verge of death. Bills and accounts-payable and Old Crow bottles that grew in rich profusion. And finally the still father-face as it looked in its coffin. Sour. Beaten. Dried out and burned to death by the sun and the sick cattle and dying dogs and the land.

And the mother, dazed, bewildered, who had been brought from Rastatt and the Rhine to Castroville and the weed-choked riverbed of the Medina just in time for World War I, when even the brown farmers in the area—who called themselves Mexicanos, thoroughly despised by the white ranchers who called themselves Texans—learned suddenly to fear and despise the German-speaking descendants of Alsatian immigrants who had been around since before Texas was a nation, much less a state. After armistice, when it was possible to be German again, his mother, homesick, lonely, had persuaded his father to bring her sister to Texas for company. Aunt Silke. Welcome to the United States, Aunt Silke. Welcome to Castroville, Texas. Welcome to a home that wasn't a home. Welcome to neighbors who after a few months for some reason began to look oddly at his father and Aunt Silke, and welcome to death, a Depression, no money, never enough money for the often dreamed-about return to Rastatt and the Rhine.

Then in his teens, with his mother desiccated and dead and deposited under the dried-out earth with his father, he and his Aunt Silke had finally left the home that was no home and had gone across the ocean to his new home, the old home of his Aunt Silke, cool and green, and cold and unfriendly. From Pearl beer and barbecue to sparkling hock and sauerbraten. From indifference with a Texas twang to indifference with a guttural accent. New home became no home, just as old home had been no home. But always work hard, never give up, Aunt Silke had urged him. This was the country which had spawned him. It could damned well accept him now. He was to force himself upon it. And so he tried. And what was his reward? A war.

First, there was the struggle to fill the gaps left by the Castroville school system, then eventually Frankfurt am Main, then one fine month of bread and cheese and cheap wine, hitchhiking through France with a fellow student named Hans-Joachim, of sketch books slowly filling with drawings of fifteenth-century castles, Hans-Joachim's hobby, and of heady war talk under bright stars. Then, on September 1, 1939, the day Germany invaded Poland, a day when all Germany sang and exulted, Dietrich did two things in a last-ditch effort to belong. He enlisted, and he married Hans-Joachim's sister Gerta. Aunt Silke raged, weeping, but he knew he was going to be dragged into the service anyway, and his stomach told him that he was going to die. But before he died, he wanted this one time to belong, to be a real part of the real Germany, and he chose Hans-Joachim's big laughing family and plump, freckled Gerta. So Aunt Silke raged and wept. So the big, laughing family stopped laughing when he was around.

For a week he had Gerta and her soft breasts, no freckles there, rounding into his hands like nesting doves, then it was away to training camp, then off to France in the spring, and, in March 1941, to more flat, dried-out earth, greedily sucking sweat and strength and life's blood. Africa. His old-home, no-home magnified, with young men in gray uniforms trudging the gray earth, following gray tanks, irrigating the desert with bright blood.

Africa. The upper edge of the Sahara. So much like the heat and yawning, greedy earth of his despised Texas youth that it made him physically ill. Sweeping back and forth for two savage months, locked in mortal combat with a cloud of dust on the horizon. The British attacking, the British retreating. The Germans attacking, the Germans retreating. Two massive clouds of dust that feinted and jabbed at each other, leaving bloody footprints and dried-out bodies in their wake, murdering and slaughtering each other in a gentlemanly enterprise for land that was useless.

And then the reprieve from war that was not a reprieve. The German intelligence officer with Oxford English who discovered Dietrich with his Texas twang, hunkered down between dunes, cursing a heavy British artillery barrage in colloquial American English. They had talked amiably and cheerfully, each pretending not to notice the smell of fear in the other, until the barrage had lifted. Dietrich had never seen the intelligence officer again, but he had felt his presence when the cryptic recall came two weeks later. Back to Germany. Back to the new-home that was no-home and to more hard work and more training, different this time, and testing and planning. And for what? To become an outsider again, to risk his sweat and his strength and his life's blood in a series of Abwehr missions to nowhere.

Dietrich still stared out the window at the overgrown yard, where the ancient black man still stood staring thoughtfully at the ancient lawnmower. A circle. Imperfect, wobbly, but a circle. Now Dietrich was back to his old-home no-home, back to go, back to where he had started. But this time it would be different. This time, somewhere along the way—in Gerta's bedroom?—he had learned the thirst for survival. This time he would not be the victim.

He moved purposefully to the bed and took the oilskin-wrapped gun from his waistband. He laid it on the coverlet, then opened his shirt and unbuckled the moneybelt. The bedsprings, as old as the house, maybe as old as the old handyman, complained squeakily as he sat down.

He unwrapped the pistol, a bulky Mauser 7.63 Automatic. They had allowed him to choose it himself, then had rigged it with a silencer. It was an oversized hand-weapon, difficult to conceal, with a chunky square magazine situated in front of the trigger guard, making it look more like a miniature submachine gun than an automatic pistol. But it was accurate and efficient and thoroughly deadly. He studied it carefully in the dim light, assuring himself that it had come through the soaking on the Amagansett beach without salt-water damage. To be safe, he broke it down, removing the barrel, barrel extension and hammer mechanism. He wiped everything carefully before reassembling it. Then he checked the stubby silencer tube and the several clips of ammunition.

Satisfied with the condition of the gun, he set it aside and emptied his moneybelt on the bed, spilling stacks of twenties, fifties and hundreds on the covers. He tried to count the money into neat stacks, but the paper bills were badly rippled and warped, like the pages of a magazine that has fallen into a bathtub. He might have trouble passing them, sea-soaked and eye-startling as they were. Perhaps he could borrow the landlady's iron later and press them back into shape. He piled the bills into uneven stacks of a thousand each and spread them across the bed. Occasionally, when he chanced across a relatively unspoiled bill, he laid it aside. He would spend those first.

When he had completed his warped piles of money, he counted them. Twenty-two thousand dollars in all. Twenty-two? How had they come up with a figure like that? Why not twenty? Or twenty-five? Of course they had been in a hurry.

He gathered the money and stuffed it back in the moneybelt, except for the small pile of better bills. Twenty-two thousand. It was too much. A few hundred would have kept him going until he could summon Dasch and Kerling. After that, money would become superfluous.

He carried the money, along with his Mauser, over to the dresser and put them in one of the lower drawers, then opened the top drawer and deposited his packet of false identification papers. He would have to go shopping this afternoon for some new clothing. And get rid of the old things, the leather jacket, the heavy trousers.

He went back to the window, wanting air, and stood there, staring down at the side yard. The lawnmower stood untended. Old Jim had apparently had second thoughts about his own mission. Yes, this time it would be different. This time he would be in control.

He would begin this afternoon.

2

Andy took his briefcase from the car and headed for the low West Wing of the White House, shielding his eyes from the bright morn-

ing sunlight. A pair of khaki-clad sentries saluted as he walked past
and he tossed a half salute back at them. God, what a hangover.
Next time he had the bright idea to kick around in the kitchen, he'd
ask Gay to lock the wine cabinet.

He entered the business wing of the White House, past another
set of guards, and crossed the big, leather-sprinkled reception lobby,
relieved to be out of the glare. A couple of the regular press people
nodded hello at him and he tried to respond with a smile. He
pushed through the far doors and headed down the rear corridor to
his office.

Two corporals stopped typing when he walked in and jumped to
attention. Andy waved them back to their typewriters. Sergeant
Huffman, Andy's assistant, was over by the window, clutching a
pair of field glasses and a walkie-talkie, chewing out a noncom on
the south lawn for spending too much time in the shade of a dog-
wood tree instead of doing his rounds. Andy could hear the noncom's chagrined response over the walkie-talkie until the sergeant
cut him off in midsquawk. He turned around and eyed Andy, then
checked his watch. "Well, well," he said.

"I overslept," Andy said. He sat down behind his desk and
shuffled pencils off his blotter. "Any business?"

Huffman picked up a clipboard. "Some coming up for Wednesday. Three VIPs from the Pacific for a medal ceremony. Couple of
war heroes and a public relations escort. They'll need passes to the
War Room."

"Did General Burrows okay it?"

"Sure," Huffman said. "If there's a chance he'll get his picture
taken, he'll okay anything."

Andy frowned at the sergeant's impertinence, then took the clipboard and initialed the requests for security clearance. "Anything
else?"

"That damned lieutenant again. The kid from Harvard. One of
the noncoms caught him goofing off in the library. That's the third
time we've found him pissing off on duty. You better tell him if he
doesn't straighten up, we're going to ship his ass to Australia."

"I'll talk to him," Andy said. He sighed and looked up at the sergeant. A thin, wiry little man with tiny feet and tiny hands.
Huffman made up what he lacked in size with military bluster. The
sergeant was career military and never let the wartime amateurs forget it, whether they were officers or enlisted men. He had been on
the job here in the White House for almost a year, months before

Andy had been assigned, and he ran the office as though it were his own personal battlefield. There were times when Andy wished for a slightly more tactful hand, particularly with all the touchy command-rank officers who wandered in and out seeking security passes, but there was no way he could handle the job without the sergeant's expertise, and he knew it. It wouldn't be so bad if the sergeant ever relaxed and took the chip off his shoulder, but there didn't seem to be much chance of that. Supercharged with energy, the sergeant fought off the rest of the world with the kind of frenzy that only the small in stature ever seem to find necessary. He reminded Andy of that bad-tempered little black Scotty that patrolled the White House corridors, snapping and snarling at everything in sight.

Andy handed the clipboard back to the sergeant and said, "I'll escort the VIPs to the War Room myself. What time are they due?"

"Between ten and ten-thirty Wednesday morning," the sergeant said. "I can take them. You're supposed to leave for the war conference at Hyde Park that day."

"I'll have time," Andy said, cringing inwardly at the thought of the sergeant roaming around the War Room, smart-mouthing the big brass.

"Yeah, okay," the sergeant said. "There's a cocktail party for the two heroes tomorrow night. I think you'll want to go to that, too."

"Tomorrow? But that's my last night. I'd better stay home and pack."

"I think you better go," the sergeant insisted. "It'll give you a chance to buttonhole General Burrows and some of the other chiefs. You're going to have to lick some ass and get us some help. That damned Calhoun is sticking it in our ear again."

Andy hesitated, frowning. He didn't like interdepartmental feuds. He said, "What's he done this time?"

"He sent out a sheaf of new memos this morning. Security arrangements for the Hyde Park conference. I got it from one of the girls in the secretarial pool. She did the routing."

"So? He's the Secret Service expert. That's his job."

"Yeah, but he left us off the list again. The memos went directly to the War Room. I know, I checked the routing list."

Andy felt his stomach sink. "Do you think he did it on purpose?"

Sergeant Huffman nodded. "Damn right he did. The bastard. He did it three days running last week, too. He knows it pisses us."

"Is it really so important that we get copies of his memos?"

"Yes, sir. It's a matter of protocol. We're the security liaison, not the damned secretarial pool. If we let him get away with crap like that, we might as well close up shop."

Andy sighed. "Okay. I guess you'd better speak to him. Tell him our copies have apparently been misdelivered and ask for duplicates."

"Not me," the sergeant said. "I complained the last three times. It's your turn, Captain. Get tough with him."

"Can't we handle it through channels? I don't want to start anything with Calhoun."

"It's already started," the sergeant said. "It's up to us to stop it."

"Couldn't I write a memo? Wouldn't that be just as good as talking to him?"

The sergeant thought it over. "Yeah, if it's a tough memo. Might be a good idea to put us on record. But make sure it's tough. Let him have both barrels. Read him the riot act."

"Sure," Andy said. He waited until the sergeant strolled back to his window and picked up the walkie-talkie, then borrowed a typewriter from one of the corporals and wheeled it to his desk.

He sat down and massaged his forehead. God, what a way to start the week. Maybe life would be a lot simpler if he insisted on a transfer to active duty. Maybe the European Theater. Or even the Pacific, if they wouldn't let him go to Europe. Anything where he could have some nice, uncomplicated carnage and get away from the guerrilla warfare of the executive hallway.

He shook his head hopelessly and rolled a sheet of paper into the typewriter. He looked up to make sure the sergeant wasn't watching, then began to peck at the keys with two fingers:

Memo: John Bradley Calhoun
Chief, White House Secret Service
From: Capt. Andrew Blaszek, U. S. Army
White House Security Liaison

It would appear that our office has been inadvertently omitted from the routing list for your latest correspondence re the upcoming Hyde Park conference. As this office is involved in the security preparations for the conference, I would greatly appreciate it if you could have someone check your files for our copies or for duplicate copies so that we might . . .

3

At 4:21 P.M. (EDT), George Dasch picked up his jacket. He started for the door of his hotel room, then paused and said to Peter Burger, "All right, for God's sake let's stop talking about it. Anyway, I've got to go out."

"You . . . you aren't going to . . . to see the . . . ?"

Dasch felt his nerves stretch even tighter, but he tried to sound reassuring. "No, I'm not going to see the FBI. I've got to think."

"Why can't you think here?"

"Because it's hot. Because the walls are too close. Because you keep sitting there with that . . . that *look* on your face."

"I'm just worried," Burger said. "Please, George, we could forget about that phone call. It isn't too late. You didn't give your right name."

"Oh stop, stop! I can't talk about it any more."

"But George . . ."

"*Please*, Peter. Let's just forget it. Just for a little while. Buy a radio. Listen to Charlie McCarthy. Get your mind off it. You're going to go crazy if you don't. We both need to be alone for a while."

"But where are you going?"

"Nowhere that will endanger us in the slightest, I promise you," Dasch said through clenched teeth. "You know that I have friends in New York, powerful friends. Something has occurred to me. Something that might help. Don't be alarmed if I'm gone for a day. Even two days. I promise, Peter, this will help. I've kept my promises to you, haven't I?"

Burger looked bewildered. "But Heinrich and Richard? If you aren't back by tomorrow, what about our meeting with them?"

"You'll have to meet them by yourself."

"But George . . ."

"One of us has to go. They'll get suspicious if we don't. Look, you don't have to make a big issue of it. Just go out to dinner with them and act like nothing has happened."

"But Heinrich will want to know where you are, why you didn't come."

"Tell him I'm meeting someone. Tell him I'm arranging transportation to recover our explosives from the beach, that ought to keep him quiet. Hell, I don't care what you say. I just have to go, that's all."

"But George . . ."

"Damn it, Peter, don't keep tearing at me. I'm doing what's right for us. Something that will assure our safety if we *do* decide to go to the FBI. We must trust each other. Don't you trust me?"

"I trust you, George, but . . ."

Dasch stepped through the door and slammed it behind him. He felt like throwing back his head and howling, but he knew that if he did, he would hear, behind the closed door, Burger howling right along with him. Like two animals caught in a trap. He hurried down the hallway. Don't push the elevator button. Too slow. Take the stairs, jump out the window, anything, anything. If only for a little while, he simply had to get out.

THE FOURTH DAY

I

The simplest test, as always, worked best. Dressed carefully, whistling "Texas, Our Texas" and carrying a bouquet of pale-pink roses gingerly over one arm, Dietrich walked deliberately down the railway siding the next morning toward one particular locomotive that seemed the site of an unusual amount of activity. Men in striped coveralls were hard at work scrubbing down and servicing the locomotive under the eyes of two white-shirted, black-tied men, who in turn were under the eyes of a foursome of men in neat business suits. Dietrich gawked openly as he walked, and one of the men with rolled-up shirtsleeves immediately came up the tracks to hail him with a, "Hey, you, where do you think you're going?"

Dietrich stopped and blinked. "Just looking around," he said in his most nasal twang. One of the business suits drifted up near the white-shirted man to listen.

"You got no business down on the tracks, fella," the shirtsleeves said impatiently. "Authorized personnel only. Didn't you see the signs?"

"No, sir, I guess I wasn't noticing," Dietrich said stupidly. He gawked some more at the locomotive, which was newish and powerful, and gestured vaguely with his bouquet, trying to look sheepish and in love and blissfully anticipatory of seeing someone who deserved to be met with a big bouquet of pale-pink roses. "You know. I guess I got here a little early. Just killing time."

"Well, kill it in the depot, kid, and stay the hell off the tracks."

The shirtsleeves turned to the business suit as if for congratulations. Hadn't he shooed this jerk away well? The business suit nodded, and Dietrich retreated, mumbling defensive apologies, as far as the concrete passenger ramps. He leaped up nimbly and leaned for a while against an empty baggage cart.

The number of the locomotive was firmly in his mind. He'd come again tomorrow, of course, to watch the President leaving and be sure that it was the right one. The intelligence report had said that the meeting was to convene at Roosevelt's family estate in New York for the first few days, then shift to Washington over the weekend on the special presidential train, which predictably would be pulled by a specially prepared engine.

Next he would need railroad maps and timetables. The President's customary route was known, but he would have to check the schedules to see when the train was most apt to pass. It would be ticklish, but not impossible.

There were alternate plans, of course. But this had been deemed the easiest, the safest. A few early preparations, an alert to the two U-boats teams, then patience. Patience and simplicity and methodical hard work. When it was done, he would dismiss the two teams and allow them to return to their original mission. Then he would make his way back to Long Island, back to wait for the submarine.

If all went well. Dietrich began to whistle again, and he moved casually, as if still meandering around, along the loading platform to the narrow, steep steps leading up into the depot. Soldiers lounged here and there, half of them eyeing a very young girl, surely not more than thirteen or fourteen, who sat glumly on a large brown suitcase. Waiting for something or someone. So were the soldiers, and, young as she was, she was the only girl around to eye.

In the crowded depot, the pickings wouldn't have been much better. The only pretty woman there was a young mother who sat staring at her white-gloved hands, studiously ignoring two exhausted, whining children who lay stretched out on the wooden bench on either side of her. No seats were vacant, and standees stared angrily at the children for taking up so much space. Dietrich walked on through the waiting room and out into the sunlight to the front parking lot, where he inserted himself into the oven that was the Lincoln coupe he had picked up earlier that morning.

The car was a nice little gray '39 Lincoln Zephyr for which Dietrich had paid $725 out of his Abwehr-provided war chest. White sidewalls. Radio and heater. Only thirty thousand miles on the speedometer. Good tread on the tires. The car papers had been made out in the name of Raymond Patterson, another identity from Dietrich's packet of identity cards.

Now a package from an art shop was locked in the trunk, and the late morning sun had had time to heat the metal top of the Lincoln to just the right temperature to bake a Thanksgiving turkey.

Baking, Dietrich sat behind the wheel and considered his next steps. It was time now to look up a public telephone and contact the two team leaders. One call to the Governor Clinton Hotel in New York, to George Dasch masquerading as George Davis. Another to a man named Wilhelm Voss, Edward Kerling's designated New York contact. He would identify himself as Richard Goethe and the two team leaders would learn for the first time that they would not be working strictly on their own, nor on those duties which had been detailed for them back at the Quenz Lake school.

He wondered how they would react. He was fairly certain of Kerling, a tough-minded, brutal man who followed orders as though they came from God himself, according to the dossiers supplied by Abwehr I. Dasch, on the other hand, might not be so eager. But he would do as he was told.

By Friday—or Saturday since he was allowing generous time for delay—Dasch and Kerling would bring their two teams to Aberdeen, Maryland, just south of the Pennsylvania border. Dietrich would meet them there. And he would explain it all to them.

He hesitated momentarily, glancing at the pink roses he had placed on the seat beside him. Despite the heat, they hadn't yet begun to wilt. Pretty roses, sturdy roses. It would be a shame just to waste them.

Not whistling now, but feeling cheerful because things had been working so well so far, Dietrich picked up the roses and re-entered the cool cavern of the depot. A row of pay telephones along one barren wall of the waiting room caught his eye, tempting him, but he preferred a phone not so openly exposed to possible eavesdroppers. He would wait. He turned to the gate area with the roses, looking for someone.

He found her in a wave of incoming passengers who struggled through the choked inlet of the waiting gate, then began to diffuse among the opposing wave of people waiting to greet them in the depot. She was alone, with no one there to meet her. She wasn't young and plump and freckled. She was tall but stooped, with salt-and-pepper gray hair and a stern face with a heavy crop of dark moles around the mouth and chin.

"Welcome to Washington, Auntie," Dietrich said gently, and he put the pink roses in her arms.

He turned and left quickly, without waiting to see the astonished smile that still clung to her face long after he started for his car and the rest of his dwindling list of errands.

2

It was a few minutes past noon when the man yawned and said, "What time is it? I'm tired."

George Dasch shuffled the cards and looked up at the bleary eyes and gray-stubbled chin of the man across the card table. Fritz, he had said his name was. A waiter on Forty-second Street. And a bad pinochle player. Dasch had already won nearly a hundred dollars from him. "Don't worry about the time," Dasch told him. "You're so far behind you'll never catch up."

"I'll catch up," the man said. "But I'm going to have to take a break in a few minutes. I'll have to call someone to take my shift."

"I'm glad I don't have to worry about things like that any more," Dasch said.

The man sniffed. "Why don't you? Out of work? Or just independently wealthy?"

"Don't ask me questions," Dasch said. "I can't answer." He riffled the cards again and glanced at the small ring of waiters who had gathered around their table to watch. Castoff men gathered around somebody's castoff table in this storefront waiters' social club with grimy windows and castoff magazines littering castoff chairs. Dasch used to come here from time to time in the old days, hating it, but coming because it was a place to go. Now it was oddly comforting. It was comforting to concentrate so hard on bids and melds that he didn't have time to think about Burger and the hotel room and the problem and what they must do. It was comforting to win with an audience watching admiringly. It was even comforting to make cryptic remarks about his background and his secrets. The puzzled looks on the waiters' faces soothed him.

"What do you mean, you can't answer?" Fritz said. "I only asked if you had a job."

"I have a job," Dasch said, "but I can't talk about it. If I talk it means death."

"Sure, sure," Fritz said. "Deal the cards."

3

At 3:27 that afternoon, the Director of the Federal Bureau of Investigation flattened his palms on the top of his desk and glowered at the pile of inconclusive teletypes from the New York office. "Seventy-two hours of intensive investigation and not one solid lead to show for it?" he barked. "Gentlemen, do you realize how inept the Bureau is made to look by this kind of incredible inefficiency? It's slipshod. That's what it is. Slipshod."

Special Agent Emerson Carter, recently brought into the case on the Washington end, sat on the edge of his chair, watching alertly. This was as close as he'd ever been to the old man, except for graduation day when he and the other neophyte agents had been paraded in for a welcoming handshake. On that day he had attempted to stop and thank the Director for giving him his chance, only to be shouldered on by senior agents whose job it was to keep the line moving. Now Carter was six years older and many years wiser in the way of agent-to-Director politics. He would sit forward throughout this meeting, looking vitally interested and always on the verge of some telling comment. But he wouldn't open his mouth. No, sir. Not unless the old man spoke directly to him first.

Jenkins, the communications officer in charge of the German spy case, shifted uncomfortably and said, "It isn't for want of trying, sir. Every investigative procedure you requested has been put into effect. We have men staked out in four locations near the beach, but no one has returned to the scene. Every known German national in the area has been thoroughly questioned. We've even interrogated most of the townspeople."

"I want progress, not excuses," the Director said. "What about fingerprints on the money they gave the Coast Guard seaman? What do the tests show?"

Good point, Carter thought. He nodded vigorously. Damned good thinking.

Jenkins shook his head. "Our experts have dusted it, sir, but they found nothing of value. I'm afraid too many people handled it at the Coast Guard station before they turned it over to us."

"What about banks? Have we checked the banks? They must have got the money somewhere."

"Sir?"

"I'm convinced they had help from German aliens on the beach," the Director said. "The money may have come from a bank or a commercial loan office on Long Island. Send a teletype to New York requesting a team to check the banks."

"Yes, sir."

"Another thing. If our people haven't been able to locate them by now, then they must be off the island. How? How did they do it?"

"We can't be sure," Jenkins said. "There were four tickets sold at the Amagansett station, but the stationmaster says they were purchased by fishermen. We have some men checking it out now, working up descriptions from the stationmaster."

"Anything suspicious there? German accents? Odd behavior?"

Jenkins shrugged. "The stationmaster seems to think it was fairly normal, except that the man who bought the tickets couldn't remember the price."

The Director leaned back in his plush swivel chair, scowling. "We're going to take a publicity beating on this. You mark my words. The newspapers and radio commentators will flay us alive."

"We've placed a news embargo on the investigation," Jenkins said. "Nothing will be released to the press until you authorize it, sir."

The Director gave him a chilling stare. "How do you keep something like this from the press? Every hysterical citizen who sees a shadow immediately calls his local newspaper to report a spy. A grocer in Cleveland calls because one of his customers buys twenty pounds of knackwurst. A woman in Kansas City reports a man who spoke German on the bus. Dallas, Chicago, Pittsburgh, you name it, the newspapers have published spy reports. Even here. Just last week the *Star* got on to that matter of the special guards on the reservoir and the Washington monument because of a sabotage scare."

"Newspapers always like to print reports like that," one of the senior agents said. "They seldom amount to anything."

"This time they may," the Director said. "Ordinarily, I wouldn't mind. I like an informed citizenry. Spy scares keep them alert. But this one could backfire on us. All we need is for one clever newsman to notice the increased activity in the New York office, or for some Amagansett people to start talking to newspapers about what we've been doing out in their town, and the entire roof could come crumbling down on our heads. Suddenly the insignificant little reports from the far corners of the country would start looking more important to the reporters and we'll be reading stories about a country full of spies, scattered from ocean to ocean, just because the Bureau was too inept to catch them."

Carter nodded. The old man was right. Those damned newspapers would blow the lid off, given half a chance. He saw a quick look in his direction from the Director and he nodded more rapidly.

Hot damn! That was it. Catch his attention, but keep your mouth shut.

The Director looked at the communications officer and said, "Jenkins, I want a personal message to go to New York this afternoon over my signature. It's time someone shook them out of their lethargy."

Carter swallowed. Panic time. When the Director sent out personal messages, legs quaked and careers toppled. The Director was famous for his personal messages.

The Director laced his fingers together and poised them beneath his chin. As he dictated, the communications officer scribbled in a steno pad:

Gentlemen:

Your recent teletype communications have been brought to my attention. I am bewildered and amazed by the lack of progress shown by your office in the matter of the German landing at Amagansett.

It appears that you have thus far developed no useful information, in spite of the time and manpower which have been made available to you. I can ascribe this only to a lack of initiative on your part. I find the situation intolerable and unacceptable.

It saddens me, but I must today inform the White House of your lack of progress. The President will undoubtedly be as disappointed as I am. Therefore, my orders to you are to be more resourceful in the future. You must henceforth follow every lead to its logical conclusion, no matter how slight. I hold you personally responsible for any embarrassment which the Bureau may suffer as a result of your lackadaisical approach to such an extreme and urgent situation.

Yours sincerely, etcetera, etcetera.

The communications officer lifted his pencil and said, "Is that all, sir?"

"Yes. Send that out immediately." He waved his hand at the circle of agents to indicate that the meeting had ended, and sat back, waiting for them to withdraw.

As the crowd started to break up, the Director suddenly turned his face to Special Agent Carter and said, "Young man, what is your name?"

Carter beamed. "Carter, sir. Special Agent Emerson J. Carter."

"There are sweat rings under your arms," the Director said. "Stop sweating. You know I don't like agents who sweat."

4

An hour later, in the cavernous file room of the New York FBI office, three file clerks were busily sorting and cataloguing the voluminous paperwork of the last several days. Mail-fraud investigations, reports on draft dodgers, detailed dossiers on people who had been proposed for security clearance, results of inquiries on suspected sabotage and malingering in war factories, correspondence, memos, schedules, depositions, activities reports.

Tucked deep in the stacks of paperwork awaiting filing was a memo typed by Special Agent Fred Shea concerning a Sunday-night telephone call from an informant who had identified himself as one "F. D. Postorius," regarding his recent arrival in the United States from Germany.

The three file clerks, like Special Agent Shea, had heard nothing about the spy hunt which was in progress on Long Island and in the environs of New York City.

At 4:29 P.M. (EDT), the Postorius memo was placed without ceremony into one of the "P" drawers and cross-listed in a file under "S" for Shea.

No copies were forwarded to Washington.

5

Much later that same evening, Andy mechanically straightened his tie, gazing in the big mirror in Gay's bedroom, and listened to the voices down the hall, where Gay had gone to check on Gaylynn. He had drunk too much at the cocktail party, he decided, but Gay had drunk even more, and she must have made too much noise when she looked in on her daughter.

Gaylynn's light little voice said, "Ugh, don't kiss me, Mommy, you smell nasty."

"That's booze, baby," Gay's voice said calmly. "Mommy's been to a party."

"Grandma says ladies don't drink."

"They do if they like to have a good time. Now go back to sleep, baby. It's way past your bedtime."

The little girl mumbled, fighting sleep as children will. "Did you have a good time, Mommy?"

"Mommy had a lovely time. She ate lovely dilled shrimp and nasty caviar, and she drank lovely rum punch, and she met two lovely young men who are going to get lovely big medals pinned on them tomorrow by the President before he goes to lovely Hyde Park. Now go to sleep."

"Didn't Andy go to the party?"

"Sure, Andy went," Gay said. "And he bought Mommy a lovely big steak after we left, and she wouldn't eat it because she was all filled up on lovely shrimp, and now she's starving again."

There was laughter from both Gays, then a smack that must have been the unwanted kiss, then the sound of a door closing. But no footsteps came toward Gay's room, where Andy waited. Instead, they seemed to go downstairs, and Andy frowned a little at his image in the mirror, staring at the Good Conduct Medal pinned on his perfectly pressed khaki jacket. It made a poor showing against all the medals that had been at the cocktail party tonight. It would look poorer still tomorrow when those two damned carrier pilots got the Navy Cross. Even his khaki looked pretty tacky against the memory of their blinding white Navy dress uniforms with the blue-and-gold shoulder boards on the tunic and women, women, women draped all over them. Not that Gay had joined the throng of both men and women who crowded around the visiting heroes. She never had to. All she had to do was walk into a room, with that ripe body and that faint, teasing aura of availability, and any man she casually glanced at would soon be at her elbow. The two young pilots from the U.S.S. *Enterprise* had been no exception. Young, hell, they were obviously just kids, probably no older than twenty-five. If that. Andy, edged out, stranded in the shallows with an elderly admiral's wife who had insisted on talking about sugar rationing, had watched the two youngsters (and Gay) as avidly as anyone else. Two youngsters fresh from the Pacific, fresh from battle, fresh from Midway. Only twelve days before, they had been right in the thick of it. There should have been something that . . . that showed. Something in the eyes, maybe. They hadn't done it all by themselves, sure, but four Jap carriers had been sunk. Shouldn't there have been something different in the eyes?

Gay came in silently, stocking-footed, carrying a baloney sandwich in one hand and her shoes in the other, and caught him staring in the mirror at his single, overpoweringly modest medal. He grinned sheepishly.

"Still dressed?" she said. She dropped the shoes on a green velvet chair and took a big bite out of the sandwich.

"I thought maybe Gaylynn . . ."

"Nah, she's asleep. Strip for action, lover."

"Gay, what does a Navy Cross look like?" he asked. She would know, of course. Her father was an Annapolis professor, and she had been raised among a sea of uniforms. The first boy she had ever slept with, she told him (and the rest of the world), was an Annapolis midshipman. It figured.

Gay shrugged. "Bronze, I guess. You don't see all that many of them. What's the matter, baby, are you jealous? I didn't do a thing, you know that. I just chatted with them a little bit." She smiled wickedly. "Why, I'm old enough to be their *mom*my."

"I'm not jealous."

"The hell you aren't. Or if you're not, you'd better be." She sighed, still smiling. "My God, weren't they gorgeous? I can't wait until I'm old enough to take up really young men. College boys. Senate pages. I wonder why they're always cuter than the House pages? After Congress, we'll run you for the Senate, baby. That'll give me easy access."

"That definitely settles it," Andy said, trying to match her light tone. "No politics for me." He took off his jacket, folded it neatly, and unknotted his tie.

She regarded him over her baloney sandwich while he proceeded to undress. Finally she said, "What's bothering you tonight? Seriously, now."

"Me? Nothing."

She studied him a moment longer, then said, "You *are* jealous, aren't you?"

He laughed uncomfortably. "Of course not, Gay. Hell."

"I don't mean of me. I mean those two fuzz-faced kids and all their ribbons and the way people hung all over them this evening. That's it, isn't it? The old social-pressure business. You hate being in Washington when there's so much going on in the rest of the world, right?"

"That's silly," he said.

"Is it? Well, I'll tell you something, baby. You've got the opportunity of a lifetime down there at the White House, but you don't take the least advantage of it. Don't you realize how much a few words in the right ears could mean to your political career?"

"I don't have a political career," he said.

"No, and you're not likely to if you don't stop wasting time. You ought to see people, talk to them, tug a few elbows. And frankly, lover, you could take a hint from those two fliers. It wouldn't hurt you a bit to go overseas and win a medal or two yourself. That's the best way in the world to win votes."

Andy had just taken off his pants. That, and her sudden attack, made him feel queerly defenseless. "For the love of God, Gay, I'm not trying to win votes. This political nonsense is all your idea. And now you want me to chuck everything and go overseas? Christ, I wouldn't even be here if it wasn't for you."

"I know, baby, you'd be fighting chiggers at Fort Sill. No, now, don't start all that frowny-frowning. You know I want you here with me, and it would be pure hell if you went off on active duty, but I'm just trying to be practical. Take Ulysses S. Grant. How in hell do you think *he* ever got to be President? By being good in business administration? No, he was a war hero, that's what. And it's going to happen again, just you wait and see. The successful politicos after this war are going to be the boys who've knocked off a few dozen Germans or Japs and come home with something to show for it."

"Like a wooden leg or a mechanical arm?" Andy said angrily. He started to pull his pants back on.

"That wouldn't hurt," she said. "But I had more in mind a string of those lovely medals on their lovely big old hairy chests. Lord, Andy, what a lot of hair you've got on your chest. Doesn't it get hot in the summertime? Come here, let me feel. Andy? Don't you dare get dressed again! Andy!"

"Knock off the shouting," he said. "You'll wake up Gaylynn."

Gay abandoned her half-eaten sandwich and leaped out of the jungle at him, abandoning clothing as she swung from vine to vine. "Put those pants down, or I'll . . . I'll . . ."

"You'll what?" he said through clenched teeth. "Call one of your little Navy heroes?" He reached for his shirt.

"I'm getting sick of this," Gay warned.

"I'm already sick of it," Andy said.

He was up to pants and half-buttoned shirt. She was down to beguilingly filled bra and panties and garter belt. Involuntarily, Andy paused and stared at her, and he saw the fresh anger go out of her eyes and a grin begin to twinkle in back of them. Slowly, watching him, she slid the panties down and stepped out of them. White lace bra straining as she sucked in her breath. White lace garter belt framing her thick blond pubic patch. Pale-beige nylons encasing her long, spraddled legs. The rest was pure Gay. In spite of himself, he felt his throat clutch up.

"Maybe we'd better change the subject," she said slyly. "Now, what can we do to get our minds off quarreling? I know. I have a good idea. I'll just trot downstairs and mix you a nightcap."

"Like that?" Andy said.

"Pooh, lover, it's a warm night. I won't catch cold. But it's an awful long walk down the stairs. And we've been on our feet most of the night. Maybe we should just . . . rest a while. Here. On the bed."

Andy reached for her. "Leave the stockings on," he whispered.

"My precious nylons? In these war-shortage days? Never. But I'll leave on my bra."

"Never," Andy said.

Gay must have had a hoard of nylons stuck away somewhere. Because she only giggled, not protested, as he backed her slowly toward the bed.

6

Just before midnight, another German U-boat, the *U-584*, surfaced three miles off the Florida Coast on a calm, starlit sea and moved within landing range of Ponte Vedra, a strip of clean, white beach some seven miles south of Jacksonville.

Unaware of the difficulties which had marred the landing from the *U-202*, the four team members on the *U-584* were worried only because they were running late. Two days out of Lorient Harbor they had been spotted by a routine British submarine patrol and had been forced to deviate from their course to a more southerly route, causing them to lose considerable time in crossing the Atlantic.

At 11:53 P.M. (EDT), the *U-584* was in position and the four German-American civilians loaded their explosive-laden crates into an inflated rubber boat and set out for the shore.

The four men were:

—Edward Kerling, 32, leader of the Florida team and a member of the Nazi party since 1928. A handsome, muscular athlete with thick brown hair and deceptively friendly gray eyes, he had lived in America for ten years before going back to Germany.

—Werner Thiel, 35, an efficient and loyal party member. He was a former machinist who had lived for ten years in Detroit, working with various American automobile companies.

—Otto Neubauer, 32, who had split his nine years of American residence between Chicago, where he first toyed with Nazism by joining the American Bund, and Miami, where he met and married a German-American girl named Anna Wolf in 1939.

—Herbert Hans Haupt, who at 22 was the youngest of them all. An American citizen with no political affiliation whatever, he had lived in the United States with his parents since he was five years old, and had left the country only because he got a girl in trouble in Chicago a year earlier.

Except for being three days late, they landed without incident.

THE FIFTH DAY

I

The War Room occupied the southwest corner of the main floor in the White House, overlooking the rose garden and the executive West Wing. The room had served many purposes over the years. It had started as a meeting place for the President and his cabinet in the early 1800s, a room of decision-making and high-level consultation. Later, when the socially proper Monroe family took up residence in the White House, it had been turned into a banquet hall. It was to remain the State Dining Room until big-game enthusiast Theodore Roosevelt moved in and turned it into his trophy room, with the stuffed heads of zebu, panther and Kodiak bear replacing the heads of state who had formerly dined there. Now, with the advent of World War II, the room had given way to maps and brightly colored pins and secrecy.

Entrance to the room was strictly controlled. A coterie of top generals and admirals were allowed easy access, because it was here that they met daily to plan the battles which would make or break the United States in the course of the war. A handful of bright young aides and assistants, most of them young Navy officers because of the President's affinity for that particular branch of service, were also allowed easy access, since admirals and generals can't be expected to stick their own pins in maps, nor shuffle their own papers.

Outsiders were practically never admitted, except on special occasions like today when war heroes had been summoned to the White House to be decorated, and Andy Blaszek made a point of leading the two young carrier pilots and their naval public information officer to the War Room himself. Andy liked visiting the War Room. He liked the heady feeling of being on the inside where all the important decisions were made. The maps with their crayon markings were nearly always days or weeks ahead of the newspaper headlines. It was like walking into a very large, very crucial crystal ball.

A polite smattering of applause greeted the entrance of the two fliers, and every man in the room, regardless of rank, rose to his feet in a gesture of respect. Andy saw more than a fair share of bleary eyes peering from command-rank faces. Most of the brass had been at the cocktail party the night before, and they drank the way they issued orders—boldly and decisively. With mandatory modesty, Andy held back as the beaming PI officer prodded his two charges forward, sending them into the maw of admiring military smiles and congratulatory handshakes.

The two young pilots looked very pleased with themselves. Why not? They deserved it, didn't they? Or did they? Andy felt his jaw muscles begin to tighten with the strain of smiling. Jesus. Was Gay right? Was he really jealous of them? He had to admit it *was* difficult, watching a couple of kids, barely out of college, reap all this awe and attention just for doing their jobs. Hell, a lot of people did their jobs these days. Andy did. Maybe it wasn't a very important job, or a very productive job, but that's the job he'd been assigned to do and he did it.

He raised his eyes to the old-fashioned rococo ceiling of the War Room. Maybe Gay was right about the other thing, too. Maybe he should request active duty. Not for the benefit of a political career; that was Gay's fantasy, not his. And not because he was particularly enamored of the prospect of facing death and disfigurement on a daily basis out in the real world with most men his age. God forbid. But he had to admit that the world out there *was* real, and he wasn't in it. Andy, in spite of his title and rank, was a nobody in the White House. Like a bright young secretary who did things for the somebodies. So near the power, near enough to be taken in by the illusion of power, but basically a small person, an onlooker. The eager, intelligent young women the system so often relegated to such jobs could at least blame the system for keeping them firmly in an inferior place, but a man didn't automatically have their gender-engendered disadvantage. What excuse did *he* have for being just a small person and an onlooker?

"Captain, I'm speaking to you."

Andy jerked, startled. General Burrows, one of the ranking warriors of the War Room dewlap brigade, was staring at him. Andy checked mentally to see that his smile was still in place and said, "Sorry, sir. I was distracted. Did you wish something?"

"Yes," the general said. "We have a few minutes before the newsreel people and the photographers are expecting these young men to appear on the South Lawn for interviews, so we're going to sit awhile and discuss the situation in the Pacific."

"Yes, sir. Would you like me to join you, sir?"

"Not right away," the general said. "We'll need coffee. Be a good fellow and run down to the kitchen for it, will you?"

Andy's jaw tightened again, but he managed to hold onto the smile. He said, "Yes, sir. Right away, sir."

He could have sworn one of the young fliers was smirking at him as he headed for the door.

2

George Dasch came back to his hotel shortly before noon that day, dead tired after thirty-six hours of continuous card playing. He felt like a fool for having done it. But he felt better. Better than he had felt since arriving in the United States. He had won nearly two hundred dollars. For the first time in his life he had all the money he needed, packed away in the leather briefcase, and then he started winning. Life was a tedious joke.

Before going to his own room for much-needed sleep, he stopped to speak to Peter Burger. He found him sitting wearily by a radio, sweating in the sticky heat.

Burger leaped excitedly to his feet. "Where have you been? You've been gone so long! Heinrich was furious at you for not showing up last night."

"To the devil with Heinrich," Dasch said. "I've made up my mind."

Burger sat down slowly by the radio. "What have you decided?"

"I'm going to Washington," Dasch said. "Tomorrow. I'll call down to the hotel desk and ask them to arrange a room reservation for me at the Mayflower for tomorrow night. Then, after a good night's rest, I'll catch the train to Washington. I'll see the chief of the FBI and tell him that you and I are anti-Nazis, and that we're giving ourselves up to save the country. We'll be heroes."

Burger swallowed. "Are you sure?"

"I'm sure. It's the only way." He looked at Burger's panicky face and said, "Calm yourself, Peter. They'll thank us. They'll reward us. We'll be celebrities, and they'll want us to go on lecture tours and help sell war bonds. They'll give parades in our honor. And the sooner we move, the better it will be for us."

"May I come to Washington with you?"

"No, someone has to keep Heinck and Quirin from getting suspicious. Don't worry, Peter. I'll take good care of you. I'll tell them you helped me to plan it. I'll say we had this idea before we ever left Germany."

"They'll call us traitors back home."

"At least we'll be alive," Dasch said. "You just keep Heinck and Quirin happy for a few days until this is all over. Explain my absence any way you wish. It won't matter much longer." He reached for the doorknob.

Burger said, "George?"

"Yes?"

"I guess I may not see you again for a while, will I?"

"Probably not."

"Then I . . . I want you to know that I . . . that . . ." He swallowed several times and turned away. "Damn it, George. It wasn't supposed to happen this way."

Dasch watched briefly from the doorway, a mixture of sympathy and disgust crowding his own dark emotions. Then he opened the door and said, "Good-bye, Peter."

3

Ellen Sue Fikinney, as usual, was having a late afternoon snack from the refrigerator, dining on the unwitting largesse of her tenants. Her mother-in-law had insisted on having the two old Miss Lillistons over for a bridge luncheon that afternoon, and the way those three old ladies always gobbled everything in sight, there was never enough left over for a martyred fourth to make a decent meal. So Ellen Sue took a slice of salami from Mr. Bornstein's pack, snitched a couple of pickles from Mr. Shales's jar, and two inches of orange juice, which she carefully replaced with tap water, from Mrs. Masur's bottle. She was trying to decide whose cheese to raid when she heard a car door slam out on the street. She quickly closed the refrigerator and hid her purloined snack in the bread box.

But it wasn't one of her regular refrigerator tenants. It was that new man, on his way in the front door, that quiet Mr. Daniels. At least that's what he claimed his name was. She wasn't so sure any more. She had called him by the name a couple of times since he moved in and had noticed a pretty fishy, slow response, as though he didn't always recognize his own name. She raised carefully plucked eyebrows and questioned the dust motes in the hot air of the kitchen. It wouldn't be the first time she had rented a room to a phony.

Ellen Sue limped—she refused to tell even her doctor, but she wondered sometimes if she could possibly be getting arthritis—to the front hall and watched as he climbed the stairs to his room. She decided he wasn't really a very good tenant. He hadn't used her kitchen privileges at all, spurning her good-natured generosity. God knows, she tried to make her unappetizing tenants feel at home, give them a little feeling that they were welcomed guests instead of just a bunch of goofy names on mailboxes. But that Mr. Daniels didn't fit in at all. He didn't have any relatives in the hospital. No friends, as far as she could see. And he was too quiet. Nobody was that quiet unless he was a pervert or had something to hide.

She looked out into the street. That new car. He'd gone and bought himself a car yesterday. Where did a man doing a little wildcatting, just drilling on a shoestring, get money for a car like that? That proved it. Something was definitely wrong with him. Maybe he was a criminal or something. Lord, you couldn't trust anyone these days. The world was moving too fast. People turned bad before you could blink. The old Miss Lillistons maintained it was Hollywood that did it. Hollywood and radio, they cawed during bridge game after bridge game. All that violence and those loose-living stars, they cawed. A body wasn't safe any more, what with the world filled with sin and evil and all the criminals running around loose, they cawed.

Of course Ellen Sue didn't believe that sort of thing, but a woman alone had to protect herself, that's what she had to do. She ought to go up to his room one of these days when he wasn't around, and take a look-see. After all, it was her home and she owed it to herself and her tenants to make sure they weren't sharing the roof with a criminal.

But not while he was up there. No telling what he'd do if she just faced him and started asking questions. Lots of criminals were crazy. Mean and crazy. She would wait. But the next time he left the house . . .

She shook her head and limped back to the kitchen, back to her waiting food cache.

THE SIXTH DAY

Thursday—June 18, 1942

1

Mrs. Fikinney had her opportunity shortly after breakfast the following morning. Hearing his footsteps on the stairs, she withdrew into the shadows of the dining room and waited, watching for him. He came trotting down the stairway, carrying some kind of large tablet and a little box of pencils. She pulled back until she heard the squeak and slap of the screen door, then hobbled out into the hallway and made her way to the front of the house, watching contemplatively as he climbed into that new car of his.

Humph. Sitting there in that fancy Lincoln. Why would any Texan in Washington just for a couple of weeks rush out and buy a car? Dressed nicely, too. He didn't have any nice clothes the day he first arrived. Now it was new gray slacks and a nice navy-blue sport shirt. Peacock. All young men were peacocks.

She watched as he pulled away from the curb, then limped up the stairs quietly, fishing in her apron for her keys. She could hear Mr. Beatty's radio playing loudly down the hall, blaring that silly "Breakfast Club" program with all the silly people marching around their silly breakfast table. She'd told him and told him not to play his radio so loud, that it disturbed her mother-in-law. She'd have to speak to him later.

She let herself into Mr. Daniels' room and drifted silently to his bed. It was carefully made up, too neat for a man living alone. Like someone who had been in the Army, or maybe in a penitentiary, trained to keep his bed neat. That almost proved it. No one his age could get out of the Army so easy these days. So probably it was a penitentiary. There were probably wanted circulars out on him right now. Maybe even a copy or two here in his room, stolen from the post office walls. Maybe hidden right there in the bedclothes.

Maybe that's why he made it up so neat, trying to disguise it. She bent over the bed and ran her fingers expertly under the sheets, probing. Nothing. She checked his pillows and the mattress, all the places that her tenants usually tried to hide things. Still nothing. He was a clever one, that Mr. Daniels. He must have worried that someone would eventually catch on to him and had used his criminal cunning to hide things more carefully.

She surveyed the room, wondering where. Mr. Beatty had taped his government check behind the radio that time he said he was broke and couldn't pay the rent. Mrs. Masur had tried to hide her hot plate on top of that priceless old chifforobe in her room, and the Polanski brothers, those dirty transvestites, had hidden their female clothing under a cushion in an easy chair. They all thought they could hide things from her, but she had shown them.

But this room didn't have any of those things. No radio. No chifforobe. Only the chairs and that marvelous old carved dresser. Her gaze lingered on the dresser. Her tenants couldn't appreciate such furniture. If she weren't so determined to hold her home intact, against the day she could once again enjoy its exclusive possession, she'd call in an antique dealer and fill her hands with gold. Could he have left them there? Reward posters right there in one of the drawers? Could he be that foolish? Or that cunning?

She floated over to the dresser and eased the top drawer open. So. Just as she thought. His clothes were all new, some with the price tags still on them. Undoubtedly an ex-convict. That would explain why he needed all new clothes. One thing she wouldn't allow in her very own house, that was ex-convicts.

Then she saw the cards. Lots of them. Driver's licenses, club memberships, draft registrations, Social Security cards. Some with the name Frank Daniels. Some said Raymond Patterson. She picked them up and thumbed through them. Other names, too. Was he letting other people use his room? There'd be none of that. Not unless he paid more rent.

She dropped the cards back in the drawer and eased it shut, then opened the next one. Shirts and things, all new like the ones in the top drawer. She poked through them and . . .

Oh Lord! A gun. Hidden down there under the shirts. She picked it up gingerly and laid it on top of the dresser. A big, ugly one. And something else down there. A belt of some kind. A moneybelt. A fat one. He really was a criminal. He'd probably been robbing banks or liquor stores or something. Or maybe he was a black marketeer.

She lifted the moneybelt with shaking fingers and pawed it open. Merciful heavens. Look at all the money. Wads and wads of money. She sifted a few bills out for a closer look. Fifty-dollar bills. Hundred-dollar bills. Lord, there must be thousands of dollars there. All wrinkled and warped like maybe he had tried to wash them off. Probably trying to get the blood off. The police. She had to call the police. They'd surely want to know about this. Unless . . .

An idea began to form in her mind. An idea so splendid, so excellent, so guaranteed of success, that it startled her. It was perfect. There was no way she could lose.

She picked up the big gun and wound the moneybelt around it and let herself furtively out of the room, smiling in anticipation.

2

The President's Hyde Park estate, a mélange of wooded hills and fields and creeks and assorted family homes clustered on the east bank of the Hudson River in eastern New York, shimmered beneath a violet haze in the summer sun.

Andy Blaszek drank it in from beneath the branches of a giant white oak tree. A great place to grow up. Trees to climb, woodchuck holes to investigate, early Dutch colonial buildings to remind one of one's heritage, sweeping gardens filled with splashes of carefully tended color. A long way from the three-room shack in Colorado with tarpaper exterior and flowered wallpaper and a narrow back yard filled with garden vegetables. Papa would burst with pride if he could see his little Andrzej today.

A caravan of cars drove through the family gate and swept slowly up the circular driveway toward what the presidential family liked to call the Big House. Even here, when the President was in residence, the punctilio of the White House followed him. A Marine band, transported from Washington to the Hyde Park estate for this special occasion, stood at attention in the circle of lawn bordered by the driveway and struck up John Philip Sousa's "Hands Across the Sea." Above them, fluttering from a tall, white flagpole, was the presidential emblem.

Andy was curious, as awed by greatness as any man, and wanted desperately to play the role of voyeur in this instant of history, but he forced himself to ignore the ranks of welcoming dignitaries and the approaching cars, and turned his attention instead to the military and civilian security arrangements. He let his eyes roam, noting the skillful placement of Secret Service men lingering on the edges of the crowd of plenipotentiaries, the military honor guard in chromed helmets and white gloves (which he himself had arranged) lining the wide driveway, the visiting British security agents who had arrived early and now scanned unfamiliar ground with nervous eyes.

As the cars drew nearer and the Marine band played louder, two of Calhoun's Secret Service minions wheeled a smiling man out of the main house onto a broad porch where he could await the arrival of the Prime Minister. Andy could no longer control his curiosity. He pressed forward, watching.

There he was in his wheelchair, waiting on the porch, the man for whom the lion's share of these security arrangements had been devised. A cripple in a rubber-wheeled buggy, dressed in a white Palm Beach suit, his cigarette holder clenched at a jaunty angle by dazzling white teeth. He was a robust, cheerful man, in spite of the ten pounds of steel which encased his withered legs and the sinus condition which plagued him in that summer of 1942. His lifestyle ledger, opened to the age of sixty, was filled with pluses and minuses. Known worldwide for his magnificent vocal cords and his splashy vote-gathering smile, yet those who knew him best said he was, at times, crudely profane and unreasonably stubborn. Wealthy and respected, loved by millions, surrounded by a cadre of influential men who responded to his every whim, yet forced to grind out his cigarette butts with the extreme care of a man in constant fear, a man who knew only too well how easily he could be trapped in the event of a fire. Commander-in-chief of the most powerful nation on earth, yet he could scarcely rise from his wheelchair without assistance. He was a defenseless cripple. He was the President of the United States.

Andy goggled, first at the man in the wheelchair, then at the cars when they came to a stop and doors swung open all up and down the line, disgorging a retinue of splendid uniforms and men in striped pants, a virtual catalogue of well-dressed Britishers dressed to fit the solemnity of the occasion. Save one. From the lead car bounded a short, chubby man in a pair of military coveralls, a pale-blue jump suit which bagged at the waist. The man grinned around an enormous cigar and brushed forward, ignoring protocol, to embrace the President. The band broke off the Sousa tune and launched into the British anthem.

Andy stood rigidly through the playing of both anthems, then forced himself to turn back to the security aspects of his job. He gazed at the line of trees backing the house, wondering briefly if John Bradley Calhoun, the senior Secret Service organizer, had remembered to station a couple of people out there. Surely he had. Calhoun was a sharp old cuss and didn't miss much.

He swung his gaze back to the dignitaries on the lawn. His attention to duty wavered slightly as his eye fell on a face he recognized among the British ranks. A young officer from the British Embassy. Hepplethwaite or Habbleweight or whatever his name was. Andy had met him at one of the diplomatic functions. The young officer had been strongly attracted to Gay that evening, had managed to be within arm's length of her all evening long. And, Andy was forced to admit, she had seemed uncommonly attracted to the Britisher, as well. They had argued about it briefly later on. He continued his security check and was surprised to note, when his eyes returned to the porch, that the President and the Prime Minister had already gone inside. Had his mind drifted that far? Jesus, he'd only allowed his thoughts to wander to Gay for an instant.

As he squinted in the morning sunshine, wondering what to do next, he saw Calhoun, the Secret Service chief, striding across the lawn in his direction, trailed by one of the younger Secret Service men. Andy promptly started to walk away, but Calhoun, rugged red face set in grim seriousness, waved him to a halt. Andy had hoped to avoid Calhoun for the duration of the Hyde Park visit, but he waited, fidgeting, as the big Secret Service man caught up with him.

"Captain, I want to talk to you," Calhoun said. He turned eyes concealed by sunglasses toward the Marine band. "Are you responsible for that?"

Andy glanced in the direction of the band, puzzled, then looked beyond Calhoun at the younger Secret Service man, as though that might give him a clue to what Calhoun was talking about. But the younger agent (what was his name? Fenson? Fenton? Andy had seen him around the White House) only looked back at him blankly. "I don't understand," Andy said. "Am I responsible for what?"

"The band," Calhoun said. "Did you arrange to have them brought up here?"

"No, sir, not exactly. I okayed it, but the request came from one of the presidential assistants."

"Why didn't you tell me about it?" Calhoun said.

"Why should I?" Andy said. "What difference does it make?"

"It makes a great deal of difference," Calhoun said. "They're a security problem. Haven't we enough strangers cluttering up the landscape without you bringing a whole busload up here for my men to watch?"

"It's the same band that always plays for the President," Andy said. He glanced uneasily at Calhoun's young subordinate. Fenton, that was it. Jerry Fenton.

"It may be the same band," Calhoun said stiffly, "but they do occasionally take on new members, you know. How can we check them out when you don't even tell us they're coming?"

"I'm sorry," Andy said. "No one told me you would want to check them out."

"If you had any security background, Captain Blaszek, you'd have figured that out for yourself." Calhoun turned to his young assistant and shook his head. "Political dilettantes," he muttered. "God protect us from dilettantes with political connections."

Andy, offended, said, "Now hold on. Maybe I wouldn't cause so much trouble if someone in your office would let me know what's going on. We got left off your memo list again this week."

One corner of Calhoun's mouth turned up. It might have been a smile, though it was hard to tell with his eyes hidden behind those ubiquitous sunglasses. He said, "So I heard. An oversight. Nothing more."

"Some oversight," Andy said. "It's happened several times in a row. How can we co-ordinate with you when we have to work in the blind?"

"Perhaps you should find another way to keep abreast of developments, Captain. I haven't got time to chase down memos and make sure they reach every unimportant office in the White House."

Andy's face tightened. "You needn't concern yourself," he said. "Several offices rerouted their copies to us, figuring we were the most logical place for them. Besides, there wasn't much new in the memos anyway. Mainly a rehash of what my office had already proposed."

The younger Secret Service man rolled his eyes and shook his head at Andy, almost imperceptibly. Calhoun was grimly silent for a moment, then said, "May I ask what you mean by that?"

"Nothing," Andy said. "Only that if we'd been on your list, perhaps we could have come up with some improvements."

"I'm sorry you don't approve of my methods, Captain. But then, the safety of the President is my concern, not yours."

"I disagree," Andy said. "As long as we use military guards here or at the White House, it's our concern, too. And it's important that we be kept informed."

Calhoun was silent for a moment, then said, "I'll look into the memo situation, Captain. I wouldn't want to offend the military. I wouldn't want to offend your sponsors, either. I don't like to offend anybody. Never know when they might come in handy. You might give that some thought yourself, just in case your influential friends ever decide to stop pulling strings for you." He swung away from Andy and drifted back to the porch.

The young Secret Service man waited until his boss was out of earshot, then said, "Dumb move, Blaszek."

"I didn't do anything. Besides, he started it. What's he talking about? What's this 'influential friend' crap?"

"Oh come on," the young agent said. "Calhoun sent for a copy of your service record a few weeks ago. You've got a big 'P' marked right across the top of the first page."

"A 'P'?"

"Sure. 'Political influence.' Someone apparently turned a few screws to get you your job at the White House. What is it, Blaszek? You got an uncle in the Senate or something?"

Andy felt the color rise to his cheeks. "No, of course not," he said. "Besides, what the hell is Calhoun doing sending for my records? I thought they were supposed to be confidential?"

"Not when you work in the White House. Anyway, he was already peeved about you and that new office of yours. He thinks it's some kind of reflection on his ability." The young Secret Service man sighed. "Look, Blaszek, maybe you aren't interested in advice, but I've got some for you. Calhoun isn't really a bad egg. He's kind of a nice old guy when you get used to him. Maybe you ought to try to be a little nicer to him. Otherwise, you might find yourself frozen out completely one of these days."

"Fat chance," Andy said. "I don't think he could freeze me out any colder than I already am."

The Secret Service man smiled wryly. "You think not? Don't kid yourself. Those memos were just a little test of authority. He hasn't touched his big guns. For example, how much have you heard about the spy landing?"

"Spy landing? What spy landing?"

"See what I mean? Some things are too sensitive to get routed around by memo. The only way you'll ever hear about them is straight from Calhoun himself. And that means you're going to have to mend your ways."

"Wait a minute," Andy said. "Back up. What spy landing?"

"Oh, it's just a little flurry down in Long Island. Some Coast Guard kid says he ran into them on one of the local beaches last week. From a submarine, he claims. The FBI is working on it."

"Why the hell wasn't I told?"

"Because you irritate Calhoun, that's why. Besides, there may not be anything to it. You know those Coast Guard people. Not enough to do, so they compensate."

"But spies? At a time like this, with the Prime Minister coming and all? I should have been told."

"It's nothing to get worked up about," the man said. "It doesn't concern you. Nor us. Even if it's for real. Let the FBI handle it. It's their problem, not ours." He glanced at his watch. "I've got to do my rounds. Think it over, chum. You know the old saying about honey and vinegar. Try to be polite to Calhoun if you want him to co-operate."

Andy watched him go, then shook his head and stared at the horizon to the south, fingering his tie nervously. Jesus Christ. Spies? From a submarine? On Long Island? That was less than a hundred miles away. And nobody had bothered to tell him? Jee-sus.

3

Atop a small hill overlooking the empty train tracks, Dietrich began a sketch of an old barn a mile or so across the way. He had the sketch pad on his lap and it was a quarter full by now of casual pencil sketches of the Maryland countryside, the sweep of terrain and farm fields, the clusters of trees under which dairy cattle grazed, an aging windmill creaking in the wind, a silo. And one not-so-casual sketch, buried in the midst of the smudged pages. A carefully rendered drawing of the narrow little railroad bridge below.

He had arrived at about ten o'clock that morning and had left the gray Lincoln down on the little farm road at the base of the hill, carrying his pad and a box of pencils up with a thermos of coffee, just as though he were a weekend artist. Earlier he had noticed a farmer watching him, a man on the road below, chugging slowly past on a John Deere tractor. Dietrich had made a big show of flipping pages in the sketch book, and had wished briefly that he had purchased an easel and canvas to be more recognizable as an artist. But he wasn't that good, and canvas and easel had a tendency to attract spectators. Not so much with sketch books. Besides, the farmer had shown little more than normal curiosity and had steered his tractor on down the road.

After three hours of sketching, stopping every time a train passed to log it in the margin of his railway timetables, Dietrich could already make a pretty fair estimate of how long it took each train to get there after its scheduled departure from Philadelphia, but he wanted a few more to make sure. Soon, just by checking his watch, he should be able to identify any train on the schedule. Or, more importantly, recognize one that was *not* on the schedule.

Not that he intended to rely solely on his ability to pick out unscheduled trains. Too many variables could foul that up, and railroad delays were too common in wartime. But once the two teams arrived and he set them about their tasks, he would have a man some twenty miles up the line, far enough to recognize the engine number of the presidential train when it passed and get word down to the assault teams that it was on its way.

Leave nothing to chance. If he had learned nothing else during his months with the Abwehr I, it was that if a superbly tailored plan can screw up, then screw up it will. In fact, he had learned that lesson on his very first mission, a sortie to England as assistant to a man whose English was faulty. They had been caught, through no fault of Dietrich's, and there had been nothing for it but to kill the two British tommies who were jeeping them in for questioning. While his partner hesitated, Dietrich had killed inexpertly but swiftly, a reflex born of panic and the will to survive. His controller, Oberstleutnant Grützner, had been interested when Dietrich's partner reluctantly reported the incident upon their premature return to Germany. So interested that Dietrich was rewarded, even though the mission had failed, with a one-week leave to see Gerta, who thought he was still in North Africa and had dutifully addressed a letter to him there every Sunday. She worried terribly, she wrote, during the hard battles of November and December 1941, and he wrote back occasionally—they wouldn't let him write too regularly—from another Abwehr training camp not three hundred miles away. He was impressed by his teachers. The letters went to North Africa for reforwarding, and one that Gerta showed him, the last time he saw her briefly, sprinkled from its pages a few grains of gritty sand.

When Dietrich returned from that first visit to Gerta, he found that Grützner had guardedly spread the word that he had a potential executioner on his hands, a youngster who thought quickly on his feet and who could pass faultlessly for American and who, with additional training and special attention, could perhaps be turned into a resourceful, efficient killing machine.

And so the Abwehr system tagged him for special drill in guns and explosives and assassination. He learned to live alone and think alone. He was given field exercises, important Nazi officials to track and analyze, plans to be set on paper. His evenings were spent in history books, studying a string of brutal ends to men of vision. His exemplars became obscure individuals like Charles Guiteau, Leon Czolgosz, Gavrilo Princip, Joseph Zangara, outsiders all, seedy, unbalanced men who blazed their way to a sudden place in history with handguns and the bombs of anarchy.

When Grützner felt he was ready, Dietrich was sent as a test on a quick visit to Ireland, this time alone, ostensibly on a mission to set up a string of coast watchers and a convoy radio warning system among the pro-German, or rather, anti-English element there. But his true mission, he was instructed, was to seek out a troublesome politician in Wexford, a man with friends in America and a weakness for American pornography, and dispatch him.

The mission was successful, thanks to an illustrated manuscript which detonated upon unwrapping, and Dietrich's new reputation as an assassin bought him another week with Gerta. No one bothered to ask him how it felt, killing coldly and purposefully, rather than in the course of self-preservation as it had been with the British soldiers in England. The system simply marked him as a man who could kill when told to, and who did it without fuss or hesitation. Grützner treated him well, but gingerly, as though he had something more important in mind for him, but wasn't quite ready to tell him about it. Dietrich accepted his changed status without comment. After all, he had killed under orders in France and Africa as an infantryman. Dietrich suspected, if he were to think it through carefully, that it would be all the same to him. But he tried to avoid thinking it through carefully. He only noted that the system seemed somehow more impressed by a man who killed in a one-to-one situation than by a lowly infantry corporal who killed only at long distance to stay alive, and he did not deny to himself that the mild new esteem he received helped soothe old aches that he wished he could forget and put behind him forever.

Grützner tested him with more missions. First to Algiers, to execute a fatuous Vichy French admiral who was suspected of treating with American military intelligence agents. Then to Switzerland to bid a permanent farewell to an American diplomat who was doubling as spy master within the neutral Swiss diplomatic community. Lastly to Zagreb, to pass himself off as an American OSS adviser and to isolate and kill a guerrilla chieftain. Each time, in spite of difficult conditions, in spite of communications which constantly broke down, in spite of chance roadblocks to carefully planned operations, Dietrich had managed to work his way to the intended victims and eliminate them.

After Zagreb turned out well, Oberstleutnant Grützner had spoken enthusiastically one snowy spring morning of a new and far more important mission, the most important of his life, and of the utmost urgency to the future of Germany.

"What?" asked Dietrich, and Grützner looked at his watch, a slender disc of gold for which his tailor constructed special watch pockets in his uniforms, and told Dietrich to get his overcoat.

Before Grützner answered, they walked four blocks through snowy streets down which traveled only an occasional military vehicle or, on foot, gray and black uniforms and the occasional housewife with market basket in one hand and big black umbrella in the other. Grützner paused and fought through the buckles, buttons and folds of his greatcoat to take out his watch again. In the process, the dagger that he carried at his side in lieu of a pistol became disengaged from his belt and fell at their feet in the newfallen snow. Grützner gestured, and Dietrich stooped to pick it up for him. "*Alles für Deutschland*" was engraved on the blade, and Grützner gazed at the engraving a moment before sliding the dagger back into its leather scabbard. "We have tentatively concluded," he said, "that you are capable of carrying out a plan that will nudge the United States out of the war. You will accomplish the demise of America's head of state, one Franklin Delano Roosevelt. Come, we may be late. We will walk this way."

Of all the questions he might have asked, Dietrich chose one, for petty assassinations were one thing and an assault on a head of state quite another. He asked, "Why me?"

"Because of your command of the American idiom," Grützner

told him briskly. "Because you have lived in America and know her customs. Because you are an excellent marksman, an inventive problem-solver, and have proven yourself an attentive student in all phases of your training. Because we are now of the opinion that you are the perfect man for the job." They had reached a more busily trafficked corner, and he paused and dug for his watch again.

Dietrich watched the Oberstleutnant's dagger. This time it didn't fall. He rephrased his question. "Why do you feel that anyone, myself included, can succeed at such a task?"

"It will be far easier than you think," Grützner said.

The man didn't act miffed at being questioned, so Dietrich risked another. "May I ask why you think so?"

"Because," Grützner said, "any man, any man at all, can kill a head of state if he is willing to die himself. History is filled with the proofs." And standing in the lightly falling snow, glancing at pedestrians hurrying by, he proceeded to synopsize one particular element of Dietrich's long studies—Alexander II of Russia, struck down by a member of a terrorist group; French President Sadi Carnot, assassinated by an Italian anarchist; Humbert I of Italy, who survived two assassination attempts and fell victim to a third; King Alexander and Queen Draga of Serbia, killed by a dissident military clique; Archduke Francis Ferdinand and his wife, murdered on the streets of Sarajevo by a Serbian nationalist.

Oberstleutnant Grützner seemed to be in no hurry now, and his list lengthened as they stood on the corner. American Presidents Abraham Lincoln, James Garfield and William McKinley, shot and killed in turn by a Confederate activist, an embittered office-seeker and an anarchist terrorist. "Even Roosevelt himself," Grützner said, "was a target. In 1933, shortly after his election, he came under the gun of an anarchist in Miami. Some foolish woman intervened and seized the anarchist's arm as he fired. The bullet struck the *bürgermeister* of Chicago, a hapless individual by the name of Cermak, and he died instead. Otherwise the Americans might never have been misled into joining this war. This, this mission, is the mission for which you have been in training since the very beginning."

Grützner's head turned as a slim blonde in a sealskin coat with matching sealskin boots went by. "Handsome woman," he said, then suddenly he came to attention, and Dietrich automatically came to attention beside him.

A black Mercedes with a military chauffeur rolled to a pause at the intersection. In the back seat, two crisp generals looked out wordlessly. Dietrich started to salute, but Grützner nudged him, so he only stood as straight as possible, staring ahead. But from the corner of his eye Dietrich could see the faces of the generals. He had seen them before, glimpses in Abwehr headquarters of two men so far above him that they never looked at him any more than at the carpets they trod on, men who were rivals, it was said, to Canaris himself. Now they looked at him, emotionlessly but deliberately, for the space of several heartbeats. The nearest general then nodded solemnly, and the Mercedes rolled on.

When the car was out of sight, Grützner turned and took Dietrich's arm, the first time he had ever touched him. He smiled at Dietrich with sudden, boyish elation. "Done!" he said. "Well done! Come, now we can go back."

Grützner continued to talk persuasively as they retraced their steps. Assassination was simple, he said, if the assassin was dedicated. True, most of the assassins he had cited had died shortly after they delivered their blows, some by their own hands, some gunned down by the victim's bodyguards, some even torn apart by frenzied crowds. But they had proved, again and again, that no man was safe from an assassin's bullet if the assassin made a determined assault.

It apparently never occurred to Grützner, much less the two generals or the general system, to ask, that snowy spring morning, if Dietrich was willing to die. They apparently assumed that he would be. But Grützner's boyish smile appeared more and more often for Dietrich, and in the planning sessions that followed he good-naturedly allowed Dietrich to include suggestions for a safe escape and return to Germany, and encouraged the experts and planning co-ordinators brought in on the operation to do the same.

But the timing was off for any tidy arrangement of a timely death for America's President. With possible approaches still narrowed down to only a half-dozen alternates, Grützner had breathlessly called Dietrich into his office on a sunny morning in late May and informed him that he was to leave immediately for Lorient, the former French naval base which Germany had found suitable as a port for its North Atlantic fleet of U-boats. Word had filtered from England that Winston Churchill was to visit the United States secretly to confer with FDR. A hated Prime Minister and a key President would be in the same place at the same time. It was too good an opportunity to pass. And furthermore, eight Abwehr sabotage men were on the verge of shipping out for the United States

momentarily. Dietrich could use them. *"Wir haben Glück. Zwei
Fliegen mit einer Klappe geschlagen."*

Luck? Dietrich flipped a sheet in his sketch book and worked on
a bird's-eye view of the immediate area, a free-hand map in which
he tried to include all the little scattered farmhouses, the crossroads,
the possible points of danger. Unfortunately, luck worked both
ways. There had been no answer from George Dasch's New York
hotel room. He had tried several times Tuesday, and again on
Wednesday, but the phone only rang and rang. With Kerling's contact it had been different. The man had listened silently, nervously,
not committing himself, but he had listened. Now Dietrich must
assume that Kerling would pass the word to Dasch. It wasn't a
healthy assumption, but Dietrich had no choice.

With luck, then, the two teams would arrive tomorrow or the
next day, and Dietrich would meet them and quickly show them
their responsibilities. Once the bridge was wired, he would split
them up. Two men to the north to block the road to Churchville;
a slightly larger group, perhaps three men, to cover the crossroads
to the south and make sure no one from the two nearest farmhouses
interfered once the countdown began; one man in Providence, up
the line to watch for the train. The other two would stay with
Dietrich, on the hill, ready to mop up any pertinent survivors once
the train had been hit. At that point, after the damage had been
done, the men on the roadblock could pull back to the bridge,
giving him a three-way crossfire. It should be easy. Even if there
were survivors, they would be badly shaken, perhaps already dying.
Dietrich and his people could sweep in quickly, before the shock
wore off, and apply the *coups de grâce*, making deadly certain that
the two major figures were thoroughly and completely out of it.
With luck.

Flickers called from the swaying treetops. Another bird wheeled
far overhead, a hawk it looked like, and Dietrich thumbed back to
his drawing of the railroad bridge. He fleshed in the abutments and
piers, trying to estimate the thickness in scale, then resketched the
upper and lower chords. From this angle the floor beams and
stringers didn't show, but he could fill them in later when he went
down for a closer look.

He leaned back and tapped the pencil against his upper lip. For
breeching, the charges should probably be placed under the ties.
Here. And here. And there. He made light pencil marks on the
drawing. And a charge along one of the piers for good measure. He

flipped the sheet over and made some simple calculations, working out the breeching formula. Wire them in common series? Or in a parallel circuit? Parallel, probably.

As he drew in the firing circuit, he heard a distant whistle. He paused and peered to the north. Perhaps five or six miles away, vaguely visible through the heat haze, he could see puffs of diesel smoke rising from the tracks. He glanced at his watch, checking the time, and made a quick mental estimate. On the basis of the earlier trains and the time it had taken them to get here, that would probably be about a 12:15 out of Philadelphia. He picked up the time-table and ran his finger down the column of southbound trains. He found a listing for a 12:17 departure. Good. Very good. That was quite close. He logged it carefully and returned to his sketches.

4

That same afternoon, Edward Kerling's four-man Florida team broke into two parts and headed north, as they had been instructed.

They had spent most of Wednesday in Jacksonville, getting oriented and making travel preparations. Then, because they were running late, Kerling passed out some of the sixty thousand dollars which had been supplied to him in Germany and ordered them to proceed immediately to their separate destinations.

Young Herbert Haupt and his partner, Otto Neubauer, left first on a two o'clock bus for Chicago. Haupt was to stay with his parents, explaining a year-long absence by saying that he had been in Mexico. Otto Neubauer was to check into a hotel and keep in touch with Haupt.

Kerling and the other team member, Werner Thiel, left an hour later by train on a circuitous route to New York. They were to find a centrally located hotel in Manhattan and settle into their roles of workaday Americans while waiting to begin their operations. When the signal came, they were to recall Haupt and Neubauer by sending a telegram to Haupt's uncle in Chicago, using the code phrase "family reunion."

They went their separate ways without realizing that the signal had already been transmitted.

5

Dietrich was dusty and tired by the time he got back to the board-inghouse and parked on the street, but he felt good. Things had gone well. It had been a satisfactory trip.

He jogged up the stairs to his room, carrying the sketch book under his arm. Tomorrow he would go back to Maryland and await the arrival of the two teams. It would take time to lay the charges, and it would best be done at night, although they could think up a cover if time began to crowd them. Perhaps as railroad workmen. Workmen were seldom questioned by anybody.

He knew something was wrong the moment he opened his door. The covers on his bed were rumpled. Not much, but enough. Someone had been here? He dropped the sketch book and the timetables on one of the chairs and took a look around, puzzled. Hadn't he locked the door? Sure he had. Then, who? The landlady? Why would she fuss with his bed?

An alarm began to burn at the back of his ears and he hurried over to the dresser. He pulled the top drawer open. There, among his shorts and socks, lay the clutter of identification cards. They had been neatly stacked when he left. He was sure of it. He was a tidy man, always had been, a legacy from his childhood and an aunt who considered cleanliness and neatness only one step removed from religion.

He picked up the cards and riffled through them. They were all there. Thank God for that, at least. He put them in his side pocket. He should never have left them lying around like that. It was a foolish mistake. And he couldn't afford foolish mistakes.

Then the enormity of it hit him. He yanked the next drawer open. The moneybelt. It was gone. And the gun. Gone. He clawed through the shirts and handkerchiefs, searching, but they were both gone. Only the silencer tube and the packet of extra ammunition remained. He gripped the tube, squeezing it in his hands, his brain in flames.

The landlady. It had to be the landlady. She had a key. She had come to his room while he was out and had poked through his things. She had taken his money. She had taken his gun. She had seen the different sets of identification.

He stuffed the silencer tube and the ammunition packet into his pocket with the identification cards and hustled down the stairs, looking for her, wondering what to do. He found Mrs. Fikinney in the kitchen, standing behind her ironing board, pressing a green blouse. Her eyes were as wild as his own, as though she had been waiting for him, expecting him.

"You took my money," he said.

"I don't know what you're talking about."

"You took my money," he repeated. "Where is it?"

"Don't talk to me about money, you . . . you war profiteer!"

Dietrich blinked. "What?"

"You heard me! War profiteer! You think I don't know? Listen, this is a patriotic house. You just pack your things and clear out, you hear me?"

"I want my money," he said.

He took a step toward her and she jerked the cord loose from the wall socket and raised the iron, brandishing it at him like a club. "Get out!" she said. "Get out or I'll call the police!"

The color drained from his face. "Mrs. Fikinney, please," he said. "You don't know what you're doing."

"Don't I?" She laughed, her eyes hard and glittery. "If you want your money, sue me. I don't have to take any backtalk from you. I saw the look on your face when I mentioned the police. Do you want me to call them? I will. I'll call them and we'll let them decide what to do about the money."

"I need it," he said. "It's very important. You don't understand."

"I understand all I need to. That money is stolen, or illegal, isn't it? And if I call the police, they'll take you away and put you in jail for a hundred years."

Dietrich began to tremble, hating what he was about to do. She was a woman, and he'd never raised a hand and barely even his voice to a woman in all his life, but she was too close to the truth, not as close as she thought, but so very, dangerously close. He started around the ironing board toward her.

She jerked the iron up over her shoulder again and said, "Stay back. I'm warning you."

When he kept coming, moving slowly, she let fly with the hot iron. Her aim was bad, but at such close range she could hardly miss. Dietrich ducked to the side, but the iron bounced off his shoulder, sending a searing jolt of pain through his shirt. He winced and staggered back as the heavy iron tumbled to the linoleum floor.

Mrs. Fikinney's hand darted beneath the folds of two ruffled white blouses on the end of the ironing board and came back into the open supporting Dietrich's big Mauser Automatic. She gripped it with both hands and pointed it at his chest.

"All right for you," she said childishly. "I've got your gun, too. You just get out of here. Right now. I'll shoot you, if I have to."

He stared at the gun. The thumb safety was still rocked forward. He sighed shakily and unplugged the dangling electric cord from the iron. He wrapped it carefully around his two hands, forming a garish garrote.

She watched him in disbelief. "Do you think I won't shoot? You're crazy. A man attacks a lady in her own kitchen, she has a right to shoot. Maybe the police will take the money away from me, but that won't do you any good."

Silently, slowly, he came at her. She closed her eyes and squeezed the trigger. Nothing happened. She blinked her eyes open and jerked the trigger again. Nothing. She stared at the gun in panic. She tried twice more to fire it at him, then screamed in terror and whirled away. The gun clattered to the floor.

He knocked the ironing board aside and leaped after her. Her screams filled his ears for another split second, then he had the cord around her neck. She fell against the kitchen counter, eyes spreading wide, her mouth frothing, and slipped to the floor. Her hands clawed at his wrists, slashing at him, but he kept his grip, bending over her, squeezing, squeezing, until her eyes rolled up under her eyelids and her hands flickered to her sides. The silvery bell began to tinkle somewhere in the house.

He squeezed and kept squeezing, even after the gurgling stopped, and might have squeezed some more if he hadn't heard the voice on the stairway. Not the old mother-in-law. A man's voice, quavery, calling, "Mrs. Fikinney? Are you all right? Is something wrong?"

Dietrich let her sag to the floor, the cord still wrapped around her neck, and stood up. He glanced quickly around the floor, looking for his gun, and spotted it beneath the kitchen table, against one of the table legs. He scooped it up.

The voice came again. "Mrs. Fikinney? What's the matter? What's all the shouting about?" Footsteps moved cautiously down the stairs, a few steps at a time. The bell kept tinkling in one of the back rooms.

The money. Where was it? Dietrich hastily hauled a couple of kitchen drawers open, scanning the contents.

"Mrs. Fikinney, I know something is wrong. If . . . if you don't answer me, I think I'm going to call the police."

Dietrich pulled back on the hammer of the Mauser and tilted the pistol up and back, freeing the safety. Then he edged to the kitchen door. He waited until a pale face leaned timidly over the banister, then fired. A chunk of plaster flew out of the wall beyond the man's head and the man jerked back. "Oh God!" the man wailed. His feet clattered back up the stairs.

Dietrich took a deep breath and tried to steady himself. He glanced longingly back at the kitchen, wondering where she had hidden the money. Surely it was in here somewhere, because this was where she had hidden his gun. But there wasn't time enough to look.

He started toward the front door, keeping the gun ready in case the man appeared again. But the stairway stayed empty. Should he climb up and find the man? No, it didn't matter. With or without a witness, the police would know who had done it as soon as they found out that one of the roomers had run away. They would get his description from the other roomers. Size and build from the clothing in his room. It was only a matter of time before the word went out. Wanted for questioning: one Frank Daniels, white male, brown hair, in his late twenties, six feet tall, muscular build. Approach with caution. Where would he go? Where would he hide? He had only the money in his pockets now. No friends. No place to sleep. And the police would be looking for him.

Let them look. They wouldn't find him. He would cease being Frank Daniels and become someone else. He would vanish into another identity and lose himself in Washington's crowded wartime sprawl. He shoved the gun in his belt and hurried outside.

The street was quiet. He glanced up at the second floor to see if anyone was watching, then moved briskly to his car. Perhaps he should leave for Maryland now. Sleep on back roads until one of the teams showed up. The money wasn't really a problem. Each of the teams had plenty of money. All he had to do was stay out of sight until one of them arrived. And forget what had happened in the kitchen to the aging lady with the young smile.

6

George Dasch arrived in crowded Washington that evening on a train from New York. The fact that he was extremely nervous seemed to attract absolutely no attention whatever. Washington was a city in flux during those early war months, and Union Station was no exception, with thousands of self-conscious overnight visitors flooding in daily—jobseekers, lobbyists, inventors, clerks, typists, industrialists looking for fat defense contracts, press agents on the prowl, a flood of servicemen in khaki and blue, a more vividly dressed flood of two-dollar whores (though wartime inflation was soon to drive the price up to three dollars). One Washington newspaper had estimated that forty-five thousand people were rolling in daily by train and bus, and another thousand a day by airplane. A solitary man like George John Dasch, in a rumpled jacket and carrying a water-stained briefcase, was scarcely noticeable.

Dasch went directly to the Mayflower and asked for his room. Because rooms were tough to get and tougher to keep, he was told that he had to be out by Monday. Dasch commented nervously that he thought his business would be completed by then.

The first thing he did when he reached his room was to run tap water in the sink and splash his face. He still wasn't certain he was doing the right thing, and now he was confused. On the train down, he had wondered if perhaps a civilian organization like the FBI might be the wrong place to start. In Germany it was the Gestapo and the German Military Intelligence who handled spy cases, and perhaps a more logical organization to take charge of this case would be the G-2 intelligence arm of the American Army. On the other hand, it was the FBI that the newspapers were always writing about. And he had heard that they never tortured prisoners.

The idea of torture appalled him. He should do something to prove to them that he wasn't a Nazi, something that would cast him in a more favorable light. He had brought the briefcase full of money, but that didn't seem forceful enough. It needed an added touch.

He dumped the money on the bed and counted it, piling the stacks of fifties and hundreds and twenties. Then he fetched a sheet of hotel stationery from the room desk and scrawled on it, "Contents, $82,350. Money from German Government for their purpose, but to be used to fight those Nazis." He studied the note and nodded. It had a nice ring. He signed it, "George J. Dasch, alias George J. Davis, alias Franz Pastorius."

Then it was time. He looked at the telephone. Should he call them now? Tell them who he was and get it over with? Or perhaps wait until after he had dinner. Surely a few more hours wouldn't matter. A nice dinner, perhaps some drinks. Maybe even a walk in the evening air. And sleep. He could wait until morning, when his head was clearer. Then call. In the meantime . . .

Just one more night. Please.

THE SEVENTH DAY

Friday—June, 19, 1942

I

It was a small story, only three paragraphs, near the bottom of page 13. A local woman, a Mrs. Ellen Sue Fikinney, fifty-three, had been found by one of her tenants, strangled to death in the kitchen of her boardinghouse. The tenant, a man named Bornstein, had overheard an argument and had gone to her aid, but Mrs. Fikinney had been slain before he could reach her. Police were said to be looking for a suspect, a man named Frank Daniels, who had taken a room in Mrs. Fikinney's establishment a few days earlier.

But George John Dasch, sitting in his pants and undershirt while he waited for breakfast to be brought to his hotel room, didn't notice the story. Nor had he any reason to. Instead, he skimmed the front-page stories nervously, merely to fill in the time. Clark Gable was in town to take an Army Air Force examination at Bolling Field and would be commissioned a major if he passed. The District rubber drive had yielded seventy tons so far. Permanent eastern gasoline rationing was to go into effect in the middle of July, according to the OPA. And the big story of the day: Roosevelt and Churchill were discussing war tasks at some secret rendezvous in the United States. Dasch paid little attention to the story, except for a line which said German propaganda broadcasts had referred to Churchill's visit as being "a gesture for publicity purposes." He wondered what German propaganda broadcasts would say about him when they heard. Perhaps he would request that the FBI not give his name to the newspapers. The authorities would owe him something for giving himself up.

There was a knock at the door and Dasch jerked involuntarily, rippling the newspaper. He cursed at his nervousness and opened

the door. It was a yawning waiter with Dasch's breakfast cart.
Dasch showed him where to put it and tipped him fifty cents.

When the waiter was gone, Dasch folded his paper and looked at
the cart. It would be nice to eat first, but he had promised himself
that he would call when the cart arrived. He had waited too long already. Besides, with the call out of the way, he could relax and eat
in comfort while waiting for the FBI agents to come. He picked up
the phone.

The call went through quickly and a male voice said, "Federal
Bureau of Investigation. Special Agent Thomas S. Creekmore
speaking."

Dasch didn't say anything for a moment. He let his brain race,
trying to find an excuse, any excuse, to hang up and postpone the
call. But there was none. He took a deep breath and said, "I would
like to speak to Mr. Hoover, please."

"I'm afraid Mr. Hoover is not available. May I help you?"

"It's very important," Dasch said.

"If it's important, I'll see that word gets to him."

Dasch was disappointed, but it didn't seem worth arguing about.
"Very well," he said. "What did you say your name was?"

"Creekmore, Thomas S. Creekmore. May I help you, sir?"

"Yes. Good morning, Mr. Creekmore. My name is George Dasch.
I'm a German agent and I'd like to talk to someone about sabotage."

There was a surprised silence at the other end, then the voice
said, "I beg your pardon?"

Dasch sighed. "My name is George Dasch," he repeated. "Also
known to your people as Franz Pastorius. I called your New York
office earlier this week. I'm the leader of the German sabotage team
which landed last week at Amagansett. I would like to turn myself
in."

Special Agent Creekmore, unlike the agent who had taken
Dasch's call in New York, was fully aware of the Long Island landing. At the mention of Amagansett, his voice became more businesslike. "May I ask where you are, Mr. Dasch?"

"Yes. I'm in a room at the Mayflower Hotel," Dasch said. "Room
351. Can you send someone around to talk to me? I'd like to get this
over with as soon as possible."

The FBI agent spoke to someone out of telephone range, then
said, "We'll have someone there in a matter of minutes, Mr. Dasch.
Two of our men are leaving now. Please stay where you are."

"Yes, thank you," Dasch said. He put the earpiece back on the hook gently, then wiped his palms on his undershirt and sat down at the breakfast cart.

He lifted the dish cover in anticipation. He had chosen eggs Benedict for his last meal, and the Mayflower kitchen, noted for its cuisine, had prepared the dish superbly. The muffin and ham and poached eggs steamed through the hollandaise sauce, touching his nostrils, begging for the touch of a fork.

The dish was still steaming, untouched and abandoned, when the FBI agents arrived a few minutes later and found George Dasch in the bathroom, throwing up.

2

Dietrich sat in the Lincoln that afternoon, watching the small train depot at Aberdeen. Four southbound trains had passed through from New York, but there was still no sign of any of the team members.

He wasn't worried yet. There was still plenty of time. Another twenty-four hours at least before the shortening hours would become awkward. But he had hoped one team or the other might appear early. There were things to be done, preparations at the bridge, escape plans to be perfected.

He was hungry. If they weren't on the next train, he would go to one of the little corner grocery stores down the street and buy a loaf of bread and a few slices of salami. That way he could eat in the car while he waited for them.

3

By early evening, Dasch's surrender and subsequent statement had prompted several quick moves on the part of the FBI. Word was passed by teletype to the New York FBI office about the three additional German suspects and their last known whereabouts. Teams of special agents were hurried into the field to find the three men and keep them under quiet surveillance until warrants could be prepared for their arrest.

The first of the three, Peter Burger, was located right where Dasch said he would be, camped out in Room 1421 of the Governor Clinton Hotel. But Richard Quirin and Heinrich Heinck were not where they were supposed to be. Dasch had informed agents in Washington that the two men were registered at the Hotel Chesterfield, the place he had recommended to them that first day in the Automat. He did not know that they had gone to the Martinique instead, nor that they had moved out of the Martinique only the night before to less expensive quarters.

The most recent Quirin/Heinck move had not been intended as an evasive action. It was, rather, purely a matter of economics—Heinck's unwillingness to shell out what he considered an unreasonable price for lodgings. Nevertheless, the two moves, first to the Hotel Martinique without Dasch's knowledge, next to a nondescript rooming house on West Seventy-sixth Street, succeeded in blocking the FBI roundup. The agents who went to the Chesterfield, expecting to find the two men, made a frantic telephone call to alert the main office. Two of the three suspects had vanished.

After hurried deliberations, a decision was made. Peter Burger would *not* be arrested. The men covering him would keep their distance and follow him wherever he went, in the hope that he might eventually lead them to the two others.

As quickly as the FBI case had suddenly opened up, it was now effectively stymied.

THE EIGHTH DAY

Saturday—June 20, 1942

I

Peter Burger left his hotel room Saturday morning at a little before eleven o'clock. It was a beautiful Manhattan morning. Clear blue skies. Minimal traffic, partially because it was Saturday and partially because of the worsening gas shortage. It was the kind of morning to make a man happy, to make a man cheerful, to make him glad to be alive. But it affected Burger not in the slightest.

Why hadn't the FBI come for him yet? George Dasch had surely gone to them by now, told them everything. Yet Burger had waited in his hotel room since Thursday night, expecting them, cringing at every footfall in the hallway. He hadn't even gone out for meals, for fear the FBI would come and think he was trying to evade them.

But they hadn't come. And now he wondered why. Had something happened to Dasch? An accident? A change of heart? Would Dasch come back to New York today or tomorrow, looking sheepish, and say that everything was okay, that they needn't give themselves up? God, that would be so good.

"Peter?"

He nearly jumped out of his skin when he heard his name. Visions of FBI agents swooping down to arrest him tumbled through his consciousness. He jerked around, adrenaline pumping. But it was only Heinrich Heinck, frowning at him from a narrow doorway. Big Richard Quirin was there, too, watching in amusement, smiling at Burger's nervousness.

"You almost walked past us," Heinck said. "Is something wrong?"

Burger took a deep breath. "No, no. Everything is fine. I guess I was thinking about something else." He looked up at the corner street sign. "I didn't realize I was this close to Forty-fourth Street."

Heinck smiled with the lower half of his face, but his eyes remained hard. "You could get us all in a lot of trouble, Peter, walking around in a daze like that. Try to remember who you are. And where you are. Stay alert."

"Sorry," Burger said. "Why did you call me? What is this place?"

Heinck shrugged. "A tailor. Our new suits are ready. I thought we could pick them up, then go for lunch. Where's George?"

"He . . . he couldn't come."

"Again? We haven't seen him for a week."

"He's been busy."

"Well, that's good," Heinck said. "It's time some of us got busy. Have you heard from Kerling yet?"

"No, not yet."

"No? That's odd. He and his boys should have arrived about Thursday. You suppose anything has happened to them?"

"What could happen?" Burger said. But he couldn't meet Heinck's eyes.

"I suppose you're right. They'll show up sooner or later." He grinned. "I hate to admit it, but George was right. There really wasn't much point in rushing into things. Richard and me have been doing the town. We went to a place called the Swing Club last night. Lots of girls. It was kind of fun."

"We ought to take Peter with us next time," Quirin said.

"Sure, why not?" Heinck said. "How about it, Peter? Want to go out on the town tonight?"

"I better not," Burger said. "I ought to stick around the hotel, in case . . . in case George needs me."

Heinck shrugged. "Suit yourself." He glanced at Quirin. "Let's go pick up our new outfits. The tailor said they would be ready by eleven. Then we can find a place to eat lunch. I'm starving."

They entered a doorway and started up the stairs together. They did not notice the three neatly groomed men on the opposite side of the street who had followed Burger to the meeting place and who now seemed totally engrossed in a window display at a nearby florist. Nor did they notice, when they left the street, that one of the three men broke away and went inside the floral shop to use the telephone.

By the time the three German-American team members came out of the tailor shop, the FBI had six men in the floral shop and an additional ten agents scattered at the two ends of the street. They did not plan to arrest the men immediately. They had decided to take each man separately, after they broke up, in order to keep any one from knowing that his compatriots had also been arrested. It was believed that each man's statement could be more clearly evaluated if he believed he was the only one who had been captured.

The FBI didn't have to wait long. Burger, worried about being away from his hotel too long, had declined the invitation to lunch and now shook hands with his two comrades and set off in the opposite direction. A number of the agents peeled away from the stakeout and followed him while the rest moved after Quirin and Heinck.

It was to be almost two hours before the agents could move in on Quirin and Heinck, on Amsterdam Avenue, where Heinrich Heinck split off from Quirin to make some purchases at a drugstore, saying he would catch up in a few minutes . . .

But for the agents following Burger, it was only a matter of moments. As soon as Burger turned the first corner, the agents began to close in. Two FBI men hurried ahead and blocked off the sidewalk and two more approached him from the rear. Burger seemed to recognize the situation before anyone even looked at him. He paled, then hesitated, then spun around and started to retrace his steps.

"Hold it," one of the agents snapped. "We're from the Federal Bureau of Investigation."

They could almost see the light go out of Burger's eyes.

2

The special presidential train rushed southward through the night, bearing the President of the United States and his honored British visitor, as well as their respective entourages of statesmen, advisers, military chiefs and personal attendants, returning to the national capital for a continuation of the strategic war talks.

Captain Andrew Blaszek, silent and preoccupied, was sitting in a special club car toward the rear of the train, sharing drinks with a few of his British military acquaintances. Presidential traveling parties were always supplied with a healthy liquor store, usually distributed during long trips for purely social purposes. It didn't pay to get pie-eyed, blind, staggering drunk, not on a presidential train where word might get back to some of the stuffy men of influence who surrounded the President. But Andy was close to breaking that

unwritten rule. He had a lot on his mind and had been stoking his
mental apparatus with the President's personal booze.

The British officers seated about him, particularly those who had
only recently met him, tried to ignore him, to talk around him. But
his brooding silence irritated them. It wasn't as though this American chap had exclusive rights to melancholia. Sitting there, completely gloomy and all. After all, rumor held that the Hyde Park
war discussions had thus far favored the American viewpoint. Everyone knew old Winnie wanted to postpone any thought of a second front in Europe, preferring rather to strike at North Africa, or
even to launch an attack at Norway in that baffling pet Operation
Jupiter he was always getting the wind up about. Perhaps this
American security captain didn't quite understand the situation. If
anyone had a right to be gloomy, it was the British chaps. Some disturbing dispatches had reached them at the President's ancestral
home. It seemed that Rommel was on the rampage in Africa again,
pushing the tommies closer and closer to Egypt. If it weren't for
those bloody brave bastards in Tobruk, the whole bleeding front
might well have collapsed by now. Yet here was this irritating Yank
officer sitting amidst them, brooding in silence as though his were
the only country in the world with problems.

But Andy's brooding had nothing to do with national chauvinism.
His mental apparatus had rejected the lofty road and had settled in
at a more personalized lower level. He didn't care what happened to
Operation Sledgehammer, or Operation Gymnast, or Operation
Jupiter. In a few hours he would be back in Washington, where he
would have to face the imminent issue of Operation Blaszek, the
White House security liaison whose records had apparently been
permanently impaired with a one-initial indictment. P. Political
influence. Why? Because he was too easygoing, that's why. He
always sat back quietly, grinning his good-natured grin, while the
people in his life decided what he should be and how he should be
it. His mother. Mr. Allenby. General Roach. General Tucker. Now
Gay. What else was somebody like Calhoun to think, when he
made no move to stop it?

Moses in the bullrushes, that was Andy. Floating from patron to
patron, brought up in a succession of palaces. In the kitchen, to be
sure, but at least they were royal kitchens. P. Take care. This man
has political influence.

Well not any more, damn it. He wasn't going to go through life
marked as a sycophant, leaning on influential props. No sir. From

now on he was going to dig his heels in and decide on his own and act on his own and be his own man. Independence, that's what he needed. No more hanging around on the inside, being shielded by a string of overly protective benefactors. And if that meant putting some treasured noses out of joint, then so be it. From now on, Andy Blaszek would stop being a hunk of modeling clay.

Well, of course, maybe not all at once. Maybe it would be enough if he just stood up to one person at a time. Like Calhoun. And the memos. If he could assert himself just this once, in this one little thing, maybe everything else would fall in place.

On the other hand, why start a fight he wasn't sure he could win?

He signaled for another drink and pressed his forehead against the dark window. Events of world importance swirled around him, but he kept his eye firmly fixed on the darkness outside as the train hurtled through the Maryland countryside.

3

Dietrich stood in the shadows on the hilltop, his hands balled into fists of frustration, and watched the train roar over the bridge, bearing the President of the United States and the Prime Minister of Great Britain.

The steel wheels of the train clacked noisily at him and his nerves screamed back at them. An uncharacteristic rage boiled up from his stomach. Rage. Frustration. An emptiness. They hadn't come. None of them. Not Dasch. Not Kerling. And now the train was past. The moment was lost.

Why?

Where were they?

What had gone wrong?

TWO

THE FLORIDA TEAM

THE NINTH DAY

I

The leader of the Florida team, handsome 32-year-old Edward Kerling, smiled easily at the desk clerk as he and Werner Thiel checked into the Commodore Hotel shortly after their arrival in New York early Sunday morning. There was plenty to smile about, and he was in a fine mood. Except for being a few days late, the Florida landing had come off smoothly. The four members of the team had reached the beach without problems, had buried their cache of explosives in the Ponte Vedra dunes, then after a refreshing midnight dip in the Florida surf, yelling and horseplaying in the darkness like a bunch of delinquent kids, they had hiked to the nearest highway and waited for the morning bus to Jacksonville.

Even Jacksonville had been fine. Kerling, a man of intense character and an overriding sense of loyalty to the Nazi cause, delighted in their ability to move around right under the noses of the Americans, without even a hint of suspicion or trouble. Swaggering around town with Thiel and the other two team members, Otto Neubauer and young Herbert Haupt. Eating in fine restaurants. Shopping in fine stores. The whole thing had been so much easier than he had expected it to be. His deep-set gray eyes were serene as he signed the register, flourishingly, Edward J. Kelly, while Thiel signed in as William Thomas.

Back in Germany when Walter Kappe had first recruited him, Kerling's first thought had been on the sacrifice of the young German soldiers who had fallen on the fields of Russia to pave the way for a better world. He knew Germany had to fight, not for the fun of it but to live, not even to save some sort of government or some ideals, but simply for room. So when Kappe cautiously mentioned a military mission to the United States, he'd maybe thought for a

brief moment of the good job he'd landed in Berlin managing the-
aters for the Minister of Propaganda, but he replied with suitable
earnestness, "I can't say no. It would look like I was a coward and
tried to stay in a place where I could earn money while the others
are fighting."

At first Kerling somehow got the idea from Kappe that the raid
was to be commando style, carried out in German uniform. A light-
ning raid, slipping into American territory and blasting the damned
Americans out of their complacency. The idea had appealed to him
greatly. What would the Americans think about that, those Americans with their flaunted national wealth and slipshod discipline?
Though he had lived and worked in the United States for eleven
years during Germany's darker Depression days, he had never
once seriously thought of applying for American citizenship. Nor
had he been sorry to leave when war clouds on the European horizon drew him back home.

But soon after he joined the Kappe group, he had been sent to
Quenz Lake where he met the others and discovered it was to be a
much longer raid, perhaps even a year or two, or however long the
war might last. He and his men, working in concert with the Dasch
team, would flit from place to place, striking at vulnerable American industries, killing, dynamiting, destroying. In time, Kappe said
he would probably come over himself, to take charge of a widening
ring of saboteurs and agents that they would help set up. In its way,
the plan was just as appealing. To sink into the bloodstream of
America and vanish, to flow with the rich, red tide like a cancerous
cell, to kill and maim with impunity, then to sit quietly at a drugstore counter with his victims and listen to them discuss the carnage
over toast and coffee, never dreaming that the man seated two
stools away was the disease carrier—these were the fond expectations which buoyed Kerling's spirit and filled him with secret elation.

A lesser man, less dedicated to the German dream, might have
despaired, however, after two days on a swaying chair car with sin-
gle-minded Werner Thiel as a conversational partner. Thiel, a
tough little man, efficient with explosives and mechanical contriv-
ances, was capable of prolonged conversation on one topic and one
topic only—gutter sex. After Kerling and Thiel split up with the
other two team members in Florida and saw their Chicago-bound
bus pull away, Kerling, concerned that passenger lists might be
checked along the direct East Coast train route, had ticketed him-

self and Thiel through Cincinnati to minimize the danger. He had succeeded only in prolonging the trip and his exposure to Thiel's one-track mind. Throughout the long, two-day trip from Florida to Cincinnati to New York, Thiel's eyes and speech had continually resided between the nearest woman's legs.

Kerling despised sex talk. He didn't particularly like women either, certainly not enough to listen to a steady stream of reminiscences about women past and speculations about women present. All his close friends were men. He liked to drink with men, to talk with men, to serve with men. They were more logical than women, better disciplined in thought and action. He was most at home in an athletic locker room or a military barracks, or off at a beer hall enjoying the easy camaraderie of like individuals, joking about men's topics, laughing, sharing. Sweat and liniment and stale beer were sweeter to him than the floral fragrances of a woman's perfume. Masculine pastimes, like sports and war, gave him more pleasure than any temporary masturbation in the loins of a woman. He had been married once, shortly after coming to America in the 1920s, but he hadn't liked it. And he had slept around with other girls after he and his wife split up. But the girls, like his wife, like every other woman he'd ever known, were always too demanding, too serious, too busy sucking up his oxygen, stifling him, to give him the kind of companionship he needed to survive. Oh, he still slept with women, used them, spurted seed into them when the pressures built up. But he didn't like them.

Perhaps he should have brought young Herbert Haupt, one of his other Florida team members, to New York with him, instead of Thiel. A fine-looking youth, wide-set eyes, delicate chin, good body tone. The kid needed an older head to protect him. That silly trouble with the girl in his home town, Chicago. Young Haupt, banging her in the back seat of a car, getting her knocked up. Then running for his life when she turned up pregnant and insisted that he marry her. A man who knew his way around would have told her to piss off. But young Haupt had fled the country, first to Mexico, then by a roundabout route to Germany, just to avoid marriage. No doubt about it, the kid needed some wiser head to counsel him.

But bringing Haupt would have screwed up their plans to use Haupt's uncle in Chicago as a mail drop when it was time to reunite the team. No, he had done the right thing. Besides, Thiel wasn't so bad. Now that the train trip was over and they had signed into a hotel, perhaps Thiel would stop talking about women and put his mind on duty.

Duty. Even now, bone-weary as he was from the two-day train trip, the secret knowledge of who he was and what he was doing in New York acted as a tonic to Kerling. He felt splendid, bursting with enthusiasm, as he strode away from the registration desk and followed the aging bellboy to the elevator, enjoying the unknowing glances he got from the various hotel employees along the way. Kerling tipped the bellboy handsomely. Take the money, little man. Keep it as a good-luck piece. It comes to you with loathing from the enemies of your country.

As soon as they were alone, Thiel yawned and said, "I'm dead. I think I'll go to bed and sleep for the next two or three days."

"That's a good idea," Kerling said. He opened his suitcase and began to unpack. "I'll wake you later. We'll go out and take in a show."

Thiel grunted assent and headed for the hallway door, tossing his room key. Then he paused and said, "What about you? Are you going to catch a nap, too?"

Kerling shook his head. "I'm too keyed up to waste a Sunday morning in bed. I'll probably go out."

"Out?" Thiel said. "Where?"

"I'll check with our New York mail drop," Kerling said, "to see if we've had any word from Dasch and the others."

"You're wasting your time," said Thiel.

Kerling didn't reply. As far as Werner Thiel knew, the two team leaders were not to rendezvous for two weeks. A meeting had been prearranged for between 12 and 1 P.M. in the grill room of a Hotel Gibson in Cincinnati, an unsuspicious spot if there ever was one, and the day of the meeting was set for July 4—a little joke of Kappe's. Kappe thought of everything, and he took good care of them. He'd even nixed their bringing a shortwave set for communication with Germany because he didn't want to expose them to risk. Instead, they were to send any information they picked up on the location of new war plants and that sort of thing in supersecret ink to a Lisbon address that was itself written in invisible ink on a handkerchief safely tucked into Kerling's pocket. The only flaw in Kappe's planning had appeared at the last minute, when he took the two team leaders aside and confided that some man under the code name Goethe might contact them and require their presence on a priority mission. Kerling had tried to pry more information out of

Kappe, but he'd seemed pretty uninformed and therefore irritable about it. Kerling had no real expectations of receiving word from Dasch or this Goethe or anybody else this soon, but duty instructed him there would be no harm in checking promptly with his chosen mail drop and at least alerting his trusted old friend that messages might arrive.

Thiel, still loitering at the door, said, "Hey, does your friend know any women?"

"I don't know. I doubt it. He likes his privacy too much to waste it on a woman."

"I don't care what he does with his privacy. I just want him to fix me up. I haven't had a piece of tail since our overnight stop in Paris."

Kerling smiled stiffly. "You know something, Werner? You're disgusting."

"Not as often as I'd like to be," Thiel said. He grinned and let himself out.

Kerling's prewar friend, Wilhelm Voss, lived alone in the East Seventies, a small one-bedroom apartment on the third floor of an old brownstone. A doctor before he retired, Voss had specialized in children's ailments and had built up a good practice in the thirties. There were those who said his retirement was premature and had been brought about when the mother of one of his young patients had caught the doctor in the examination room committing decidedly unmedical acts upon her seven-year-old son. Kerling had heard the rumors back in the old days before he left the States, but he discounted them. He had always found his friend to be a mild, soft-spoken man with a preference, much like his own, for solitary living and quiet conversation. There had never been a hint of bizarre sexual behavior in all their years of friendship. Kerling was convinced that the spurious charges of aberrant appetite on the part of his friend had stemmed from some of the more envious Jew doctors in the neighborhood. It was the way Jews worked.

Kerling checked the street carefully after descending from the taxi outside his old friend's apartment building. He had been warned before leaving Germany that the American Government might set up some kind of surveillance on German citizens still living in the country. Actually, there was probably no reason to worry. If the German High Command was correct in its figures, there were some eight million Germans still residing in the United

States, and it was extremely unlikely that the American G-Men could mount an effective watch over even the smallest portion of them.

Satisfied that the street was clear, he climbed the stairs to Dr. Voss's door and knocked. A Sunday newspaper lay on the hallway floor in front of the door. Someone moved inside and a soft voice said, "Yes? Who is it?"

"A face out of your past," Kerling said.

The door opened a few inches and a short, gray man in a faded maroon bathrobe looked out. Rheumy eyes blinked, then blinked again in sudden recognition. "Edward? Edward Kerling?"

Kerling smiled. "Hello, Willie."

The door swung wider and Wilhelm Voss ran a hand through sleep-tousled hair. "My Lord, Edward. I thought you were in . . . Where did you come from?"

"Surprised?" Kerling said. "Surely you didn't think a little thing like a war could keep me away." He walked in and looked around. The apartment was untidy and smelled of age. He frowned to himself in disappointment. His friend had always been so meticulous in the old days.

"I thought you were in Germany," Voss said. He stooped awkwardly and picked up the newspaper, then closed the door.

"I was," Kerling said.

"Then, how did you get here?"

"You don't want to know," Kerling said. There was a gray stubble on the old man's sunken cheeks, three or four days old. And deep lines spreading across the once-handsome face. Apparently the times had not treated him well. Kerling shook his head and said, "Aren't you glad to see me?"

"Of course I am. You know I am. But . . . Why did you come here? What if someone were to see you? Things aren't so good these days, Edward. They all hate us."

In the old man's eyes was fear. Paranoia. Perhaps it would be wise for Kerling to conduct his business quickly and leave. He said, "I'm in town with a friend, Willie. He's waiting for me now. I only came by to say hello and tell you that we might get some messages. I gave your name and address. Will you keep the messages for us if they arrive?"

"Messages? What kind of messages?"

"Just an occasional communication from our . . . relatives. Don't worry about them, Willie. Just keep them for me until I come by to collect them."

"Would they be phone calls? A . . . a phone call came. About five days ago. But it wasn't for you. It was for someone named Kelly."

Kerling stiffened. "Who was it from?"

"A man who called himself Goethe. I . . . I thought it was a trick. They do that, you know. The FBI. It happens all the time. A butcher on Lexington Avenue told me so. They persecute us. I wrote it all down in a letter to myself, denying any knowledge, and sealed it. I was afraid they would come to question me about it, and I wanted evidence that I was not involved."

"Where is the letter?" Kerling said.

"I put it away," the old man said. He laid the Sunday newspaper on a precariously cluttered couch, from which it promptly slipped to the floor. He moved to a dusty old roll-top desk near the window and opened its front, and rummaged through a rat's nest of bills and newspaper clippings, then hesitated and drew out a half-empty bottle. "Would you like a glass of sherry, Edward?"

"No, it's too early. Get the letter."

"Yes, of course. Too early." Voss set the bottle reluctantly back in the open maw of the desk and pawed through the cubbyholes, then extracted an envelope. He held it out in shaking fingers. "I didn't know the message was for you," he said.

Kerling took it and ripped it open. It was dated Tuesday, the day he and his men landed in Florida. It was a short note, recalling briefly the content of the telephone call, interlaced with almost hysterical denials on the part of Wilhelm Voss that he had any knowledge of the matter. A man calling himself Richard Goethe, the last-minute code name Kappe had given them, had instructed Voss to tell Edward Kelly that he and his men, as well as George Davis and his men, were to meet Goethe in a small town in Maryland. Aberdeen. Two days ago. Damn.

"Are you sure you wouldn't like a sherry?" the old man asked.

Kerling shook his head impatiently, feeling defensive. It wasn't *his* fault the U-boat had been late in landing. Could they possibly think it was his fault? Among the data Kappe expected them to send him in his silly damned invisible ink were reports on any questionable acts committed by the other men on the mission. And worst of all, Dasch and his men had undoubtedly received the same message and were already there by now. They were probably embarked on something fantastic, and Kerling and his men were missing it. Of all the terrible luck. Now it was too late. At least for Maryland. No telling where they were by now. Nothing to do but wait and hope for another message. If it was important, Goethe would contact them again. Perhaps in the next day or two. Kerling would have to get the team geared up and ready to move. Quickly. He would have to send for Haupt and Neubauer today.

"If . . . if you don't mind," the old man said, "I think I'll . . ." He let his voice trail off and reached back into the desk, bringing out the sherry bottle and a small glass. He poured himself a shot and downed it.

Kerling grimaced. "You never used to drink in the morning, Willie. What's happened to you?"

Voss gestured vaguely. "I don't drink too much, Edward. Honestly. It's just that I have so much on my mind. I have debts. Never enough money. You know how it is."

Kerling thought for a moment. Then he folded the letter and put it in his pocket. "Perhaps I can do something about that," he said. "I have plenty of money. More than you could possibly believe. If you're willing to do a few favors for me, perhaps I can relieve some of your financial problems."

"Favors?" Voss set the sherry bottle down carefully. "What kind of favors? I wouldn't want to get in any trouble."

"There will be no trouble," Kerling said. He opened his wallet and peeled some large bills out of it, fingering them slowly so Voss could see them.

The old man rubbed his hand across his whiskery mouth. "Are you sure?" he said. "The FBI is everywhere. If this is something against the law . . ."

"There will be no trouble," Kerling repeated. "I merely wish you to send a message for me. And to lease a car for my friend and me."

"Lease a car? I . . . I suppose I could do that."

Kerling smiled and handed him the money. "We'll need it in a couple of days," he said. "We may be leaving town and we'll need transportation. Just as soon as you send the message for me and a couple of friends join us from Chicago."

"What kind of a message?"

"A telegram," Kerling said. "Over your name. I want you to get dressed and go to the Western Union office and have them send it right away. It's to go to a man named Artur Haupt. In Chicago. It should say that the family reunion has been set forward. Tell them to come to your house. And include your address."

"Family reunion? My address? What does it mean?"

"Never mind what it means. They'll understand."

"But the FBI? What if they arrest me?"

"Forget about the FBI, Willie. You're perfectly safe. Our presence in this country is completely unsuspected. The FBI knows nothing."

Voss hesitated, then went to his closet, taking off his bathrobe.

2

Sunday morning traffic in wartime Washington was so sparse that Dietrich had no difficulty in driving down Pennsylvania Avenue slowly enough to study carefully the classic ten-pillared profile of the big white presidential mansion across the street from Lafayette Park. It was set back from the street at the far edge of a sweeping lawn, protected from traffic noises by ranks of weeping birches and maples and bald cypresses. A flower-rimmed fountain hissed serenely in the center of the lawn, spraying the hot morning air with wind-blown mist. Squirrels scampered at the base of two giant seventy-foot trees. The place and the morning looked deceptively peaceful.

It was futile to go on cursing the inefficiency of the Abwehr II amateurs they had assigned him, but the train would have been so quick, so simple. Two for the price of one. Now, if he were to look at things at all practically, he would have to admit the wisdom of falling back on the original plan of a single target, Roosevelt. Churchill wouldn't be here much longer. A dreamer might hope for a lucky break, but a practical workman would face the fact that his chances for getting them both were practically nil.

Dietrich circled the park and again drove slowly past the iron fence surrounding 1600 Pennsylvania Avenue, studying the massive white building with its porticos and pavilions and two unattractive wings, architectural afterthoughts tacked onto either end of the main building. He tried to visualize the cripple who was now safely back inside, tucked away in one of the many rooms of power, perhaps reading or relaxing over his stamp collection or sitting at lunch in his rubber-tired wheelchair, or even taking the air out in the rose garden with his infamous British house guest. What would the man think, what would either of them think, if they knew how close to death they had come?

But he mustn't waste time thinking of might-have-beens. The failure of the train scheme, no matter how it had happened, would inevitably sully his own record and diminish the commendations of his masters, but it was useless to think of that, too. He would have to try again to contact Kerling and Dasch. He would tell them to hold their positions until he had a new plan organized. But this time he would be certain. He would demand an explanation of their failure to show up in Maryland, or he would cease to rely on them. And he had to know if he could rely on them. He had to know whether to design a plan for one team or both teams. When it came to that, he even had to consider the possibility that Oberstleutnant Grützner might expect him to go ahead with the assignment even if no assistance at all were forthcoming from the truant teams, but there was no point in worrying about that either. He had problems enough without borrowing more needlessly.

His plan must be precise this time, with no loose threads of knowledge. Historical assassinations generally took one of three basic forms, the first and most common being the lone man, working fanatically, seizing the first opportunity to shoot or stab or bomb at close range. The second, just as felicitous, but extremely complicated, was to infiltrate the household of the intended victim. Chances of escape increased considerably with this approach. Only two years earlier it had been used by a Stalinist agent who called himself Ramon Mercader to reach the inner office of Leon Trotsky long enough to bury an alpenstock in Trotsky's brain. But Mercader was a fool and had not provided himself with an escape mechanism, and now was rotting away in a Mexican prison. The third method, perhaps the most complicated of all, but one which offered the surest chances of success and escape, was a paramilitary operation, a handful of carefully selected men who acted as a single unit, lay in wait, struck quickly, then withdrew to vanish into the countryside.

The third method was preferable, obviously. But he had attempted it with the train and had failed. Therefore, he concluded, he must fall back on the next surest method, the infiltration of household, preferably infiltration with paramilitary diversion. He would create a footnote to history. Someday, perhaps, his own name would join those of the Booths and the Mercaders, as an object lesson to some fledgling political killing machine.

Church bells pealed in the distance as he cruised around the park once more, intent on one more look at the big white building. He reached into his shirt pocket for a Lucky and thumbed the dashboard lighter. Yes, infiltration. If he was to seek the quarry in his own den, then the first priority would be to locate a safe lair of his own, one from which he could sally at leisure. He couldn't just go to a hotel or another rooming house. That was too risky. No, he would sleep in the car again tonight, out of the city on some country lane, as he had done last night and the night before. Then, tomorrow, with the city alive again, he would scout around for a safe refuge and begin the hunt.

He slowed down as he approached the northwest White House gate. A small group of tourists, dressed in their Sunday best, stood outside the gate, peering through the bars, as though they hoped to catch a glimpse of the President. Dietrich gazed at them impassively through the open car window. Here was a country at war, struggling for survival, yet these people found the time and inclination to travel and enjoy their summers as though nothing had happened. It seemed frivolous somehow. Even arrogant.

Beyond the tourists, on the other side of the closed and locked iron gate, loomed a squat, ugly boxlike structure, a guardhouse. A handful of armed men stood around it, restricting entrance to the asphalt driveway which entered the White House grounds and curled through the trees to the executive West Wing.

Dietrich took a last drag from his Lucky Strike and threw it away. Here at least was a sign that all was not roses and manicured lawns for the cripple who lived within. In a way, the presence of armed guards hovering beside the iron gate both pleased and troubled Dietrich. It pleased him, oddly, because it was proof of the vulnerability of his quarry, visible proof that someone in the White House recognized the danger which might lurk outside their iron-fenced little world. Someone was afraid. And Dietrich felt they had no right *not* to be afraid.

But it also troubled him. It troubled him because now, with the decision made, he knew he would have to find a way to go through this gate. And time was growing short. The *U-202* would return for him in less than two weeks. Unless he found a way in, quickly, and finished off his quarry, quickly, he would have the new and unwelcome task of finding another route back home.

3

Herbert Hans Haupt, a tall, broad-shouldered young man, had finished Sunday lunch and was now comfortably enthroned in the biggest chair in his uncle's living room, his feet on a leather hassock, being shown off by his mother to her dearest friends. All through lunch he had talked, watching their faces as they hung on his every word, his mother and father, his aunt and uncle, his two nieces, and the Voigts and the Pluskats, all soaking up his fiction about living in Mexico for the past year, about getting homesick for Chicago and wanting to see them again and catching the bus from Laredo. It was nice, being treated like a returning hero. While his mother and his aunt oversaw the cleaning up of lunch dishes, and his father and the other men smoked their pipes in exile in the back yard, he was assigned to sit with the other visiting dignitaries, Mrs. Voigt and Mrs. Pluskat, the center of attention, nothing pressing to do, unless you counted his obligation to meet Otto Neubauer later that afternoon at the movie theater. It had been a good homecoming.

It was, in its way, odd that he should be involved in a homecoming at all. Of all the eight men who made up the Florida and New York teams, young Haupt was the least likely prospect for a project of assault and destruction. Unlike the others, most of whom ended up in Germany because they believed in the German cause and wanted to contribute to the war effort, young Haupt had reached Germany through a series of stumbles and accidents, a weird collection of mishaps which began a year earlier when his girl friend of the moment, a pretty young widow named Hedda Weglin, announced to him that she was pregnant.

Haupt, who had just turned twenty-one, had no desire to get married at that tender age, particularly to a woman who had already been another man's wife. And, since he was scheduled to register shortly for the draft anyway, he decided the easiest way out would be simply to disappear. So he had quit his job and talked a friend into joining him and the two of them had headed south in a 1933 Chevrolet, armed with a hundred and sixty dollars and the optimism of youth.

The second in his series of odd turnings came when Haupt and his friend discovered that they would not be allowed to work in Mexico without work permits. Their money slipped away quickly. By the end of their third week in Mexico, they were all but broke. They might well have returned to the United States, had they not been introduced to a man from the German Consulate. In the course of their discussions with the German official, they learned of an adventurous-sounding job opening in Yokohama, where they were told there was a monastery which habitually hired German citizens. The official said the German Consulate would pay their passage if they were interested. It seemed an exciting solution, so they sailed for Japan on July 26, 1941, in the company of a dozen other young Germans.

The third mishap in Haupt's personal maze came when he and his friend discovered that the so-called monastery was actually a labor camp for dissident Japanese. They backed out of the jobs they had been offered and were informed by German officials that they must therefore pay for their passages from Mexico by training to be able-bodied seamen on a German liner berthed at Kobe. As soon as they were considered ready, they were transferred to a German freighter bound for Germany. Haupt served as an oiler. His friend did duty as a cook's apprentice.

The fourth accident of fate, and one which removed any chance for Haupt to turn back, was that the freighter arrived in Bordeaux in Occupied France on December 11, 1941, the day Germany declared war on the United States. Haupt and his friend, immediately suspect to German authorities because of their American citizenship, were kept on the boat for three days before they were allowed to come ashore. After a brief fling in Paris, Haupt went to his grandmother's house in Stettin while his friend caught a train to visit relatives in East Prussia.

Wartime Germany was no kinder to Haupt. He couldn't work without a work permit, just as he had been barred from working in Mexico. Worse, the Gestapo continually questioned him. They considered his Mexico story too absurd, too naïve to be real. For three months he bounced between Gestapo headquarters and his grandmother's house, growing progressively more despondent.

Finally, in March of 1942, he received a letter from a man named Walter Kappe, who claimed to be a magazine editor interested in doing a story on Haupt's brave flight to freedom. After so much apparent doubt from the Gestapo, Haupt was eager to meet with this man who seemed willing to believe him, so he borrowed train fare from his relatives and headed for Berlin to keep the appointment suggested by Kappe.

Kappe talked to him about his background, then turned the questions to Haupt's current difficulties—the harassment by Gestapo officials, the lack of available work, Haupt's dependence on his grandmother. Maybe he should go back to America, Kappe suggested. Haupt nodded. Yes, one pregnant girl at home now seemed far less troublesome than his difficulties away from home, but how could a return be accomplished? Never mind, Kappe told him. It could be done, but it would call for the performance of a few services for the Fatherland. It would take strength, imagination and a will of iron. Did Haupt think he possessed such qualities?

Mrs. Voigt leaned across happily and patted Haupt's knee. "It's so good to have you back, Herbert. Your poppa and momma missed you."

"I missed all of you, too, Mrs. Voigt."

Mrs. Pluskat, who liked being the center of attention herself, regarded him with a colder eye. "Did you find any of the gold you were looking for in that Mexico?" she asked.

"A little," Haupt said. "Enough to buy some things for Momma and Poppa tomorrow." He thought of the money Kerling had given him down in Florida. A hell of a bankroll. He had pulled it out earlier when they were alone for a minute and had offered his uncle Artur a fifty-dollar bill with the little but lofty joke that they should have ice cream for dessert. His uncle had pushed the money back, apparently thinking it was a fiver or something. But Haupt had insisted he take it. When his uncle finally realized the bill was a fifty, he almost choked. Haupt got a real kick out of that.

Maybe Haupt should take his uncle aside later, when all the visitors went home, and explain the whole scheme to him. Not in so many explicit terms, but at least a general explanation. After all, Uncle Artur was supposed to be the message contact in Chicago. That had been decided back at Quenz Lake, during training. The Florida team depended on his uncle's co-operation. He would have to know enough to avoid any foolish mistakes once the messages started coming through. Besides, his uncle seemed suspicious already. Why not? He was smarter than the rest of the family. A Bundist before the war. Made good money. Had the biggest house. It wouldn't hurt to talk to him. Uncle Artur could keep things to himself.

Mrs. Voigt patted his knee again. "Such a muscular young man you have become. That Mexico was good for you."

"That comes with age, Stella," Mrs. Pluskat said disparagingly. "A boy grows no matter where he may be."

"Nevertheless," Mrs. Voigt insisted, "he's handsome. That Hedda Weglin would eat her heart out to see him now."

"Stella!" Mrs. Pluskat said. "Such a subject to bring up!"

Mrs. Voigt looked flustered. "I did wrong? I shouldn't mention Herbert's sweetheart?"

"Don't worry, Mrs. Voigt," Haupt said. "I don't mind." But inwardly he winced. Hedda. Hedda and the baby. What if she found out he was home and decided to raise hell again? Kerling had estimated that it would be at least a week or two before any messages came. Time enough for Hedda to hear about him. Time enough to start the old trouble again. Hell, he didn't even know yet whether he was the father of a boy or a girl. None of the family had mentioned it yet. Probably afraid of worrying him. That would be funny. To find out about the baby, then give Neubauer a cigar at the movie house this afternoon. Hey, Otto, it's a boy. He looks just like me.

He smiled at Mrs. Voigt. "How is Hedda? Have you seen her lately?"

"She's fine," Mrs. Voigt said. "You got nothing to worry from her. You never did."

"I guess she used to come around to see Momma a lot when I was gone, huh? She used to be pretty crazy about me."

Mrs. Pluskat claimed the floor. "She hardly ever came. Too ashamed, that one. And well she should be."

"How, uh, how is the baby?"

"Baby! Such a lie! There was no baby. A miscarriage, she told everyone. If you ask me, there was no miscarriage. There was never a baby. It was a trick. A trick to make you marry her."

"No baby?" Haupt said. "You mean I went to Mexico for nothing?"

"You can't be sure, Gretchen," Mrs. Voigt said. "There might have been a baby. Maybe there really was a miscarriage."

"No. It was a lie. Her mother put her up to it. Herbert was wise to go to Mexico until the lie was exposed."

Young Haupt leaned back in the easy chair. No baby. Son of a bitch. How about that? All that worry for nothing. Well, in that case, maybe it wouldn't hurt to go by her place later and say hello. She was a hell of a good lay. Maybe they could start up again. He might even dangle the idea of marriage in front of her. It would make a damned good cover. A married man, settled down. No one would suspect him of being a secret saboteur.

He was on the verge of asking Mrs. Voigt if Hedda still lived in the same place when the doorbell rang. He heard his aunt calling from the kitchen for his uncle Artur to go to the door.

"You see?" Mrs. Voigt said. "Already the word spreads that you are back from Mexico. This will be some of your old school friends, come to pay their respects."

"Or the FBI," Mrs. Pluskat said.

Haupt's stomach jerked. "The FBI?" he said. "What do you mean? Why would the FBI care?"

Mrs. Voigt dismissed Mrs. Pluskat's comment with a wave of the hand. "She worries for nothing, Herbert. Your mother told us they came to see you, last December, when you were gone, that's all."

"Why?"

Mrs. Pluskat said, "It was to see why you didn't register for the draft."

"Oh, now, Gretchen, don't make it sound so awful," Mrs. Voigt said. "They came looking for Ernst Zuber's son, too."

"What did Momma tell them?"

"That you were in Mexico," Mrs. Voigt answered. "What else?"

"Did they seem angry?"

"No, why should they be angry?" Mrs. Voigt said. "It isn't against the law to go to Mexico. Besides, it was nothing special against you. They are interested in all Americans. They told your mother to tell you that you must register for the draft when you came home, that's all."

"Maybe I should go down and talk to them," young Haupt said worriedly. "It's better than having them come look for me. The last thing in the world I want is to get the FBI mad at me."

"Maybe you shouldn't go," Mrs. Pluskat said. "Your mother showed them the cable."

"The cable?"

Mrs. Pluskat raised an eyebrow. "You don't remember? You sent your mother a cable. From Japan, it said it was. I saw it myself. How did you do that, Herbert? How did you send a cable from Japan when you were still in Mexico?"

The cable. Good God, he had completely forgotten the cable. After his arrival in Yokohama, he had sent a playful cable, telling them where he was. It had never occurred to him at the time that he would be coming home so soon and under such strange circumstances.

Okay, think of something. What to say? There was no sense in denying it. Mrs. Pluskat had seen it. So had the FBI, apparently. But he couldn't change his story about Mexico. Not this late. That would be too suspicious. What would Kerling say in a spot like this? He was the smart one.

He smiled and said, "The cable. Yeah. Well, don't tell me anyone believed it about the cable? You see, I, ah, I met some guys in Mexico City who were on the way to Japan, and I paid them twenty pesos to send the cable as a joke. That's all it was, a joke. I didn't realize it would create a misunderstanding. I'd already forgotten about it."

"You see?" Mrs. Voigt said to Mrs. Pluskat. "Didn't I tell you it was a mistake? Didn't I tell you Mexico was far enough from home without going to the other side of the world?"

"Some mistake. What's the FBI going to think about it?" Mrs. Pluskat said.

"Oh, the FBI has probably forgotten all about it," Mrs. Voigt said. "They haven't been around for more than six months now."

Haupt's uncle leaned around the corner and watched them for a moment, then said, "Herbert, could you come out here for a moment? I need a strong young man to help me."

"Sure," Haupt said, happy to get off the subject of the cable. He smiled at the ladies and said, "I'll be right back."

In the hallway, his uncle took him by the elbow and led him into the empty dining room. He looked very serious. He said, "Herbert, what is going on? What is the reason you have come back?"

Haupt dropped his eyes. "I can't tell you, Uncle Artur. I'd like to, but I can't."

"It has something to do with the war, hasn't it? You are an intelligence agent. That's why you've come back. To spy."

Haupt looked up suspiciously. "What makes you think so? I didn't say anything like that."

"The doorbell," his uncle said. "It was a Western Union boy. With a telegram."

"Telegram?"

His uncle nodded. "From New York. I don't know anybody in New York, Herbert. But it was addressed to me, so I opened it. It makes no sense to me. Were you expecting a telegram?"

"Well, I . . . I might be getting some messages. I gave them your name and address."

"That's what I thought. Are you sure you don't want to tell me about it, Herbert?"

"I can't," Haupt said. "I'm under orders. I . . . Look, all I can say is that it's very important. You'll have to trust me."

Haupt's uncle looked grave. He took the folded telegram from his vest pocket and held it out to Haupt. "All right, Herbert. Here it is. I will ask no more questions. I will not even ask which side you are working for. I don't want to know. Now you read your telegram while I go back outside and keep your father company."

"Thank you, Uncle Artur."

"Don't thank me. I'm not doing it for you. I do not approve. But I will say nothing. For the sake of your mother and father, I will say nothing."

Haupt wet his lips and watched his uncle walk away. The old bastard. What the hell kind of Bundist was he, anyway? Didn't approve? Who the hell cared whether or not he approved? This was a young man's war, not a war for old fuddy-duddies.

He unfolded the telegram and immediately frowned. God. The code phrase. Family reunion. Already? No, it wasn't fair. Kerling had promised. At least a week or two before anything would happen, Kerling said. God, he'd just got home. He'd barely had time to say hello to his parents. He deserved more. Time with his family. Time to straighten out his affairs. Time to rest. A few days to get used to the idea. He couldn't just leap into action right away. It wasn't fair.

He lowered the telegram. And Otto. What about Otto? He glanced at his watch. He was due to meet Otto Neubauer at the Chicago Theater in just a little over three hours. Three hours. How could he face him? How could he tell Otto that the word had already come for them to gear up and get moving? Otto was tired, too. Otto needed the rest as much as he did.

4

"What's in the package?" one of the FBI technicians said, looking up from a spectroscope as Special Agent Emerson J. Carter entered the crime lab, bearing a paper-bound parcel.

Carter shoved the parcel across the table. "Personal belongings of our German informer," he said. "Clothing, mainly. The important thing is the handkerchief. It's got some kind of secret writing on it, he tells us. Addresses or something. He says they gave it to him back in Germany to help him contact the Florida team."

Carter was bone-tired. He had been working all weekend, acting as backup man for Special Agent Grover in the continuing interrogation of George Dasch. As the technician unwrapped the parcel and began to examine the handkerchief, Carter drew himself a cup of coffee from a big urn near the bulletin board. He started to drop his nickel into the change cup, then decided the Bureau owed him something for keeping him down at the office over the weekend, so he glanced over his shoulder to see if the technician was watching, then clinked his nickel against the side of the cup and slipped it back into his pocket. He carried the coffee to a stool next to the technician and sat down.

"I hear the guys in New York caught three more of them," the technician said.

"Yeah. We just received a summary of their early statements on the teletype."

"Have they started talking?"

"Not much. They're too scared, I guess. They've only been in the country for a week or so, and they can't figure out how we got onto them so fast."

"What do I use to bring out the writing on this hankie?" the technician asked.

"Ammonia, we think. At least that's what the informer says. He couldn't remember at first. He's still pretty confused. Not very bright, either. You should hear him in those interrogation sessions. He's been running off at the mouth almost nonstop since we pulled him in, but none of it makes much sense. I pity the poor guy who has to organize his statement."

"Any of it relevant?"

"Not much. Stuff about that training camp in Germany. A whole hell of a lot of anti-Nazi talk about how he had been planning to give himself up even before they shipped out on the submarine. But when it comes to the meat, how we're going to get a quick line on these other four guys from Florida, he comes up a big fat zero. We've got all the names. Descriptions, too. But it won't do us a hell of a lot of good unless you come up with the addresses on that handkerchief."

"I'll do it right away."

"Good. Push it, will you? The old man is screaming for results."

The technician grinned. "You're getting pretty thick with the old man, aren't you? I hear you sat in on one of the strategy sessions the other day."

Carter nodded. "Yeah, I was there. Grover set it up for me. Hell of a good session. The old man clicks off ideas like a machine gun. He asked me to stick around afterwards, you know."

"No shit?"

"Sure. After the session ended and the others started out, he told me to stick around for a chat."

"Man, that's great. What did he say?"

Carter put his nose in his coffee cup. "Oh, just the usual thing. He said he'd heard I was doing a good job and told me to keep it up."

5

It was a standard man's white handkerchief, except that when exposed to ammonia fumes, red lettering appeared across its white folds. Names and addresses. Three sets of them. One was a Lisbon address. The other two names and addresses, of more immediate interest to the FBI, belonged to a man named Artur Haupt in Chicago and one Wilhelm Voss in New York.

It took the technician less than an hour to complete his tests and type up his report. By late afternoon, the Chicago and New York addresses were on the teletype to respective FBI offices, with instructions that both men were to be watched on the off chance that they might lead agents to the missing members of the Florida team.

As Artur Haupt's name and address clattered into the Chicago FBI office, his young nephew, Herbert Haupt, carried a bag of popcorn into the rear of a darkened theater and waited until his eyes adjusted to the dimness. On the screen, George Sanders and Paul Lukas held a whispered conversation in clipped German accents, something about setting up an undercover spy system in the United States.

Young Haupt swept his eyes across the few occupied seats, looking for the team member who had accompanied him to Chicago, Otto Neubauer. He spotted the back of Neubauer's head, dark hair slicked back, wide ears flaring in silhouette, sitting about halfway down, next to the aisle.

Haupt finished his popcorn and dusted the salt from his fingers before starting down the aisle, just in case Neubauer offered him a handshake. He didn't want any wisecracks about eating popcorn at a clandestine meeting. The guys were always kidding him about being too young for this business anyway. When he reached Neubauer, he leaned over and whispered, "Hey, Otto. It's me. Move over."

Neubauer grinned up at him, then slid over a seat. "Hey, kid, good to see you. How's the family?"

"Okay," Haupt said. "Except my mother. She wasn't too keen on me leaving the house this afternoon. I told her I was coming off to see one of my old high school chums."

"I guess they were glad to see you."

"You better believe it," Haupt said. "I really knocked their eye out, too. Caught a cab from the bus station and rode up in style. You should have seen my old man's face when I tipped the driver."

"Don't throw money around unnecessarily," Neubauer cautioned. "We can't afford to attract too much attention."

"I'm not throwing it around," Haupt said. He was silent for a moment, remembering the fifty-dollar bill he'd pressed on his uncle, then he put it out of his mind and sneaked a glance at Neubauer in the darkness.

Neubauer was a pretty good guy in his way. Big, sturdy. A real Nazi, too. He had come to the States back in 1931, when Haupt was only an eleven-year-old kid, and worked in restaurants and ships all over the country. He was a good cook, they said, and even ran one of the food concessions at the Chicago World's Fair back in 1934. Then he joined the Bund, and later the Nazi party, and went back to Germany, where he had ended up fighting on the Russian front after the war started. Haupt envied him that. Otto had shown him the scars once back at Quenz Lake, shrapnel tracks all over his hip and leg where an artillery shell had cut him up. He even had a fragment in his cheek, a deep scar on the left side of his mouth which made him look tough. Haupt envied him the facial scar. It was just deep enough to make him look interesting, the kind of thing that made girls squirm.

Neubauer turned his head. "What are you looking at?"

"Nothing," Haupt said. "How's the movie? Any good?"

"Not bad," Neubauer said. "The Nazis are evil, crude and stupid. And working against them is Edward G. Robinson, the kindly, gentle government man. He never does anything wrong. Pretty true to life."

Haupt giggled. Then, "You check into a hotel yet?"

"Yeah. I'm at the LaSalle. It's a dump, but it's handy to the Y. I can work out on the barbells every day and keep in shape."

George Sanders simpered and sneered and told secret agent Francis Lederer to get hold of thirty-five blank American passports for the German spy ring. His interest caught, Haupt watched as

Lederer made a phone call to the New York passport office and pretended to be the Secretary of State, requesting that the blank passports be delivered to him at the desk of a Manhattan hotel.

"Hey, that's pretty neat," Haupt whispered.

"He'll never get away with it," Neubauer said. "The government man is too clever. I don't suppose you've heard anything from Kerling yet?"

Haupt started. "Why do you ask?"

"I don't know. I just thought maybe he'd let us know when he got to New York safely."

"He wouldn't bother to tell us anything like that," Haupt said. "He'll save the messages for something important."

Neubauer sighed. "I guess it's too early for the important stuff."

"Yeah, I guess it is," Haupt said.

As Neubauer had predicted, German spy Lederer walked into a trap when he went to the hotel desk to pick up the passports. Government agents dragged him off to the FBI office where Edward G. Robinson, puffing contentedly on a pipe, broke him down with trick questions.

Lederer was a fool, Haupt decided. A spy with any sense would have seen what the FBI man was up to. He would have kept his mouth shut and waited for a lawyer. That was the trouble with spies. They were always rushing into things.

He glanced at Neubauer in the darkness and began to wish for another bag of popcorn. Something to keep his mind occupied through this fictional toppling of Nazi dominoes.

THE TENTH DAY

I

Dietrich hadn't been able to see it from his car the day before, but a small black sign with gold-leaf lettering was fastened to the bars outside the east gate. The inscription said:

WHITE HOUSE TOURS
Tuesday–Saturday
10 A.M. to NOON

Dietrich braced one hand against the iron fence and peered through the bars at the hedge which flanked an asphalt driveway to the East Wing. Tuesday. Too bad. He'd wanted to begin by taking a close look at the inside of the building. Not that it really mattered. According to the new tour guide booklet he had bought after breakfast, the White House tours were usually restricted to just a few of the public rooms on the ground floor.

Still, it would have given him a chance to seek possible diversionary gambits for the Kerling and Dasch teams. The teams. At least there was some progress on that score. Dietrich had placed his calls again Sunday afternoon, using two different phone booths on the outskirts of Baltimore. Dasch still wasn't available. Mr. "Davis" had checked out of the hotel, a man's voice had told him, but if he would leave his name, there was a possibility . . . Dietrich had hung up quickly. If Dasch had seen fit to go against orders and change his hotel, he must have feared he was being watched. Perhaps that explained why Dietrich had been unable to get him before. Dasch had probably been lying low.

But the Kerling phone call had been more successful. This time Kerling's New York contact seemed less wary. Mr. "Kelly," the man said, had arrived in New York that very morning and had expressed concern at having missed the first message. No, the man hadn't been told what had caused the delay, and yes, he would certainly see that a second message reached Mr. "Kelly" and tell Mr. "Kelly" to reach Mr. "Davis." The contact was to meet with Mr. "Kelly" and an associate on Tuesday evening. He would relay the message at that time.

That would do it. If Kerling could locate Dasch and bring him in on it, Dietrich could set up a full-scale operation. Perhaps he would have Kerling and Dasch take the White House tour when they arrived. He wanted at least two or three men inside the building to create a distraction. Another man waiting with a getaway car. Yet another, perhaps, ready to lay a false escape trail for the police, or at least ready to broadcast false calls on the police bands to create confusion. He could do it without them if he had to, but it would be so much easier with help.

Another group of tourists, like the ones he had seen from his car yesterday, paused along the fence to his left and aimed cameras through the iron bars. Dietrich turned his back and walked along the fence to the north. At the corner he turned west, following the fence, staring at the sweeping grounds and the big, elegant white building. Something like a hundred and thirty-two rooms, the tourist booklet said. And twenty bathrooms. How does a man in a wheelchair use a bathroom? Does he have Secret Service agents trained to lift him off the wheelchair and deposit him on the commode? To wipe his bottom and zip his pants? Or does he have a removable potty which attaches beneath the wheelchair seat?

Gaining entrance was the big problem. Sure he could go in as a tourist. Stand in line with several hundred people, carrying an explosive device of some kind, inching forward a few feet at a time until they let him in. Ask one of the swarms of White House policemen where would be a good place to put a demolition device to make sure it was below the President's bedroom. After all, the White House police were supposedly trained to answer questions, all kinds of questions. He smiled a little at the thought. A White House policeman, crisp and polite, thinking it over, saying, "Well, sir, I'd suggest the Red Room. If the President sleeps with his wife tonight, you're out of luck. But then, Eleanor hasn't slept with him for years, so if he follows his usual pattern, you should be just about right. What's that? Your tourist booklet shows his bedroom as being above the Blue Room? Well, now, that scale is off a bit. I'd say the Red Room, perhaps near the east wall. You just put your bomb in that antique desk and move along. There are other people waiting to come in. After all, as the President says, his house belongs to *all* the people. It isn't fair to dally."

Actually, it wasn't as silly as it might sound. He *could* do it that way. It was an old building, structurally unsound. If he could find a way to bring the bomb in, a way that was unlikely to be noticed, he could set a charge that would rip the place to pieces. Perhaps an incendiary, something that would turn the building into sheets of flame. The President was completely helpless. Unless he slept with Secret Service men at the foot of his bed.

Dietrich ran his hand along the dark fence bars, watching the soldiers patrolling the grounds. One could lure one of the enlisted men aside, corner him, kill him. Armed with the proper papers, one could become a temporary White House sentry oneself. It wouldn't take long. Time enough to get behind the West Wing, within sight of the Oval Office. Then the enlisted man's rifle off one's shoulder, a shot through the window, and it would be all over. Except for a single thing. Once one fired the shot, they would come at one from all directions. They would cut one to pieces before one covered twenty feet. No, he had no wish to be a dead martyr. Success was important. But so was survival. He'd rather take them together.

He would need a longer time inside, time to analyze the situation, time to set up his escape. He needed an almost permanent access, something which would allow him to come and go at will, without being noticed. A job of some kind. Gardener? Cook? A place that size, with such huge grounds, so many people to service, was bound to have rather large professional staffs. Could one create an opening for oneself by arranging "accidents" for some of the regulars? But what if the Secret Service checked out kitchen and garden employees? Surely they did. How long would it take to set up a credible background as a loyal dishwasher or stable lawn mower? And even if one could manage, would menial jobs give one the access needed?

Perhaps as a radio technician. This President liked the sound of his own voice, liked to talk to groups, to officials, in person, on the radio. Perhaps Dietrich could wangle a position as a technician and wire his microphone for electrocution. A presidential fireside-radio-barbecue. "Good evening, my fellow Americans-s-s-s-z-z-z-z-z-z-z-z-z!"

No, it would have to be some other way. Perhaps as a working member of the executive wing. He had watched the people coming in and out of the working northwest gate, showing their ID cards to the gate guards. Army officers, businessmen, newspaper reporters, photographers. None of them seemed to excite the guards. It was almost as if they were invisible people. Suppose he were to seek entrance as a newspaperman. Somewhere among the identity papers prepared for him back in Germany was a press card, made out on one of the Pittsburgh newspapers. But it would never withstand the checking he would undoubtedly face in getting into the White House. One call to Pittsburgh and it would be all over.

Still, if he had the run of the West Wing, his job would be made quite simple. Close enough to the President to spit on him. Within easy access of West Executive Avenue for a quick escape. He could have Kerling and his men prepared to cover his withdrawal, while the Dasch team worked at the other end of the grounds, creating a distraction.

He paused a few feet short of the northwest gate and lit a cigarette, watching the guards from the corner of lidded eyes. There must be a simple way to go through that gate without being stopped. This afternoon, immediately after he worked on the next step, a quiet place to live and hide, he would do some research, ask some questions. Surely there was a procedure, a viable procedure, for a man who was willing to take chances.

2

Inside the barred fence, inside the big white building, Andy Blaszek poked his head through the press secretary's office door and grinned reluctantly at the receptionist. He said, "Hi, Cora. It's me again."

The receptionist, a tall, busty girl with chestnut hair, looked up from her desk and arched an eyebrow. "Well, well," she said. "Our shy friend from the back hall. What is it this time, another request for those greedy generals of yours?"

Andy nodded weakly. "Yeah, sort of." He looked nervously across her shoulder at the closed door to Steve Early's inner office. "Is he in?"

She shook her head. "He's with the President."

"Good," Andy said. He came farther into the room. "I need a favor, Cora. The *Post* ran a shot of General Burrows last Thursday. With those two Navy fliers who came in for medals. He wants prints."

"Oh, my God. Burrows again? I thought sure the admirals would freeze him out this time. How does he do it? Is it that wavy gray hair and his dimpled chin?"

"I think he just happened to be standing around at the right time," Andy said. "Look, Cora, the general wants ten eight-by-ten glossies of the one that ran, and six each of everything else the photographer got. I called the *Post* this morning, but I guess I talked to the wrong person. Could you send a request for me?"

"I suppose he wants them for free?"

Andy tugged at his tie. The knot seemed unnecessarily close. "If it's too much trouble . . ."

"Never mind," she said. She flipped open a steno pad and made a note, then tapped her teeth with the pencil. "Do you suppose the general will sulk if we pare the number a bit?"

"Don't pare it too much," Andy said. "I think he plans to send them to some camp newspapers." He tugged at his tie again. Now the damned thing was off center.

"Here," she said. She rose from her desk chair and stepped in close and adjusted the knot, breathing warmth and invitation. She said, "Sometimes I think you need a mother, Andy. I almost wish you were unattached. I'd put in for the job myself."

Someone cleared his throat discreetly at the door and Andy jerked back, afraid it was Steve Early, the press secretary, returning from his briefing with the President. But it was only one of the Secret Service agents, grinning through the door at them.

It was the young one, Fenton. The man who had talked to Andy after his encounter with Calhoun at Hyde Park. He smiled wickedly and said, "I didn't mean to interrupt. This will just take a second, then you two can carry on."

The receptionist, not at all nonplused, said, "What do you want, Jerry?"

"A list of the European correspondents who wanted to talk to the Prime Minister this afternoon," he said. "Calhoun wants us to check them out. Can you lend it to me for a few minutes?"

"I think the British security people have already okayed it," she said.

"Yeah, I know. But Calhoun wants a double check."

She nodded. "I'll get it. Stick around, Andy. I want to go over that picture request again." She went into Early's inner office.

Fenton grinned. "Sorry about that," he told Andy. "Hate to mess up another guy's play. Maybe you should have closed the door."

"I wasn't making a play," Andy said. "She was fixing my tie."

"Sure," Fenton said. "Say, did you hear the latest on that thing we talked about the other day?"

"What thing?" Andy said.

"The spies. Those Germans who supposedly landed from a submarine. I told you about them at Hyde Park."

"Oh. Yeah. What about them?"

"Well, it turns out there really *were* some spies. The FBI picked up a bunch of them Saturday. Four in all."

"You're kidding."

"No, straight poop. It seems one of them caught a train down here last Thursday and gave himself up. Then after he talked, they caught the other three hiding up in Manhattan."

"One of them came to Washington?"

"Yeah. Spent the night at the Mayflower, just as bold as brass. Calhoun got a brief on it this morning. The FBI honchos say there are four more, from another sub. They're hunting them now."

Andy's eyes widened. "In Washington?"

"No, no, they're not in Washington. The Hoover boys think they're in Chicago, or maybe New York. They've got a lead of some kind."

"But why did the first one come to Washington? Why didn't he turn himself in to the New York bureau?"

"Hell, I don't know. Spies aren't exactly my specialty."

The tall receptionist breezed back into the room and handed a typed list of names to Fenton. "Get that back to me as soon as you make a copy," she said.

Fenton mumbled his thanks, and started for the door. Then he hesitated and looked back at Andy. "Look, maybe I shouldn't have mentioned what I just mentioned. It's still kind of hush-hush. Let's just forget it, okay?" He glanced at Cora and hurried out.

"What was that all about?" she asked. "Did he make some smart crack about me?"

Andy shook his head slowly. "No, we were talking about something else. Listen, uh, Cora, could you do me another favor?"

She arched an eyebrow at him. "Are you trying to take advantage of my good nature, Captain?"

"No, honest. This time it's a small favor. Could you go through the stacks and pull copies of the local papers for me? I'd like a copy of each for the past couple of weeks."

"Is this for General Burrows?"

"No, this is for me."

"That's good," she said. "Personal favors are the kind I do best. What's up? You starting a scrapbook?"

"Not exactly. It's something Fenton said. A man came to Washington last week. I've got a hunch about it. I thought I'd look through the papers and see if I can spot anything to back me up."

"That sounds mysterious. Who's the man?"

"Just a guy," Andy said. "Would it be much trouble?"

"Not at all. Hang on, I'll go get them."

"No, wait," he said. He grinned in embarrassment. "This is something I'd like to keep to myself for a while. Could you wait until noon to send them down? Sergeant Huffman will be out to lunch then, and I can stick them in my desk without having to answer any questions."

She tossed her head, making the chestnut curls jiggle. "Captain, for you I'll bring them down my very own self. Particularly if the mad, bad sergeant will be gone."

He knew she was kidding. At least he thought she was. But he blushed anyway as he thanked her and left the room. He'd have to make sure his staff had plenty of work to do. He wanted at least one of the corporals around when the lunch hour came. Safety in numbers, they say.

3

At noon, Dietrich walked up Connecticut Avenue to Farragut Square and embarked on the second search he had been impatiently waiting to begin, the search for a safe place to live. Farragut, like all of Washington's small, centrally located parks, was an oasis of green surrounded by tall buildings and the day's commerce. And, like all the city's centrally located parks, it was a favorite lunch and lounge haven for the legions of poorly paid government girls who worked in the neighborhood.

He paused in the center of the square by the statue of American naval hero David Glasgow Farragut, pretending to read the inscription, all about the Civil War battle of Mobile Bay and Farragut's famous "Damn the Torpedoes!" cry. But his eyes moved swiftly from side to side, sweeping past bright beds of petunias, azaleas and flowering crab apples that now were flowered out, to the lavishly blooming young women dotting the open park.

The war had taken most of the men, all but the very young and the very old, and left thousands of government jobs vacant. There were, according to official estimates, some eighty thousand young women in the city to answer the call, girls from north, south, east and west, lured to the capital by jobs which brought them an average of $1,560 a year. Young and pretty, most of them, they invaded the parks daily at lunchtime, sprawling in groups on the grass and on park benches, soaking up the noon sun and giggling over sandwiches and fruit from brown paper bags.

As far as Dietrich was concerned, they might all have been pressed from the same mold. There was a depressing sameness about them, a herd look. They were mostly quite young, ranging in age from nineteen to twenty-five. They were nearly all wearing hats, all wearing the same bright-red lipsticks, and mostly bare-legged, thanks to the nylon shortage. Perhaps as many as 80 per cent of them wore two-piece flowered dresses, with exaggeratedly padded shoulders. White, high-heeled sandals seemed to be the only fashionable footwear, and all the skirts fell only slightly below the knee, exposing a lot of bare calf. About the only noticeable difference was in the hair styles. Even so, he saw a conformity in the division, with about half of the girls wearing upsweeps and the other half letting it fall to their shoulders.

He set off down one of the crosswalks, strolling casually, watching for a likely candidate. A few of the seated girls stared at him openly, even hungrily, a condition aggravated by the scarcity of eligible young men in wartime Washington. A trio of young women lounging near a box hedge whispered as he approached. One of them winked and mouthed the words, "Hubba, hubba," but Dietrich ignored her. Girls wrapped in the safety of groups were too hard to cut out of the herd, no matter how brazenly they might appear to welcome it.

He finally spotted one who seemed right. A small, carefully dressed brunette sitting on a bench near the southeast corner of the small square, chewing on a sandwich. Three members of a motley flock of park pigeons bobbed agitatedly near her feet, but she ignored them and was staring at him, indicating interest. She was pretty, a point which made her easier to take. And best of all, she was wearing a wedding ring, which meant she wasn't likely to be sharing a room with other girls.

He took a napkin-wrapped fistful of broken toast, pilfered from the coffee shop where he'd eaten breakfast, from his pocket and went over to her. "Excuse me," he said. "Do you mind if I share your bench and your pigeons?"

"Oh, please, you really shouldn't feed the pigeons," she said, but she gathered up her lunch sack and scooted a few inches to make room.

"Don't you like pigeons?" he said.

"It's not that," she said softly, almost apologetically. "But once you start feeding them, they get to expecting it. They depend on you. Then what happens if you go away somewhere and you're not around to feed them? I feed the birds at my apartment, and I always worry—what if I go somewhere? They'd starve. Wouldn't they?"

Dietrich smiled and sat down on the bench. "Are you planning a trip?"

"Oh no," she said. "I never go anywhere, except just home to Baltimore some Sundays."

She sounded so sad that Dietrich's pleasant mask became one of his rare, sympathetic smiles. So young and eager and so carefully dressed, and nowhere to go. And she was eager, and quick to try to strike up a conversation. Good. That meant she was agressive. On the prowl, probably. A husband in the service. Time on her hands. She had narrow but mobile and well-formed lips. Expectant brown eyes. Her hair, more brown than black and carefully coiffed, rolled to her shoulders. She had combed a three-inch bang across her forehead above the right eye, a kind of restrained imitation of Veronica Lake. She wasn't one of the two-piece print girls, but rather wore a silky patterned blouse with a big bow dangling from the throat, covered by an expensive-looking light-green summer suit jacket with the inevitable padded shoulders. Her nose was a shade too prominent, but on the whole he found her to be quite attractive.

She was aware of his look of appraisal and she reduced her sandwich munching to dainty nibbles. "Oh well, it really wouldn't hurt to feed the pigeons once or twice," she said. She nodded at his napkinful of toast. "Go ahead. I guess I spoil these anyway. I always give them my sandwich crusts. You don't come here often, do you?"

He opened his packet of toast bits and tossed a few on the sidewalk. The three pigeons pecked greedily, and a half-dozen more of the park pigeons promptly fluttered over to join them. "No, I'm new in town," he said. "Just got in this morning."

"Oh? Where are you from?"

He scattered more toast. "San Antonio. I take it you're from Baltimore?"

"Yes. But I've been here nearly six months."

The air stirred and the whole flock of park pigeons flew in a low, tattered cloud to compete with the bickering first-comers. "My name is Raymond," he said. "Raymond Patterson. My friends call me Ray."

"Mine is Sarah. Sarah Miller."

He grinned at her. "Hello, Sarah Miller."

She smiled back, a gay, very pleasant smile. One of the pigeons at their feet, a gray like most of the flock, snatched up a crust from under the beak of the gray next to it and skittered off a few feet, followed by two more grays and one timid pigeon that was an odd shade of reddish brown. Dietrich threw another crust toward the brown, but it wasn't fast enough and another excited gray got it.

"This is a crazy town," Dietrich said. "I've been all over, looking for a place to stay. I've never seen a place so crowded. Must be the war."

"Yes, it's hard," she said. The brown pigeon ran in little circles, peering at the ground, and Dietrich fished out more toast, but this time, throwing carefully, he nevertheless succeeded only in hitting his brown pigeon on the wing, and it skittered away from the food it so desperately appeared to want.

He frowned. "Even when I locate a place, I'll probably have to share it with two or three other guys. That's what the rental agent told me. Too expensive, otherwise. But I guess you know that. You probably have roommates yourself."

"No, I live alone."

His stash of toast was gone. The brown pigeon had gotten none. Dietrich tried to concentrate harder on the girl. He had chosen well. He turned his head and let his eyes roam over her. Good body. Hips maybe a shade plump, but narrow waist. Probably good breasts, too, though it was hard to tell through that dangling bow and the suit jacket. He said, "You're very pretty, Sarah Miller. Did you know that?"

She smiled demurely, her eyes on the pool of hopeful pigeons still at their feet. "No I'm not."

"Nonsense," he said. "You should be proud of being pretty. Frankly you're the prettiest woman in this park."

"I'm too short," she insisted happily. "I always wanted to be five-foot-seven, but I'm only five-three." She looked at the sandwich in her lap and said, "Would you like to share my lunch?"

"As a matter of fact, I was about to suggest you feed your sandwich to the pigeons and let me take you to lunch," he said.

"Oh, I couldn't let you do that."

"Sure you could. Look, I'm new in town. You're the only person I've met so far. I'd deem it a favor if you'd join me. You could tell me a little about the city. Maybe give me a hint or two about where to look for a job."

"I'm really not very hungry," she said. As she spoke, she laid the sandwich cautiously in her lap and slipped her hands unobtrusively under the paper bag. Her hands worked at each other, doing something out of sight.

"Come on," he said. "You wouldn't want to starve the poor pigeons. They're still hungry."

"I'm afraid they're always hungry," she said. A moment later, when she thought he wasn't looking, she opened her purse and dropped something inside. The wedding ring.

"Then let's feed them and go find a restaurant." He reached for the sandwich in her lap, letting his finger brush her thigh. She sucked in her breath nervously and watched while he shredded the sandwich and tossed it on the ground among the pigeons.

Off to the side, the brown pigeon bobbed indecisively, wanting to rush in but blocked by a feathered wall of grays. Dietrich stood and held out his hand to Sarah. He wished suddenly he hadn't dumped her sandwich so carelessly. Now there was nothing left for the dumb brown pigeon. But it was its own fault. To the cowardly go no spoils.

4

At his desk in the Chicago FBI office an hour later that afternoon, Special Agent Morris Goodall sat studying a file folder and wishing he hadn't chosen stuffed peppers for lunch. Across from him, chatting amiably, was a young German-American named Herbert Hans Haupt, explaining his absence of a year and a cable from Japan which he said his mother had shown to FBI agents back in December.

"So you see," young Haupt said, spreading his palms cheerfully, "the joke I played on my mother may have caused some confusion. Actually I was in Mexico the whole time. I only got back to Chicago day before yesterday."

Agent Goodall nodded in boredom and made a mark in the file folder. It was a slim folder, containing only a few necessary statistics and a summation of the December visit to Haupt's house. There was only the vaguest reference to the cable.

"That explains a lot," Goodall said. He glanced at his watch. A coffee break wouldn't be a bad idea. He snapped the folder shut. "It was good of you to come in, Mr. Haupt."

"Well, I didn't want anyone to think I was a draft dodger. It's just that I was out of touch down there, and I didn't know I was supposed to register."

"Are you registered now?"

"Oh, sure. I went by my Selective Service office this morning before I came in to see you."

"Well, that does it then," Goodall said. "Thank you, Mr. Haupt. You've been very helpful." He stood up, to give the young man the idea.

"Good," Haupt said. He stayed in his chair. "Like I told my mother, I wouldn't want to cause any trouble over some simple little misunderstanding. I was off in the hills, you understand, prospecting for gold. I hardly saw a living soul all year, except for a bunch of Indians."

Agent Goodall raised a skeptical eyebrow. Gold? Indians? That was about the fishiest excuse he'd heard all month, and he invested five minutes firing questions at the increasingly confused and stammering little jerk sitting on the other side of the desk. Finally it all began to come out: a pregnant girl, ten or twelve other guys who might have been the father, flight, then finally return after the girl's convenient miscarriage.

When young Haupt finally got to his feet, he looked red in the face but relieved, and Agent Goodall had delivered a stern little lecture about making incomplete and misleading statements to the FBI. It was just a standard lecture, but after the kid left, Goodall stood tapping the file against his fingers, then laid it in his out basket. One of the secretaries could return it to the file room, where it had resided for months until Haupt came in and announced himself. Only another idiot kid who had let personal problems take precedence over his draft registration. Unless he was purposely trying to duck the draft. But that would be hard to prove. Besides, he had come in and admitted the oversight. That would probably get him off the hook for good.

But Goodall couldn't move away from the desk. He intended to. He had every intention of wandering off to the coffee room for a much-needed bicarb and a little break in the routine. Something was holding him back. Some odd, unformed thought nagging at the back of his mind. What was it? Something else fishy about the Haupt kid?

He stared at the file folder again, almost picked it up. Haupt? Was there another file on him somewhere? An APB or something? The name was familiar. Why?

He picked up a telephone and buzzed an inside number. He got an answer after two rings. He said, "Harris? This is Goodall. Listen, something is bugging me. Haupt. Herbert Haupt. Mean anything to you?"

"Haupt?" the telephone voice said. "Let's see. Yeah, we got a tele-type yesterday from Washington. Man named Artur Haupt. Part of that spy search."

Goodall's Adam's apple bobbed. "That's it," he said excitedly. "I knew I'd seen the name. This kid was just in with some story about being in Mexico for the last year or so. You suppose they're related?"

"We can check that out easy enough. You got an address?"

Goodall snatched up the folder and flipped it open. "Yeah, it's right here, in his file."

"Good, we'll send some men out to ask some discreet questions. If there's a connection, we may have a breakthrough."

"He just left the office," Goodall said. "Hang on, I'll send some one to bring him back."

"No, abort that!" the voice said. "Orders from the top. Put a tail on any suspected person and let him go. There are still three men unaccounted for. He might lead us to them."

"Right," Goodall said. "What about the file, then? Do you want it?"

"Yes. Bring it down."

Goodall hung up, feeling nervously pleased. He tucked the slim file folder under his arm and headed for the doorway.

The six-month-old case of Herbert Hans Haupt, unregistered draft-age citizen, one of 37,486 such cases to be investigated by the FBI in 1942, had just been reopened.

5

Andy was in Gay Cogswell's big, overfurnished living room, thumbing through one of the backdated newspapers, when Gay came down from her bedroom to join him. He was so engrossed that he didn't hear her at first. His collar was loose, his tie and tunic flung across the arm of one of her easy chairs, and his discarded shoes were lying on their sides under the coffee table.

"Good Lord," she said, "aren't you ready yet?"

Her voice startled him and the newspaper shook momentarily in his hands. He folded it quickly, intending to shove it back in the pile with the others, then realized it was too late, that she was watching him, so he laid it, as casually as possible, on the coffee table and looked up at her. She was dressed in a simple, chic dress of white linen, her tan glowing splendidly against it. A deeply slashed neck, which she filled abundantly. A little white leather purse in which she kept her cigarettes. Linen wasn't a sexy material, not great to touch like the silks and chiffons she sometimes wore to parties, but she looked marvelous in it. He said so.

"Thank you, lover." She kissed him on the cheek, then glanced at the newspaper he had been reading. Distractedly, she said, "Come on, let's go. It'll take us half an hour to get to the Hieberts' house and we're already running late."

He watched her eyes linger on the newspaper. "Sure," he said quickly. "Let me get my shoes on."

But she slid onto the couch next to him and pulled the paper closer. "Andy," she said, "why are you reading an old newspaper? Didn't today's *Star* come?"

"Yeah, it's in the hallway," he said. He kept his head down, tying his shoelaces.

"Then, why are you reading this?" She saw the other newspapers on the floor. She leaned over the couch arm and lifted the top three newspapers, one by one. "They're all old newspapers," she said, puzzled. "What are you looking for, baby?"

"Oh, nothing in particular," he said. He had finished his shoelaces and it was time to straighten up, but he knew she was watching him, waiting for an answer, so he untied the right shoelace and started again.

"Andy, I only wangled this invitation for your sake. Two Democratic National Committeemen will be there tonight."

"I know, I know. I'll be ready in a minute."

"But you hadn't even started getting ready," she said. "You were so involved in that newspaper that I could have walked in and dropped a pillow in your lap without disturbing you. Why? What's so special about last week's news?"

He sighed and sat back. "It sounds kind of silly now."

"What sounds silly? What are you up to?"

He grinned sheepishly. "Hell, honey, it's embarrassing. I was talking to one of the Secret Service guys this morning. He told me the Germans had landed some spies by submarine about a week ago. We got to talking about it, and . . . Jesus, I don't know, all of a sudden I got this idea that maybe some of them are here in Washington."

"Spies? In Washington?"

"Yeah, I know. It sounds dumb."

"I don't think it sounds dumb. Not at all. What better place for them to come?"

He looked at her, wondering if she was making fun of him. She looked serious enough. He nodded and said, "Yeah, that's what I thought. You see, one of the spies gave himself up. But he didn't do it in New York, where the rest of them were. He caught a train to Washington. I started wondering why. According to the guy I was talking to—his name is Jerry Fenton, I don't think you've ever met him—there are four more spies, still running loose somewhere. I got to wondering if maybe they aren't right here, in Washington. I mean, hell, look at the timing. They land last week, and just about the same time, the Prime Minister flies in for discussions with the President."

"And the newspapers?" she said.

"Well, I guess I figured if there really were spies in Washington, maybe I could spot something to prove it. They wouldn't come here for a vacation. So if they were up to anything, maybe one of the newspapers might have stumbled onto it and reported it. You know, without realizing what it really meant."

"Have you found anything?"

"A couple of things." He picked up one of the newspapers. "Here, look at this. The air-raid practice last Wednesday. Someone was shining lights near the capitol building. The cops tried to catch him, but he got away. Here's another, in the Saturday paper. I thought I really had something here. During the Saturday drill, someone set off two explosions near the Supreme Court building. Damn near scared Justice Jackson to death. But it turned out they were only simulated explosions to make the drill more realistic."

"Are you sure they were only simulated explosions? Perhaps they were real and that's only a cover story to avoid creating panic."

"No, I suspect it's true. Apparently the FBI thinks the remaining spies are in Chicago and New York. If they had an unexplained explosion here in town, they might not be so quick to make up their minds."

She kicked off her shoes and tucked her feet on the couch next to him. She looked interested. "Anything else?" she said.

"Yeah, a few things." He flipped through the newspapers. "Here's one. A man with a camera, trying to get pictures of the machine-gun emplacement on top of the Lincoln Memorial. He drove off when one of the sentries started to question him. And there's a whole string of crimes and muggings from the police blotters. I found one that really interests me. Here, let me show you."

He dug through the pile and pulled a newspaper from the bottom. As he spread it across his lap and turned to a story on the inside pages, she leaned closer, following his pointing finger. "A murder?" she said.

"Yeah. A woman strangled to death in a boardinghouse last Thursday. That's the day this informer from New York came to Washington, see? The very same day."

"Couldn't that be a coincidence?"

"Sure. But on top of that, the man the police are looking for, the man they think did it, only moved into the boardinghouse on Monday. That's pretty close to the time the first German U-boat supposedly put the spies ashore. See how nice the timing works out?"

"Wow!" she said, and the enthusiasm in her voice startled him. She pulled the newspaper from his hands and said, "We ought to make notes of everything we find. There's a tablet in the desk. Fetch it, will you, lover?"

"Notes?" he said.

"Sure. We'll go through all the papers. There's bound to be more. Wow, just think, Andy. What if you're right? Think what a feather in your cap this would be. We'll prepare a brief on it, and you can take it to someone important. Think what instant visibility it will give you."

"Uh, Gay . . ."

"It wouldn't surprise me," she said, "if the President himself took a hand in this. And once *he* hears about you, you're on your way."

"Gay, I'm not doing this for visibility. I'm only . . ."

"Get the tablet," she said. "You can call each item out to me and I'll make an entry on it. How far back shall we go? When did the submarine land?"

"I'm not sure," he said uncomfortably. "Probably the weekend before last."

"Probably?" she said. "That's not good enough. Find out tomorrow. We'll need to know exactly so we can prepare a solid brief. Do you think we ought to look over the New York newspapers, too? No, I guess not. We're trying to prove they're in Washington, not New York. Get the tablet, Andy. Hurry."

He pushed to his feet, feeling distinctly uneasy. The whole idea had seemed far-fetched to him, so much so that he had been almost ashamed to tell her about it. But at least it had been *his* idea. Now she had taken the ball and was running on her own. He felt like a crackpot inventor, shunted aside by some massive industry that had figured a way to make money on a mild, harebrained inspiration.

He could hear her turning pages behind him as he searched the desk, finally finding a Big Chief tablet that Gaylynn must have used for school. The pages stopped turning. Gay was crouched over another story, her long blond hair hanging down on both sides of her intent face.

"Honey?" he said. She glanced up at him, saw the tablet and waggled her fingers, gesturing for it. He tried again. "Honey? What about the party? Aren't we going?"

She said, "Oh, don't be such a bore, Andy. Don't you ever think of anything but parties? Look, here's another. Two suspicious men seen loitering near the reservoir. They would try to poison the water system, wouldn't they? Here, give me the tablet."

He sighed and handed it over.

6

Sarah lay on her back, submitting passively to the pounding thrust of his loins. His face was blank, not contorted in an agony of pleasure like Ben's. The beginnings of lines around his eyes and his mouth, lines that had made him look so manly in the park this afternoon, faint threads against dark skin, filled with sweat as he drove deeper and deeper into her. His broad chest, so much broader than Ben's, heaved with each thrust and his hand clutched her right breast, kneading and twisting as he approached completion.

She closed her eyes, seeking darkness. They'd forgotten and left the light on, it had happened so fast. God, how could it have happened at all? She hadn't intended to let it go this far. Nor had he, she could tell. Lunch had been lovely, a French restaurant no less, and after they'd found out they both loved the beach but hated the way seaweed sometimes brushes your legs, loved Glenn Miller but were cool to Gene Krupa, found crêpes scrumptious but loathed even the thought of eating snails, he had met her after work and driven her home, just a gesture of friendship between two lonely people. They'd fed her birds and laughed about the lurking way the flock, mainly sparrows, gathered on the telephone wires to wait for the grain she scattered. Then they'd eaten their own scraped-together dinner of grilled-cheese sandwiches and cantaloupe in her kitchen, listening to Vox Pop, tippling a bit from a bottle of chilled white wine she luckily had in the fridge. Nothing had been said, nothing untoward had occurred. Yet they had ended up in bed as surely as though it had been planned in advance.

She tried to think back. When had it changed? When had it stopped being a friendly meal and pleasant conversation between casual acquaintances and become a race for the bedroom, with all the scrambling to get out of clothes and the hands groping and the touching and the kissing and the wetness, the disgusting wetness, between her thighs? She had flirted with him, certainly. Flirtation was expected. And he was a strikingly handsome man. But to have him push her down on the bed and spread her legs and put that thing in her. God, what would Ben think? Here, in his own bedroom.

Not that she was a saint. Merciful God, she was no saint. She had betrayed Ben before. First it was that boy, that Lester Whitehead, back when her parents were first telling her that she ought to marry Ben. It made her so wild, the way her parents seemed so stuck on Ben, just because his father was in real estate and played golf regularly at a country club. Who cared about golf? She let Lester do it to her in the bed of a pickup truck at the senior picnic, while Ben was off with some other boys trying to buy more beer, and she told Ben about it three or four months later, by God she did, and nothing had ever made her more furious than listening to him decide to forgive her. Then Ben did it to her, after they were married. Three or four times a week, whether she felt like it or not. And after Ben shipped out with his unit and she'd stubbornly had her way with him, with her parents and his parents and had patriotically stayed on in Washington, she had done it again. Twice. Once with Mr. Cooper from the office, and the other time with that sailor she met at Katie's party. But Mr. Cooper and the sailor had been mere accidents, times when she'd let her imagination run away with her and thought, to hell with it, what if the Germans dropped a bomb on them tomorrow and she'd never been with a real man, a man she could fall really sincerely in love with, but neither Mr. Cooper who'd left his shirt on the whole time nor the sailor who kept grunting like a pig had been the man. No, they'd just been one-night stands in hotel rooms, and left her feeling sticky and disappointed and still waiting for the rapture. Love was supposed to be rapture, not just someone your parents liked, like Ben. Ben. Now she'd sunk to letting a strange man make love to her in Ben's own bed. God, what kind of a woman was she? Suddenly panicked, she began to count. Lester. Ben. Mr. Cooper. The sailor. Now this man she had met in the park. That made it five men. Five different men. Good God, was she one of those nymphomaniacs? Five different men!

She tensed up so much that the pounding her body was undergoing became painful. Usually, even with Ben, it really felt rather nice. Not that any of it ever *was* nice. The movements were so ludicrous, the positions grotesque. She could never quite stop from comparing it to those disgusting pornographic comic books, the ones the rough girls used to pass around the cafeteria in junior high school, with Popeye and Olive Oyl and the disgusting things Wimpy would do if Olive Oyl offered to pay him with a hamburger. *She* wasn't like Olive Oyl, no, she couldn't be. *She* tried to accept it as a victim, rather than reveling in it.

She pushed Ben from her mind and looked up at the man's face, hovering above her, eyes now closed as tightly as hers had been, teeth now bared as he weaved back and forth. Did he think she was a cold fish, too? She tried to wiggle her hips in time with his thrusting penis, but she had no sense of rhythm and almost lost him. His other hand found her left breast and he squeezed, holding onto both breasts, guiding her as though she were a mounted horse and her breasts were the reins, helping her to slide into the proper galloping beat. She rode out the race passively, counting the strokes as they neared the finish line, then felt him go rigid, like a jockey standing up in the stirrups. His seed spurted into her and she thought, oh God, I forgot my diaphragm. Oh God. What a time to think of it. But at least it proved she hadn't been planning to let it go this far.

He collapsed across her and rolled to the side, breathing in fits and jerks, his face relaxed, soft and childlike. She touched his skin, so warm and firm. He smiled at her, his eyes still closed.

"Ray," she whispered. "Ray, dear."

"Yes?"

"How was it? Was it good?"

"Beautiful," he murmured. "You?"

"Oh yes," she said. "Yes."

THE ELEVENTH DAY

1

Dietrich sat in bed the next morning, distracted, and watched her zip up her yellow broadcloth skirt and reach for a yellow leather belt. She paused in front of the mirror and touched her bangs lightly for the eighth time—or was it the ninth?—then puckered her lips and applied a rich red lipstick. She saw him staring at her reflection in the mirror and she flashed him a shy smile. He smiled back.

"Raymond?" she said.

"Yes."

"Do you think I'm tall enough?"

"Just right."

"No, I mean it. Only tall girls can wear clothes really well. Do you really think I'm tall enough?"

"Yes, I really think you're tall enough."

"Do you . . . do you still respect me after last night?"

"Respect you? You darling. I may erect a monument to you."

"I never brought a man here before," she said.

He reached for a cigarette and lit it. He tried to look serious as he said, "I know that, Sarah. And it pleases me."

Something was bothering her. There was a hint of moisture glistening in her brown eyes. She said, "Ray, I'm sorry. I lied. Not about bringing a man here. That's true. I never have. But I've . . . I've been here with a man. My husband."

Oh, so that's what it was. The husband bit. He pulled the cigarette from his mouth and summoned a look of surprise, even shock. "Husband?" he said. "You're married?"

The moisture welled up and tears began to overflow her lower lids. "Yes. Please don't hate me, Ray."

He wondered how to play it. Hurt? Guilt? Maybe just a touch of guilt. That would ease her conscience. He shook his head, pretending confusion. "My God. I'm sorry, Sarah. I didn't know."

"Oh no, it wasn't your fault," she said. She hurried to the bed and perched beside him, clasping his bare shoulders. "You had no way of knowing, Ray. It was my fault. All my fault. I let you think . . . Oh, Ray, you must despise me."

He returned her embrace awkwardly. "Don't be silly," he said. There was a catch in his voice. "What happened last night, just happened. No one is at fault."

Now the tears really came, a free flow that flooded her cheeks and spilled across her mouth. "I'm not that kind of girl, Ray. Honest I'm not. I love him. I really do. And I've tried to be faithful to him. Oh God, I'm a terrible person."

"No you aren't," he said. He glanced at his watch over her shoulder. He needed to bring this to an end pretty soon, to get her on her way. It was vital that he get going on his own day's work.

She raised her wet face and gave him a salty kiss. "Oh, Ray, you're so good. It can't be wrong, can it? Nothing that feels so good can be wrong."

"No, it isn't wrong," he said.

"I wish I could believe that," she said. She cupped his face in her hands. "Oh, Raymond, my darling. I'm falling in love with you. You must know that, don't you? I couldn't have done it with you last night if I weren't falling in love with you."

His eyebrow went up a fraction of an inch and he controlled an urge to laugh. Instead, he said, "Of course you couldn't."

"It's true," she said. "Some girls might go to bed with just anybody, but I'm not like that. I gave myself to you because I'm falling in love with you, and you're falling in love with me. It's a sacred trust. A bond of our love. You wouldn't respect me if it were any other way. And I wouldn't respect myself."

"I know that," he said. "Look, sweetheart, shouldn't you hurry? You'll be late for work."

"In a moment," she said. She stroked his cheeks. "The important thing is that we mustn't hurt Ben. It would just break his heart if he knew. This moment is ours. For now, there's only us, you and me. But we can't forget Ben, do you understand? Someday, some sad, dark day, this will have to end."

"I understand," he said.

She smiled. "You're so good," she said. "So gentle."

He pushed her away and patted her cheek. "You'd better hurry," he said. "You don't want to miss your bus."

She pouted a little, and he noticed that, like the landlady, she had a faint, downy mustache. She should have it removed or bleach it or something. He watched it unwillingly as she said, "Bus? Aren't you going to drive me?"

"There's nothing I'd rather do," he said. "But I can't. I'm running short of cash. I've got to go out and find a job."

"You could wait a day or two. I've got some money in the bank. Not much, but enough to keep us going. And I'm getting a good salary."

He shook his head. "I don't take money from women."

She nodded understandingly. "Yes, of course. That's one of the things I like about you, Raymond. Principles are important to you. You're so honest, so sweet." She stood up and smoothed the yellow skirt, then reached for her purse and opened it. "Do you need any money for gas?"

He hesitated. "Well, maybe a couple of dollars."

She handed him a twenty-dollar bill. "Will you . . . will you be here when I get home?"

"Sure."

"Do you promise? You won't just go away and not come back?"

He smiled gently. "I promise. I'll be right here."

"Lovely. I'll see you tonight." She paused briefly at the bedroom door. "Oh Lord, I forgot to feed the birds. Will you do it for me?"

"Sure," he said.

"They get one coffee can full of grain in the morning."

"I'll take care of it."

She gave him one last brave smile, then she was gone.

Dietrich raised his eyes to the ceiling and sighed. Thank God she had finally gone. Five minutes more of that cloyingly sweet romantic garbage and he would have been sick. Falling in love, for God's sake.

Yet, in spite of the touch of tears and the sticky dialogue, he found her attempt to romanticize their sexual effort of the night before oddly touching. She couldn't accept the fact that they had simply engineered themselves a good old-fashioned fuckfest. No, she had to embellish it, make it palatable, ease her conscience by convincing herself that she was falling in love with the stranger who had ended up in her bed.

Hell, she had nothing to be ashamed of. It wasn't even as though she had plunged into the activity with any sense of enjoyment. As a matter of fact, she had lain there last night like a stick, making him do all the work. Except toward the end. For a moment or two, there toward the end of it, she had given him a couple of amateurish wiggles. It was a good sign. Perhaps when her feelings of guilt wore off and she stopped freezing up, he could even teach her to enjoy it. Then maybe they would be more comfortable with each other. Maybe even learn to like each other a little bit.

He hadn't once thought of Gerta, nor tried not to think of her. There was no need. His young wife was different, separate, from all the other compartments in his life. With Sarah, he was just a good workman, contentedly doing his job. But he thought of Gerta briefly now and wondered, as he'd wondered before, just what she did on the six days a week when she wasn't dutifully going to church with her family and writing him her Sunday letter, and more to the point, what did she do with her nights? But it didn't matter. He had decided long ago that only the time they spent together mattered. Could he still somehow bag both a president and a prime minister, he had no doubts that the war would end quickly and he could soon be home with her seven nights a week. But that would have to wait. His last night's work over, it was time to embark on his day.

Dietrich's first stop that Tuesday morning was at the corner of Fourteenth and F Streets, some two blocks east of the White House. He studied the buildings until he determined which one was the National Press Building, then counted upward to the thirteenth and fourteenth floors. That was where he would begin. The National Press Club.

The Press Building, built in 1926, was nothing more than a shabby office building, filled with news offices and information facilities rented to wire services and small newspaper bureaus and big-city correspondents assigned to the Washington beat. But the top two floors, the thirteenth and fourteenth floors, were different, plusher, filled with an exclusive warren of dining rooms and game rooms and reading rooms and lounges. The private social club of Washington journalists. A place where reporters could escape the pressures of a pressurized wartime society and dawdle over social drinks with their peers. A place where Dietrich could launch his alternative solution to the problem set aside for him back in Germany.

He crossed the street and entered the lobby, feeling in his pocket for the Pittsburgh police press pass which had been prepared for him in Berlin. Assumption of a newsman's identity was a common practice for Abwehr agents. Legitimate newsmen often suspected or knew far more than they could prove or print, and they were a fair information source. Besides, newsmen could go almost anywhere and see almost anybody in the pursuit of news, and it provided a good cover. His own pass had been included in his packet only against the possibility that he might need a method to cross police lines at some point in the operation, but today it also enabled him, with no particular difficulty, to get past the National Press Club's protective checkpoint at the thirteenth-floor reception desk by claiming to be a visiting reporter who wished to use the facilities temporarily. A man passed his press card without question, sending him through the doorway into the select chambers. He was instantly impressed by the trappings—paneled walls covered with mats of famous front pages, original drawings by noted editorial cartoonists and comic-strip artists, photographs of notable Club members standing shoulder to shoulder with instantly recognizable world leaders, bronze plaques proclaiming what he assumed to be important newspaper awards.

He was equally impressed, when he reached the small cocktail lounge off the reception corridor, to see how many early-bird journalists were already bellied up to the bar. He had been told that journalists were heroic drinkers, but he was nevertheless surprised by the sizable crowd clustered around the mahogany bar so early in the morning. It was here that Dietrich hoped to find a man. Not a specific man by name. But a man who would fit a specific list of qualifications.

He found a small gap toward one end of the bar and wedged himself in, smiling as the men on both sides politely made room for him. The two newsmen on his right were arguing about sports, the point of contention seeming to be whether or not it was worthwhile to continue the sham of major league play when all the stars were in military uniform and only rejects could take the field.

"Listen, sport, I just saw the best baseball game of the season, and you know what made it the best?" proclaimed one of the two arguers, an overweight bald man with a florid face. "Some Navy chief bosun's mate named Bob Feller. Pitched five innings for Norfolk against the Army all-stars. What's the point in watching cripples and 4-F's at Yankee Stadium when the best ball is being played on service fields?"

"Oh yeah?" countered his opponent. "What about Joltin' Joe? He's still in a Yankee uniform. And he plays a pretty fair brand of baseball."

Dietrich tuned them out. He had never shared the American fetish for sports. There were too many practical ways to keep one's body in tone without resorting to manufactured crises. It was almost as though Americans were addicts, unable to suffer through a full day without heavy dosages of baseball scores and a shot or two of synthetic courage extracted from some playing field.

A bartender worked his way down to Dietrich, mopping leftover spills with a wet rag, and said, "What'll you have, sir?"

Dietrich had intended to order coffee, but the heavy drinking traffic changed his mind. Coffee might seem out of place. "Brandy and soda," he said.

The bartender reached for a glass. "You're new, aren't you? Don't think I've seen you in here before."

"Yes. I'm new."

"Thought so," the bartender said. "I know most of the boys by sight. You need anything, you ask for me. They call me Phil."

Dietrich stumbled momentarily as his mind ran quickly over the many names in his kit, trying to remember which name was on the Pittsburgh press card, then he said, "I'm Dave. Dave Pastor."

"Good to meet you, Mr. Pastor. You thinking about joining us? I could introduce you to a couple of guys, get your name put up for consideration."

"I thought I'd hang around a few days first," Dietrich said. "Just to see if it's worthwhile."

"Oh, it's worth it," the bartender said. "It's kind of a second office for some of the guys. Drinks are big. Cheap. Food isn't bad, either. And you can pick up most of the government handouts right out in the reception hall. Couple of people never even leave here, except to go home every now and then to sleep and change clothes. Beats working, they tell me." He set Dietrich's drink on the bar. "Remember, you need anything, you ask for me."

The bartender shifted his attention to the sports argument and Dietrich turned to gaze around the bar. Literally dozens of newsmen. Most of them regulars, probably. He couldn't deal with a regular. He would need a newcomer, someone unlikely to be missed. Someone new to the city, someone assigned to the White House. Preferably from some small, relatively obscure town, though time and chance might not permit him to be that selective.

The man on Dietrich's left fluttered a newspaper, a quiet signal that Dietrich was crowding his elbow. Dietrich smiled an apology and narrowed his stance. Then a headline on the man's paper caught Dietrich's eye. An Axis victory. Tobruk had fallen. Rommel and his Afrika Korps had the British on the run. The whole North African front was falling apart. Dietrich quickly looked down at his drink. A feeling of elation swelled through his chest.

But the moment of inner cheer for his desert comrades faded as his eyes moved furtively back to the newspaper and glanced over the first paragraphs of the story. The disastrous turn of events in Libya had caught the British off guard. British Parliament was gravely disturbed. Prime Minister Churchill faced a vote of censure in the House of Commons. The story went on to point out that the Prime Minister, who was said to be somewhere in the United States for top-level war discussions, might well be forced to break off the talks in the next day or two and return to England to face the expected challenge to his authority.

Dietrich scowled and sipped at his drink. He had never expected to be sorry to read of a German military success, but he was. His chances to add Churchill's body to the funeral bier of the American President had already faded almost beyond reach, but that story, if true, finished them. The Prime Minister would be leaving any day now. And Dietrich had only begun his search for the right man.

2

At almost three o'clock that day, Andy Blaszek stole a glance at the wall clock. He still hadn't had a chance to make his phone call. It was as though Sergeant Huffman knew he wanted to be alone and was determined to thwart him. The feisty little sergeant had bustled about the office all morning, yapping and snapping at the heels of the daily chores, creating a major emergency out of the fact that two of the military guards were out with summer colds, then zestfully meeting his self-created emergency. Andy thought he might have a moment of privacy at noon, but the sergeant had decided to skip lunch in order to redo the entire month's rosters. Now the afternoon was waning and it was beginning to look as though Andy

would either have to place his call to the FBI with the sergeant still
floating somewhere in the background, or give it up as a lost cause.

The truth was, he was perfectly willing *not* to make the call. He
didn't really have that much to go on. Just the list of entries that he
and Gay had pulled together last night. He would know more tomorrow. Earlier, when the sergeant hit the mimeograph machine,
cranking the assignment sheets noisily around the mimeograph
drum, Andy had placed a hasty call to the Washington police and
used the noise to muffle his request for an appointment with one of
the D.C. city detectives, a chance to check the details on a few of
the assorted crimes that Gay thought might be worth looking into.
He managed to get only tentative agreement for a meeting the next
morning, but he did manage to hang up just seconds before the
mimeograph run was completed.

So why not wait until after the trip to the police station before
calling the FBI? Maybe he would have more to tell them then. But
he knew he couldn't wait. Calling the FBI had been Gay's idea
(breathlessly, "Call Mr. Hoover, lover. Tell him what we've come
up with. If anyone can help, it will be Mr. Hoover, right?"), and
she was sure to ask him about it when he got home. Last night, surrounded by scattered newspapers and fortified with martinis, he had
accepted her suggestion gladly. Of course, the FBI. That was the
proper agency for news this stupendous. Spies in Washington? Call
Mr. Hoover and tell him. The FBI would pick them up in a trice.
But somewhere, between the martinis and actually picking up the
telephone, a night of sober sleep and the cold light of day had intervened and he felt foolish. Call the FBI and tell them an amateur
sleuth in the White House had reached a rather fantastic conclusion
about their missing spies? And do it in front of the cynical sergeant? It was to laugh. And Andy wasn't much in the mood to be
laughed at, not by Huffman or anyone else.

On the other hand, why should he care if Sergeant Huffman
heard him make the call? It wasn't as though he was breaking any
rules. Far from it. Far-fetched though his theory might be, it was
still entirely within his purview. Danger to the White House was
his faithful concern. If he smelled the possibility, it was his duty to
pass it along. The sergeant would have to approve. Damn it, he
would call right now.

He reached for the telephone, to test his resolve, but the sergeant
looked up at him from across the room and his hand swerved to his

pack of cigarettes. He shook one out, frowning, admonishing himself for the failure of will, and tamped the end on the desk surface. The sergeant's gaze returned to the details of work.

Maybe the sergeant would go to the bathroom, Andy postulated. Wiry, tough little bastard though he was, his kidneys were mortal. And Huffman had been drinking coffee most of the afternoon. The sergeant was sure to head down the hallway to the john sometime. If Andy could at least place the call and ask for the FBI Director while the sergeant was out of the room, then it wouldn't matter so much if the sergeant came back before the call was completed. He would hear only the tail end of the conversation, not enough to know what it was all about, nor to whom Andy was talking, nor even, for that matter, whether Andy had placed the call or was responding to a call from someone else.

He dragged on his cigarette, feeling foolish. Such subterfuge. Such careful planning for the benefit of one tiny phone call. What the hell was getting into him? Who was the master in this room, anyway? The sergeant looked up at him again, frowning as though he had read Andy's thoughts, and Andy busied himself, thumbing through a sheaf of last week's reports.

Three cigarettes and two false starts later, Andy got his chance. The sergeant stood up abruptly, shifted his weight uncomfortably from minikin foot to minikin foot, and muttered something about taking a leak. He breezed from the room and Andy grabbed the telephone.

The call went through smoothly enough, but then the delays began. Andy asked for the Director and was clicked off to another operator. He asked for the Director again, identifying himself as a caller from the White House, leaning on his title for support. Another delay. Andy pulled out the Big Chief tablet with the newspaper entries marching down the ruled lines in Gay's flowing hand. He drummed the tablet with his fingers. He began to watch the door. Finally, a cultured voice said, "Yes? May I help you?"

Andy breathed his relief. Salvation. The sergeant was still unlimbering his kidneys. He put on his best face and his best telephone voice and said, "Good afternoon, Mr. Hoover. This is Captain Andrew Blaszek at the White House. I'm calling in reference to . . ."

The voice cut him off politely. "This is Special Agent Lawson. What can I do for you, Captain?"

"Lawson?" Andy said. "I asked for the Director."

"The Director isn't available," the cultured voice said. "May I help you?"

Andy watched the door. Still no sign of the sergeant. "Perhaps I didn't make myself clear," he said. "I'm the internal security liaison at the White House. I think I may have something of importance to discuss with the Director."

"I'm sorry, Captain. The Director is tied up. If you would care to discuss your business with me, I'll be happy to relay it to him at first opportunity."

"Oh, I see," Andy said. "Is that the way it usually works?"

"Yes, sir. The Director is a very busy man. I'm sure you understand."

"Yes, I guess so. Well, I'm calling in reference to . . ." He pulled the school tablet close to the telephone as he spoke, intending to give the FBI man a full rundown on what he had, but before he could get it out, Huffman scurried into the room and plopped down behind his typewriter again. Andy swiveled in his chair and looked out the window.

"Yes, sir?" the voice said. "You're calling in reference to what?"

"The spies," Andy said softly.

"The what, sir? Could you speak up? I'm afraid we don't have a very good connection."

Andy cleared his throat. "I'm calling about the spies," he said. "The Nazi spies. The men who landed a couple of weeks ago. From a submarine."

There was a cold silence on the phone, during which Andy was certain he could feel the sergeant's eyes on the back of his neck.

The telephone voice said, "That information was supposed to be restricted, Captain. May I ask how you heard about them?"

"That's my job," Andy said. "The point is, you only have four of them in custody. I wonder, have you given any thought to the possibility that the others may be somewhere in Washington?" He heard the sergeant's chair squeak. Oh damn, he was coming over here.

"I see," the voice said. It sounded weary. "Perhaps we're in a better position to make that kind of determination, Captain. Why don't you just leave it to us."

"Yes, well, I just thought . . . I mean, I've been working on it, and wondered if . . . You don't think the Director would be interested?" The sergeant reached over his shoulder and took the tablet. Andy snatched it back.

The voice said, "I'm sure the Director will be gratified at your interest in Bureau affairs, Captain. I'll see that he hears about it. In the meantime, you may rest assured that we have the situation well in hand. We expect arrests momentarily."

"In Washington?" Andy said hopefully.

"No, Captain. Not in Washington."

"I see. Well, if the Director decides to look into it, you might have him call me. I have a few notes that I . . . Well, there's probably nothing to it, anyway. I just thought it might be a good idea to be on the safe side."

"We appreciate your interest, Captain."

"Yeah. Well, thank you very much for your attention."

He hung up quickly and reached for yet another cigarette, trying to avoid the sergeant's gaze. But the sergeant wasn't to be put off. He moved around Andy's desk until he was directly in Andy's line of view. "The Director?" he said.

Andy nodded and blew smoke. "FBI," he said. "Business. It's still pretty hush-hush."

The sergeant's eyes went to the Big Chief tablet again.

"I was working on it at a friend's house," Andy said. "There was nothing else to write in." He puffed nervously. The sergeant was staring at Gay's handwriting. He looked disapproving. The sergeant always seemed to recognize Gay's handwriting. The two of them didn't really seem to care for each other, though they had only met a couple of times in passing. Andy had often wondered why. He leaned forward and shut the tablet. "She took notes while I thought out loud," he said.

The sergeant nodded. "Spies," he said. "In Washington." He rolled the words out slowly, as though tasting them. The first traces of a grin appeared at the corners of his mouth.

"It's a definite possibility," Andy said. "I'm checking into it now."

"Spies. In Washington," the sergeant said again. "From a submarine." The grin was firmly in place now. "Fascinating, Captain. Fascinating."

Mercifully, he restrained himself from outright laughter. He merely carried his grin back to his typewriter and plunged himself back into the duties of the office. Almost twenty minutes passed before he allowed himself one sharp guffaw, an explosive chortle sandwiched between finishing one report and preparing carbons for the next.

Andy gave him a hard look, but the sergeant never bothered to raise his eyes.

3

That evening Edward Kerling and Werner Thiel sidestepped through the crowded tables of a New York restaurant and headed for the rear. A string quartet, composed of men in their fifties and sixties, filled the air valiantly with music, trying to boost Bach above the din of conversing diners, clattering platters and noisy, surly waiters. An elderly man, seated at a table against the back wall, saw Kerling and Thiel coming and waved his hand in greeting.

"That old man?" Thiel whispered hoarsely. "Is that Voss?"

Kerling nodded. "His name is Willie. You'll like him."

"But he's a queer," Thiel said. "Look at him. He's wearing make-up."

Kerling said, "Hush. He'll hear you."

Voss jumped to his feet as they drew near. "Edward, how are you?" He gestured. "Sit down, sit down, both of you. My, you look splendid this evening, Edward. Where did you get that suit?"

"In Florida," Kerling said. "Willie, I want you to meet my business associate, ah, Bill Thomas. Bill, my old friend, Wilhelm Voss."

"Hello," Thiel said awkwardly.

"Hello, Bill. Any friend of Edward's is welcome. Please. Sit."

As they took their chairs, Kerling said quickly, "My name is Kelly. You recall that, of course."

"Yes, of course," Voss said. "May I order a sherry for you?" He signaled for a waiter.

"I'd rather have a beer," Thiel said. He glanced from Voss to Kerling, looking puzzled.

"Anything you want," Voss said. "This is a celebration." He signaled again, more actively, until a waiter broke away from a disdainful group by the kitchen door and slouched over to their table.

Kerling sat back and watched while Voss rattled off the order. Thiel was right. His old friend was wearing make-up. Not much. Just a faint dusting of powder along the cheeks and temples. A touch of rouge. A modest trace of foundation cream to disguise the puffiness around the eyes. The end result was mildly successful. Voss looked better this evening than he had on Sunday morning. Not just his face, but his whole demeanor. Gray hair carefully in place, combed and oiled. Brown suit immaculate. A handsome striped tie nestled under the wings of his shirt collar. This was more like the Willie Voss of old. The successful doctor. The sophisticated gentleman. Kerling felt a stirring of rekindled friendship.

The waiter wandered off sullenly with their drink orders, and Kerling said, "Tell me, Willie. Have you heard anything from our friends in Chicago?"

"Friends in Chicago? You mean . . . Oh, the telegram. No. Nothing. Not yet."

Kerling frowned. "It's been two days. Are you sure?"

"I've been right by the telephone," Voss said. "No word at all. But I do have another message from Mr. Goethe. I told him I would be seeing you tonight."

"Goethe?" Thiel said. "Who's Goethe?"

"One of our people," Kerling said. "Kappe warned me we might be hearing from him. What did he say?"

Voss smiled. "Well, first he seemed awfully relieved to hear that you had arrived. He told me to tell you that you are to hold your position until he contacts you again."

"Then we aren't too late," Kerling said. "Wonderful."

"Too late for what?" Thiel said.

Kerling didn't answer. He cocked his head at Voss and said, "Is that all? No explanations? No instructions?"

"Yes, he did have an instruction. He says he has been unable to reach a Mr. George Davis. Something about his having checked out of his hotel. He asked that you try to get in touch with the man and tell him the same thing I've told you."

"Dasch?" Thiel said. "This guy knows about Dasch, too? What's going on?"

"Possibly something very important," Kerling said. "We'll have to get busy. We need to find Dasch, if we can, and send another message to the boys in Chicago. We've got to get geared up fast. The word may come at any moment. Willie, did you arrange the car?"

Voss nodded. "Yes. You can pick it up whenever you wish."

"Excellent. When we finish dinner, my friend and I will leave you. You go back to your apartment and wait by the phone. The next message could be very important."

"Please," Voss said. "Can't we wait until later before you talk of leaving?" He smiled at them, his eyes shining. "It's so nice to have you both here. I haven't been out like this in months. It's like a party."

"Jesus," Thiel muttered. He swung around in his seat and stared at the crowded tables.

Voss blinked and glanced hesitatingly at Kerling. "Have I said something wrong?"

Kerling shook his head. "Don't worry. He's just a little nervous. What's the specialty of the house here? I'm in the mood for something special."

Thiel suddenly turned back and stared at Wilhelm Voss. "Did anyone follow you here tonight?" He sounded edgy.

"Follow me?" Voss looked startled. "I don't think so. Why do you ask?"

Thiel leaned toward Kerling. "Don't look up," he whispered. "There's a man behind me. The other side of the room. At a table. Just keep looking at me for a moment or so, then turn your head slowly. Near the kitchen. Dark-blue suit. Young fellow. Wavy hair."

Kerling nodded and let his chin drift slowly to the side. "Yes, I see him. He's reading the menu."

"He wasn't reading the menu a moment ago," Thiel said. "He was watching us. There was another man with him. Big man. Broad shoulders. He went up front to the pay phone. See him?"

Kerling shook his head.

"He was there a moment ago," Thiel said. "Come on, let's get out of here."

Kerling put a hand on Thiel's arm and said, "Relax. It doesn't mean a thing."

"Relax?" Thiel said. "A man stares across the room at us and you say relax? Have you forgotten who we are?"

"I know who we are," Kerling said. "But no one else does. Believe me. No one has any reason to follow Willie. Nor to stare at us. No one knows anything about us." He patted Thiel's arm, then glanced at Voss. The older man looked jumpy, too. Kerling smiled reassuringly and said, "Don't worry, Willie. It's nothing."

"I'm not worried," Voss said nervously.

Thiel nudged Kerling and said, "He's back. The one who went out to the telephone."

Kerling sighed. "Stop it, will you? Believe me, we're absolutely safe. Sit back and enjoy yourself. This is supposed to be a celebration. Let's order dinner. Where's that waiter? I'm famished."

An hour later, shortly after Kerling and Thiel shook hands with Wilhelm Voss and left the restaurant, they were surrounded and placed under arrest by six FBI agents. Thiel groaned and surrendered without a word. Edward Kerling, stunned by the sudden appearance of the FBI men, resisted briefly and was subdued only after one of the agents hit him and knocked him against the side of the building. Then he and Thiel were quickly hustled into waiting cars and driven off.

It happened quickly. No one in the restaurant noticed the scuffle on the sidewalk. When Wilhelm Voss came out five minutes later, the street was clear. He adjusted his suit coat and pulled on a pair of slim, brown kidskin gloves. He was allowed to depart uncontested.

But two men, one with wavy hair and one with broad shoulders, came out a moment later and followed him, continuing their surveillance.

THE TWELFTH DAY

I

Andy Blaszek sifted through piles of clothing the next morning with eager hands. All new, every item, some still in boxes with sales slips. And the slips were all dated last week, *after* the submarine landing. No old clothing. None at all. It was as though Frank Daniels, the man from the rooming house, had never existed before he moved in.

A police property officer came into the small, airless room, mopping perspiration from his neck, and said, "Lieutenant Savage just called. He's got that money in his office now. You can come back up and take a look at it when you're finished here."

"Good," Andy said. "Tell him I'll be ready in a few minutes."

The property officer nodded. He laid some additional items on the table and said, "These are for you, too. The papers we found, and an artist's sketch book. The guy was apparently an artist of some kind. Remember, you can't take any of this out of the property room."

The property officer wiped a handkerchief across his forehead and cheeks and frowned at an immobile fan sitting on top of a filing cabinet. "Sorry about the busted fan," he said. "Damned thing died of old age a couple of weeks ago. Can't get replacements these days. Guess we'll have to suffocate for the duration."

"I don't mind," Andy said. "I feel great." He picked up the artist's sketch book and thumbed through it. Landscapes, country scenes, a bridge. All rendered with a kind of amateurish flair. Good drawings, but undisciplined, as though committed to paper by a fair artist with no formal training. The bridge, for example. All parallel lines with no vanishing point, more like an engineer might draw than an artist. And a layout of the countryside, kind of a bird's-eye view of the fields and roads, with farmhouses and barns and crossroads carefully sketched in. There were figures on the back of one of the sheets, some kind of algebraic computation. Odd. It meant nothing to Andy. Perhaps he should have one of the White House photographers come over to make some copies. Maybe someone who knew a little more about mathematics could figure it out.

Next he turned to the collection of papers. There was a city map, fairly new and unmarked, and a couple of recent magazines. There were some cash receipts, including dinner checks. And a set of railroad timetables.

Andy turned the timetables over in his hand. Penciled notations in the margins. He frowned, puzzled. Each notation was opposite a train, but the times indicated in the margins had nothing to do with the departure and arrival times of the trains they matched. Rather they all appeared to be times somewhere in between the two, primarily on trains running between Philadelphia and Washington.

Trains? Between Philadelphia and Washington? His skin tightened. He had, himself, recently been on a train that ran between Philadelphia and Washington. A train bearing the President and the Prime Minister. Could there be a connection?

He looked around to make sure the property officer was gone, then tore a blank sheet from the artist's sketch book. He folded it to make it less obtrusive, then tried to calculate the times from the margins of the timetables, looking up frequently and guiltily toward the door. When he was done, he stared at his results. Somewhere in northern Maryland, most likely, but it could be anywhere between Baltimore and the Pennsylvania border. He couldn't pinpoint it any closer than that.

Would it help him to know exactly where the notations had been made? Possibly. He turned the folded sheet over and copied the list of trains, plus the marginal notations. He could take these to someone at Union Station later, someone who knew the running times better. A railroad expert. Maybe they could narrow it down for him.

He stuffed the sheet in his pocket and leaned his head out the door. The property officer was sitting in front of another fan, one that worked, holding his chin high. Andy told him he was done and the officer came to lock things up.

Then he went back to Lieutenant Savage's office. Savage, the overworked, overbored city detective who had agreed to see him,

was waiting behind his desk, sitting guard over a bulky manila
envelope which Andy surmised held the money.

The money was apparently the thing most confusing about the
boardinghouse killing. When Andy had first called from Gay's
house that morning to make sure the tentative appointment was still
on, Savage had explained it to him. A wad almost twenty thousand
dollars thick, hidden in the landlady's flour tin. The police had no
reason to think it belonged to the suspect, but they had talked to
other roomers and were fairly certain it had not belonged to the
landlady, either. She had a notorious reputation among her tenants
for prowling their rooms and picking up anything of value that
wasn't nailed down. And she certainly had no such ready cash a few
weeks earlier when a tax notice on her house fell due. To the con-
trary, she had raised rents in an effort to scrape up the tax money
and had almost lost the house.

So the money, they theorized, might well have come from the
missing suspect's room. One of the roomers claimed he heard money
mentioned in the argument downstairs. It was certainly a worthy
motive. Twenty thousand dollars, serially numbered, stuffed in a
can only a few feet from where she was choked to death.

Yes, Andy could take a look at it, but only in Savage's office with
the detective standing at hand. They'd had some problems with
money disappearing from police protection, and now they only
brought it out in the presence of veteran upper-echelon officers.
Not that they didn't trust Andy or any of the lower-paid officers in
the property room. It was just a matter of procedure.

Savage, a hulking, gray-haired bull with his own heavy summer
cold, sniffed into a handkerchief as Andy came in and said, "Find
what you were looking for, Captain Blaszek?"

Andy nodded. "Yeah, I think so. Although the guy didn't leave
much trace of his life before he moved in, did he?"

Savage dabbed at his nose, rough and red and tender from blowing, and said, "Nope. That's what makes it so tough on us. We've
looked for him. Damn, we've looked just about everywhere. But the
sonofabitch has flat disappeared."

"You have a description?"

"We've got two or three. He's a tall, dark, average, good-looking
guy, apparently. But he might as well be a walking potato for what
good it does us. The world is full of tall, dark, average, good-looking people. One of the boardinghouse people told us he may have a

car. Someone heard the landlady muttering about it. But no one recalls seeing it."

"You've looked for him, I guess?"

"Oh hell, yes. We've done the usual. Hotels, motels, rooming houses. Nothing. Either he changed his name and appearance, or he's skipped town. Why is the White House so interested in this fellow, Captain?"

"I'm not at liberty to say, for the moment," Andy lied. He wasn't sure how far he could push the detective's willingness to co-operate once the man learned that he was working on a personal wild hair of his own. "Is that the money?" He nodded his chin at the manila envelope.

"Yeah, this is it." The detective picked up the envelope and unfastened the flap. "Sorry about the condition of it," he said. "It's kind of hard to look through. Watersoaked, or something. My men assure me it was that way when they found it."

"Watersoaked?" Andy said.

Lieutenant Savage shrugged. "That's what I'd call it." He spilled the bills out on the desk where Andy could see them. They were uneven bills, warped and wavy to the eye, stiff to the touch. "We think they were dry by the time the landlady stashed them. Otherwise the flour would have stuck to them."

"What could cause that?" Andy said.

"Beats me. Looks like someone gave the whole bundle a good bath."

"Could it be salt water?"

Savage raised an eyebrow. "I guess so," he said. He picked up one of the bills and smelled it. "I don't know how anyone could tell the difference, myself. Why do you ask?"

"Just wondering," Andy said. "Suppose a man carried that kind of money in the surf. Wouldn't that be the result?"

"You mean go swimming with a roll of bills like this? Why the hell would anyone do a thing like that?"

"It's a possibility," Andy said. "I can't say anything just yet, Lieutenant, but we think this man may be part of a group. A group that came ashore from a . . . well, from a boat. Could you get someone to test the money and see if it's salt water?"

"Hell, I don't know if that's possible. I guess I could check with our lab and see. It may take a while. Can I give you a call?"

"Yes, thank you. You have my number?"

"Yeah. White House, right?"

Andy nodded. He climbed to his feet and watched while the detective gathered up the bills and stuffed them back in the envelope, then held out his hand for a good-bye handshake. The detective sneezed as Andy walked out the door.

Holy Christ, Andy thought as he headed down the stairs for the street. Gay would go out of her mind with glee when he reported on this. It all fit. The new clothes, the watersoaked money, even that business of the notations on the timetables. Unless, of course, it was all a matter of coincidence. Coincidence? Maybe a coincidence here and there, but that many? Not likely.

He came out of the police station and looked at his watch. The morning was almost shot. Huffman would surely make some kind of wisecrack about him coming in this late. Particularly if he hit the telephone immediately to try the FBI again. Maybe it would be better, at least until he was sure the coincidences weren't coincidences, if he called from a street booth before he went to the office.

He scouted up a pay phone and dug for a nickel. After the same long delays as yesterday, during which he again identified himself and asked to speak directly to J. Edgar Hoover, the cultured voice came on again.

Andy sighed. "This is Lawson again, right?"

"Yes, Captain. May I help you?"

"No. I want to speak to the Director."

"I'm sorry, Captain. Nothing has changed. You'll have to talk to me."

"But something *has* changed," Andy said. "I've got evidence now. You guys are looking in the wrong place. The other four spies are here in Washington."

Lawson's voice seemed to have a smirk in it. He said, "Captain, I shouldn't be telling you this, but we picked up two of them last night. In New York. So you see, your information source isn't as up-to-date as you might wish. Nor, I fear, is your evidence."

"In New York?" Andy said. He felt his stomach sink. "Are you sure?"

"I'm sure, Captain. Furthermore, we have a third under surveillance, and we expect him to lead us to the fourth, momentarily. Again, not in Washington."

"Maybe you've miscounted," Andy said, seizing straws. "Damn it, one of them is here. I've got the goods on him. So there must be more than eight of them."

"Yes, I see," Lawson said. "That's very interesting, Captain." But his voice was totally uninterested.

"Listen," Andy said. "I want to talk to the Director about this. I'm not just some ordinary citizen calling. I'm a working member of the White House staff, charged with protecting the safety of the President of the United States. I may not be able to influence the Director's decision on the matter, but I can damned sure see that he hears about it. I'll go through channels, if I have to."

Now Lawson sounded faintly dubious. He said, "I'll relay your message to him, Captain Blaszek. That's all I can promise."

"You do that," Andy said. "You tell him I'm on my way to my office right now. If he's interested in hearing the details, he can call me and ask for them. I'll wait there for his call."

He hung up and pressed his forehead against the glass pane of the telephone booth. The goddamn idiots. What made them so sure they knew everything? After all, what was there to prevent the Germans from having landed nine, or ten, or even eleven? Or more. A whole army. But no, the FBI was a sharp outfit. If they said there were eight men, then there were probably eight men. One of them was still missing, Lawson had hinted. Maybe that was it. The eighth man was in Washington and the FBI was simply looking for him in the wrong place. Soon they would realize their error and turn their search to the capital.

But he couldn't get the thought out of his head. How *could* anyone be sure there wasn't another? It wasn't as if old J. Edgar could pick up the phone and call German intelligence and say, "By the way, you didn't happen to send a ninth spy over this time, did you?"

He slouched out of the booth, frowning sternly, but then reaction set in. Maybe he shouldn't have been so forceful about it. What if J. Edgar got mad? There were those who said he was the last person on earth you ever wanted to get mad at you. Even the President was a safer enemy. Maybe Andy should have explained a little more about why he thought there was a spy in Washington, instead of just losing his temper and sounding off on the telephone like a lunatic. For that matter, he wasn't sure he *could* explain his feelings, even if he tried. Watersoaked money. Big deal.

He shielded his eyes from the sun and headed for his car. Might as well get to the office and sit by the phone, just to see what would happen. He had a hunch it was going to be a long wait.

2

Herbert Haupt slid into the movie seat beside Otto Neubauer and leaned back. It was only their second meeting since arriving in Chicago. Flickering images, this time of Walter Pidgeon and Greer Garson touching in gentle embrace, danced on the screen and the music swelled.

"Where have you been?" Neubauer whispered. "I was beginning to think I'd have to sit through this damned movie twice."

"I've been busy," Haupt said. He glanced at Neubauer. "I'm seeing Hedda again."

"That girl you knocked up?"

Haupt frowned. "I didn't knock her up," he said. "She lost the baby."

"Oh. I'm sorry."

"Hell, I'm not. She's more fun this way. I think I'm going to ask her to marry me."

"Is that smart?"

Haupt shrugged. "It'll make a great cover. We can use her, too. As a courier, maybe."

"We don't need a courier," Neubauer said. "And we don't need problems. You better talk to Kerling before you do something dumb like getting married."

"It isn't dumb," Haupt said. He sulked for a moment, then said, "I bought a car, too."

"A car? I thought I told you not to be so free with money."

"We'll need a car," Haupt said. "As soon as we get word from Kerling and Thiel, we'll have to have a way to get to them, won't we? Besides, it's a nice car. A convertible. You'll like it."

Neubauer shook his head worriedly. "I'd hoped we might have heard something from them by now."

"We aren't going to hear anything until something important happens," Haupt said. "It wouldn't surprise me if we didn't hear anything for another week or so."

"Perhaps the four of us should have stayed together," Neubauer said. "I don't like being out of touch like this."

"Don't worry. He'll send for us. Maybe I'll have a surprise for you later this week."

"What do you mean by that?"

"Nothing. I've just got a hunch, that's all. I'll bet he sends for us in a few days."

"I hope you're right."

Haupt fidgeted and said, "You aren't getting nervous, are you, Otto?"

"No, not really. It's just that I don't have much to do to keep myself occupied. Working out on the barbells at the Y, some calisthenics in my hotel room, but how long can you keep busy at that? It's different for you. You have your family."

"Yeah, well, they're kind of a pain in the ass. I don't have it as good as you might think."

Neubauer patted Haupt on the knee. "Buck up, kid. We'll hear from Kerling one of these days, then we'll get some action started. Look, I'm going back to my hotel. This movie is boring. Get in touch with me Saturday. Come by my hotel and pick me up in that new car of yours. We'll take a ride. I'm registered under the name Henry Nicholas."

"Sure, Otto. Sure, I'll do that."

Haupt watched him go, feeling a faint sense of guilt for lying again about the message. Then he slumped back in his seat and cursed to himself. Nuts, it wasn't as though he was keeping anything important from Otto. Kerling had only sent the one telegram. If he was serious about it, he would send another. Haupt wouldn't ignore a second message. That would be irresponsible.

Haupt didn't see the two FBI men who came strolling into the darkened theater from the lobby and took seats to the rear of him, where they could watch him.

Equally unknowing, however, were the FBI men. One of them had lingered in the lobby long enough to report in by telephone and to cover his colleague while he went to the bathroom. That single call of nature, combined with an adherence to reporting procedures, had cost them.

They had missed Otto Neubauer.

3

The FBI Director scowled and toyed with a ragged paper napkin which had been brought in with his dinner tray. "Could this military person be right?" he asked.

"Well, it's hard to say, sir. We've had Haupt under surveillance for three days now, and still no sign of the eighth man."

"What's his name?"

"Blaszek, sir. Captain Andrew Blaszek."

"No, I don't mean him. I mean the eighth man."

"Oh. Otto Neubauer."

"Could he be in Washington?"

"Possibly. One of our people intercepted a phone call Sunday meant for Dasch at his New York hotel. The long-distance operator said the call came from Baltimore, which could indicate some action down this way. But we assumed it was merely one of the Florida team members calling en route to either New York or Chicago."

"Why do you think the missing man is also in Chicago?"

"Well, Dasch has indicated under interrogation that both the remaining members of the Florida team were to establish themselves in Chicago, but that could have changed."

"Perhaps we should check it out," the Director said. "I don't believe it for a minute, but I'd hate to get caught with my pants down."

"Yes, sir. Shall I get Captain Blaszek on the phone?"

"No! I'm blasted if I'll talk to him. If there's a spy in Washington, then it will be the Bureau that uncovers it, not some damned military outsider. There'll be no contact with him whatever."

"Sir? Wouldn't it be wise to ask him what led him to his conclusions?"

"No. Anything he can find, we can find. Put a team on it. Today. Use Special Agent Grover. And that protégé of his. The new man. What's his name?"

"Carter, sir. Emerson Carter. He isn't actually a new man. He's been with the Bureau for six years."

"He's a new man until I say he isn't," the Director said. "I'm leaving for New York tomorrow morning to oversee the interrogation of the three spies we caught last week and those two men we picked up last night. Tell Grover I want a report ready by the time I get back. If there's a spy in Washington, I want to know it."

THE THIRTEENTH DAY

Thursday—June 25, 1942

I

At midmorning on the third long, nerve-racking day of his Press Club vigil, Dietrich found a likely prospect sitting in the corner dining room. He twisted around in his chair and said, "Excuse me, did I hear you tell George that you were new in town?"

"George?" the man said.

"The waiter," Dietrich said.

The man, a sandy-haired fellow in horn-rimmed glasses, smiled. "Oh, right. Yeah, I just got in a couple of days ago."

Dietrich laid his breakfast napkin aside. "I thought so," he said. "I know most of the fellows who hang out at the Press Club, and I didn't recognize you. My name is Dave. Dave Pastor."

"Bob Sheppard," the man said. He leaned over from his table to extend his hand. "I work for the *Denver Chronicle*. How about you?"

"I'm an old wire-service hack," Dietrich said. "So you're from Denver, are you? Funny, I never saw so many new newsmen in town. Must be the war. We get eighteen or twenty new people a week in here. Can I buy you a welcome cup of coffee? I believe I heard you say you'd be covering the White House beat, so I guess we should get to know each other."

The man responded eagerly to a friendly overture, and within two minutes he and his coffee cup were sitting at Dietrich's table, fresh coffee steaming in the cup. Dietrich's smile froze slightly as he saw the waiter's name tag said Charles, not George, but the other man didn't seem to notice. Without missing a beat Dietrich continued, "Maybe you ought to consider joining. I could introduce you to a couple of guys, and get your name put up. It's really a pretty good deal for a newsman. Drinks are big and cheap. Food isn't bad, either. And you can find most of the government hand-outs out there in the reception hall. Some of the guys never leave here, except to go home now and then for a change of clothes. It's kind of like having a second office."

The man laughed. "Sounds a pretty lazy way to do a job."

"Beats working, they tell me. I don't do it that way myself. Too much competition at the White House."

The newsman's interest quickened. "You work at the White House too?"

"Sure. That's why my ears came up when I heard you say you would be there. Have you picked up your credentials yet?"

"No, I haven't had time. I'm going out of my mind just trying to find an apartment. God, this city is crowded."

"You ought to get busy on it," Dietrich said. "I hear the credentials office may set a quota."

"Really? I hadn't heard that."

"Well, it may be just another rumor. But I wouldn't take any chances, if I were you. I'd go over right away."

"Thanks for the tip. Maybe I should call and ask for an appointment this afternoon."

"I'd do it this morning," Dietrich counseled. "It shouldn't take long. Unless they've gotten tougher, all they have to do is document your newspaper affiliation and check to make sure you're here on a legitimate assignment. They can handle that with a couple of long-distance calls to Denver. You ought to have your card by lunch-time. Then you can relax and take your time finding an apartment."

"Say, thanks. I'll get right on it."

Dietrich raised his coffee cup and sipped. Perhaps his luck was changing. For the past two days it had been all bad. A few prospects, but none of them had panned out. One man had seemed perfect, but his newspaper had assigned him strictly to coverage of the War Production Board and had no interest in the White House. Another had come close to filling the bill, but had too many close friends in Washington for Dietrich to take a chance. And on top of the failures, he kept hearing Press Club rumors about the departure of the Prime Minister. Apparently the entire British cortege was scheduled to leave this very day, due to the weekend German victory at Tobruk. So Churchill was out of it. Well, to hell with him. There would be other agents to deal with him, back in London. And for Dietrich there was still the President, the prize plum.

No, he wouldn't become discouraged. Now, after all the bad

strokes against him, things were looking up. Kerling on standby in New York, waiting for the word. Probably the Dasch team, too. And this newsman looked promising. Dietrich looked across his cup and said, "Do you have any friends in Washington?"

"Not exactly. There are a couple of guys here that I met once at a Sigma Delta Chi convention, but we aren't exactly friends."

This was a crucial point. Dietrich tried to keep his face just looking amiable and interested as he said, "Maybe I know them. Does either of them work at the White House?"

"No, I don't think so. One works the departments, I think. The other covers the Hill for a Sacramento paper. I ought to look them up."

Dietrich set his cup down. "Sure," he said. "In the meantime, let me show you around. I guess you'll be busy clearing up the accreditation business today, but tonight we'll go out on the town."

The man shook his head. "Thanks anyway, but I wouldn't want to be any trouble."

"What trouble? I remember how it was when I first got here, not knowing anybody. We'll knock around a little tonight, then tomorrow I can introduce you to a few people over to the White House and around. It will make things easier for you later, when you need good news contacts."

"Hey, terrific. I sure would appreciate it. It's tough, coming in cold on a beat."

"Don't I know it. Listen, about tonight, I know a couple of girls. Dictationists down at the office. Real whistle bait. We'll take them out to dinner. What do you say?"

The newsman grimaced. "I'm a married man, Dave. I don't really fool around very much."

"Married?" Dietrich said. He could feel this one slipping away, like the others. "Where's your wife?"

"In Denver. She'll be up to join me in a month or so, after I find us a place to live."

Dietrich relaxed. "Well, if she isn't here, what difference does it make? We don't have to do anything spectacular. Just squire the girls around for a few hours, buy them a few drinks. It would be an act of kindness. The town is full of girls, with not nearly enough men to go around. Come on, Bob, let's do the noble thing and take them out for some laughs and just let nature take its course."

The newsman looked tempted. "I guess it wouldn't really hurt. I'm getting pretty tired of that damned hotel."

"Good man. I'll pick you up at your hotel at six. Where are you staying?"

"The Roger Smith. Listen, Dave, about the girls . . ."

"What about them?"

"They won't be upset if we don't . . . you know."

"Let's just wait and see," Dietrich said. "When you get a load of the big, stacked blonde I have in mind for you, you may want to change your mind."

The man smiled uncomfortably, then shrugged and said, "Well, what the hell. A good newsman never goes into anything with a closed mind, does he?"

"That's the ticket," Dietrich said. He drained his coffee, watching the man over the rim of his cup.

2

Sitting stiffly on the edge of his bunk, George Dasch looked at the simple severity of his surroundings, the bare white concrete wall, scrubbed clean of any graffiti left by prior prisoners, the shining chrome faucet in an undersized porcelain sink which served as handbasin, tub and drinking fountain, and listened to the approaching footsteps. It was the gray-haired one again, and the young one. He could tell. Odd, but he could always recognize the different footfalls, as though his hearing had heightened over the past week. Something about the way toe and heel clicked in the dim corridor outside his cell, echoing, chipping away at the silence.

He composed himself, letting his face relax, waiting for the figures to appear outside his door, waiting to see if he had guessed correctly. Then there would be more questions. There were always more questions. Almost a week of it now. He emptied his mind, readying himself. He would be, once again, the friendly, co-operative informer, ready to tell everything, ready to immerse himself in betrayal. He would be helpful, cordial, obedient, even servile. Soon they would recognize that he was being completely honest with them. Soon they would stop treating him like a traitor and give him the respect a patriot deserved.

A uniformed turnkey and two men in civilian clothing stopped outside his cell. Sure enough, it was the older man, Mr. Grover, dressed in a striped seersucker suit, and the younger agent, Emerson Carter, who had brought him a pack of cigarettes last time. Dasch closed his eyes, listening to the click and scrape of the heavy key.

He heard the iron door swing open. He opened his eyes and smiled brightly.

"Good afternoon, Mr. Grover. And you, Mr. Carter." It was clever of him to remember their names. It made them more like friends than prisoner and interrogators. He started to get up, but the man in the seersucker suit waved him back to the cot.

The door swung shut and the older agent sat beside him on the cot and let his breath hiss sadly. "Well, Mr. Dasch. It appears that we have a problem."

Dasch looked at him. "Problem?" He swung his eyes to the younger agent, standing by the cell door. "I don't understand. What problem?"

"It appears you haven't told us the complete truth," the older man said.

"What? But yes. Yes, I have. I've told you everything."

"You said there were eight men, right?"

"That's correct. Eight men. Mine and the four men in Edward Kerling's team."

"We've accounted for six," the agent said. "And we have another under surveillance in Chicago. But we're missing one."

"He's there," Dasch said. "In Chicago. I told you. That's the way the Florida team was set up. Two in Chicago and two in New York. You watch that boy, what's his name, and he'll lead you to the other. I told the agents yesterday."

"We're not so sure any more," the agent said. "We got a call yesterday from a man at the White House. He says one of them is here. In Washington."

"In Washington?" Dasch looked confused. "No, of course not. He was supposed to wait in Chicago until Kerling sent for him."

"Are you sure?" the agent said. "There was no mention of sending a man to Washington?"

"There was no reason for it," Dasch said. "We were sent here to . . . to sabotage bridges and factories. There was no reason to come to Washington."

The older agent looked at the younger one and sighed. "We think you're lying, Mr. Dasch. And you know what that can mean. It'll probably be a firing squad for all of you."

"No! No!" Dasch said. "I wouldn't lie. I've told you everything. Everything, haven't I?"

"You didn't tell us about the man in Washington."

"But there is no man in Washington. Not unless Kerling changed his plans. You just keep watching that boy in Chicago. You'll see."

"Perhaps there are more than eight," the agent said. "Perhaps you lied about the number."

"No, there were only eight. I should know. I knew everyone who trained at Quenz Lake. It's like I told you. There was . . . there was an instruction. We were told to wait for a message, to tell us when to begin, but that's the only unusual thing that happened after our training."

"A message? How could you get a message unless there was another man here somewhere?"

"We assumed it would be from Europe. Or South America. No one suggested to us that it would be anything else. Please, you must believe me. I've told you everything there is to know."

"I'd like to believe you," the agent said. "But it isn't easy." He stood up. "We may want to discuss this further. Search your memory in the meantime."

"Please," Dasch said. "There is something I would like to ask."

"Oh? What's that?"

Dasch dropped his gaze in embarrassment. "Could you . . . could you make them give me back my belt? My trousers keep falling when I stand."

The two agents looked at each other and the older one shook his head. "Sorry. We can't do that."

"I won't hang myself," Dasch said. "I have no reason to hang myself. I believe in what I'm doing. I'm trying to help you."

The man shook his head again and called for the turnkey.

Dasch waited until the two agents were out in the corridor and his cell door clanged shut, then he sank back on his cot and began to shake.

The older agent cocked his head at Emerson Carter and said, "Well, what do you think?"

"I think he's telling the truth."

"So do I. Damn that captain at the White House. They're all the same, these amateurs. Outsiders, always sticking their fingers in. This one is a waste of time."

"It's too early to tell," Carter said. "Maybe we ought to go by and talk to him. See what he's got."

"Who? The captain? Not a chance. The Director expressly forbids it."

"It would be a lot faster," Carter said.

Grover shook his head. "You don't understand how strongly the Director feels about extrabureau interference. God, I'd hate to be in that captain's shoes. The Director will probably have him investigated for subversive activities."

"But what if the man is right?" Carter said. "Shouldn't we talk to him and find out what set him off? It's dumb to start from scratch when all we have to do is talk to him. Heck, that doesn't make any sense."

The older agent gave him a hard stare. "I'd keep that kind of thinking under my hat, if I were you. The Director doesn't think it likely that any brass-polishing military man sitting on his ass in the White House can come up with something that the entire machinery of the Federal Bureau of Investigation would have missed. I happen to agree with him."

"I didn't mean the Director was dumb," Carter said quickly. "I just meant the whole idea was dumb. One phone call. That's all it would take."

The older agent frowned paternally. "Carter, there's one thing you should always remember. When the Director says 'frog,' most of us take a great big jump. When he says 'defecate,' you can hear earnest groans all up and down the halls. And when he says this joker in the White House is off his rocker, we reach for straitjackets. You better get smart and join the team, friend. Otherwise you can kiss your pension good-bye."

Carter swallowed. "So what do we do?"

"We check around a little more, then we tell the Director that he's right and we can ignore this lead."

3

That evening, Dietrich parked his gray Lincoln near the Roger Smith and hurried into the hotel, carrying an inexpensive zippered briefcase and a brown paper bag with a bottle of Bourbon in it. He was running late, what with having spent much of the afternoon scouting up a suitable location for what he was planning as the evening's culminating activity. It was nearly six-twenty by the time he knocked on the newsman's door.

"Who is it?"

"It's me," Dietrich called. "Dave Pastor."

The door swung open and the Denver newsman looked out, smiling nervously. His sandy hair was wet and plastered straight back from his forehead and he was wearing a bow tie. "Hi, Dave." He flicked a nervous glance into the hallway. "Where, uh, where are the girls?"

"We'll pick them up later, when they finish their shift," Dietrich said. "Say, nice room. Expensive?"

"My paper picks up the tab," the newsman said distractedly. He glanced into the hall again, then reluctantly closed the door after Dietrich. He seemed disappointed that the girls hadn't arrived, and at the same time relieved.

"Sorry I'm late," Dietrich said. "I had to file a couple of stories before I could break loose. Did you go by to see about your White House accreditation?"

"Yeah. It took a little longer than I expected. I've only been back about an hour."

"Good," Dietrich said. "Well, let's celebrate." He deposited the briefcase on the dresser and stripped the brown paper bag off the bottle. "I thought we could have a few belts while we wait for the girls to get off," he said.

"Sure, terrific," the newsman said. "Glasses are in the bathroom. Hang on, I'll get them."

Dietrich turned for a quick survey of the room. Bed, chair, dresser, lamps. A suitcase on a bench in the corner. Wallet, keys, loose change on the bedside table. Dietrich started toward the wallet, but the man came back into the room.

"Do we need ice?" the newsman said. "I can call room service."

Dietrich carefully kept his eyes from the wallet. "Nah, but we could use some cold setups. Didn't I see a Coke machine down the hall?"

"You're kidding. You drink Bourbon with Coke?"

Dietrich grinned again. "Only among friends. Would you mind?"

"It's your stomach," the newsman said. He scooped up some change from the bedside table and headed for the door. "Make yourself comfortable. I'll be right back."

As soon as the newsman was out the door, Dietrich grabbed up the wallet and went through it, looking for the new White House press card. He found a number of cards which might be useful later —driver's license, Denver press pass, Sigma Delta Chi card, Social Security, some kind of church membership, assorted other identifications which would be less helpful, some pictures of a pretty woman with upswept hair, a snapshot of the newsman with the same woman and a spotted dog. Some money, too. That would help. But no White House card.

He could hear the chunk of the Coke machine down the hall, so he knew he still had time. He dropped the wallet and crossed to the dresser, going quickly through the drawers, checking to see if the man had stashed the card elsewhere. The top drawer contained socks and handkerchiefs and a carton of Chesterfields. The next drawer contained shirts and underwear and a brown bathing suit, plus a copy of *Sun and Sea*, one of those nudist magazines with the airbrushed pubic patches, turning male and female alike into sexless sausages.

There was no White House card in the bottom drawer either, but he found a number of things which he rapidly determined might be valuable: a scrapbook of clippings under the newsman's by-line, Robert H. Sheppard; a couple of letters of introduction from a Denver editor named Capers, authorizing him to represent the *Denver Chronicle* in Washington, D.C.; and carbons of interviews with two Colorado politicians that Sheppard had already worked up, showing the format he used in sending copy back to Denver.

Dietrich quickly scooped up the whole pile and opened his brief-case. He lifted the Mauser Automatic with its fat silencer tube and stuffed the papers beneath it, then zipped the case shut. He picked up his Bourbon glass just as the newsman came swinging back into the room with three bottles of Coca-Cola.

"You're my kind of host," Dietrich said. "You want some?"

"God, no. Water will do me fine."

"Coming right up," Dietrich said. "How did it go today?" he asked as he mixed the drinks. "Any trouble getting through the credentials committee?"

"Not really. Oh, they're pretty tight on security. Lots of checking and double-checking. I'm glad I don't have to pay their long-distance phone bills."

"But they cleared you?"

"Sure. No sweat about that."

"That's good," Dietrich said. He rasied his glass in toast and sipped, then said, "I hear they've come up with a new card, different from our old ones. You mind if I take a look at yours?"

"Sure, once I get it," the newsman said. "Boy, were they busy today. Lots of people with gripes. There must have been twenty reporters in and out while I was there, bitching about one thing or another. They told me to come back in the morning to pick it up."

"In the morning?" Dietrich said sharply.

"Yeah, they needed some kind of signature or something. They said they'd have it ready by eleven." He pulled a slip of paper from his shirt pocket and looked at it. "Man named Chesser. Don't bother to come early, he said. It's like taking a number at a bakery, isn't it? The red tape in this town is fantastic."

Dietrich took a healthy swallow of his Bourbon and Coke. Could he wait? Could he put the whole thing off until tomorrow? Probably not. He'd made too big a thing of the girls. If he tried to improvise now, or back out, he might blow the whole thing. He forced a smile. "It's been a long day," he said. "How about you? Have you started filing any stories yet?"

"A couple. I'm not really due for a week or so, though. They told me to take my time and get settled in first."

"How do you send your stuff?" Dietrich asked.

"Night wire, mainly. I'm supposed to hold the budget down. I guess I'll shoot them a few thousand words every couple of days." He smiled sheepishly. "Mainly follow up on wire-service stories if I can find a fresh angle. You know."

"Yeah, I know," Dietrich said. He sipped again. "I kind of miss the old newspaper grind since I joined a wire. The *Chronicle*—say, I think I met some guy from the *Chronicle* once. A guy named Capers. Is he still there?"

Dietrich led the man into a rambling conversation about his paper, suffering patiently through the anecdotes and accounts of memorable practical jokes among his Denver coworkers and listening closely to anything about the man's background and how he handled his copy. It wasn't likely that Dietrich would need any of this, but it seemed safer to soak it in, just in case. He kept the drinks coming while the newsman reminisced. By the time Dietrich built the third drink, he realized that the newsman's capacity for liquor might well outstrip his own, so he adjusted the odds, slugging the newsman's drink while simultaneously easing off on his own. The dark Coke mixer helped to hide his subterfuge.

The newsman chattered away, growing more and more relaxed, and finished his fifth drink in record time. He glanced at his empty glass and blinked, obviously beginning to feel the effects. He said, "Enough of this goddamn shoptalk, Dave, old pal. When are we going to get to the girls?"

"Pretty soon now," Dietrich said, slurring his words. He

checked his watch and said, "Oooh, yeah. Just about time. Let's take the bottle, huh? We may want to loosen them up a little."

The newsman pushed unsteadily to his feet and said, "Sure, terrific." He weaved over to the dresser and picked up the bottle, then slapped his pockets. "Little old wallet. Mustn't forget my little old wallet." He stuffed it in his pocket and staggered before Dietrich.

On the elevator, Dietrich said, "Let's play it cagey, Bobby. We may want to bring the girls to your room later, so hide that bottle under your arm and let's walk out separately. That way no one will know we've got a party going."

"Good thinking," the newsman said. He tapped his forehead and winked.

At the lobby, Dietrich held back and let the newsman weave across the carpet alone, then followed at a safe distance. He waited until they were outside before catching up.

The newsman snickered. "Did they see us?"

"Not a chance," Dietrich said. "Come on, let's get going. That's my car, over there."

"Hey. Little old Lincoln. Not bad, old pal. Not bad at all. They must pay you wire-service jokers pretty well."

"Yeah, it's okay," Dietrich said. "But I've had it a couple of years now and it's beginning to wear out. Hell, I was just on the verge of trading it in when this damned war came along and messed me up."

"That's sad," the newsman said. "That's really tragic. Frigging war. A real damned shame."

Dietrich helped him in the car, then went around and climbed under the steering wheel. He carefully set his briefcase between them, where he could get to it.

They headed west, toward Georgetown. After a few blocks, the newsman said, "Hey, old pal. I thought you said these girls worked downtown? This isn't the way downtown."

"We're going to pick them up at their place," Dietrich said. "You know how women are about getting dressed up."

The newsman giggled. "And getting undressed, too. Eh, old pal?"

Dietrich drove carefully until he reached Rock Creek Park, then turned north, looking for the isolated area he had scouted out that afternoon. He found the turnoff shortly after they passed Dumbarton Oaks, a narrow dirt road that wound down into a concealed glen filled with elms and oaks and dogwoods. He bumped along the dirt road to the end, then pulled off beyond the road and drove into a stand of tulip trees. He yanked the emergency brake and shut the engine off.

"I don't see any houses," the newsman said. "Hell, I don't see anything. Where are we?"

"We're not there yet," Dietrich said. "I thought maybe I should give you the lowdown on these girls first. They're really something special."

The newsman uncapped the Bourbon bottle and took a swig. "Well, lay it on the line, old pal. Are they horny? You know, I'm beginning to feel better about all this. You want a drink?"

Dietrich shook his head. He reached down and unzipped the briefcase and pulled out the Mauser.

The newsman saw the gun and laughed. "Hey, what's this, old pal? A game?"

Dietrich pointed the gun at the newsman. "Get out," he said.

The newsman grinned, then let his mouth droop a little. He looked puzzled. "I don't get it," he said.

Dietrich leaned across him and levered the door open, then shoved him. The newsman toppled out backwards onto the ground.

"Hey, watch it, Dave," the man said. "Jesus Christ, you almost made me spill the booze. What's got into you?" He started to get up.

"Sit still," Dietrich said.

The newsman looked confused. "My God, Dave, are you serious? What is this? Money? Is that what you want?"

"No, it isn't money," Dietrich said. He leveled the gun.

"This is crazy. My God, Dave. Don't point that thing at me. Take what you want. Take my money. Take anything. But don't hurt me."

"I'm sorry," Dietrich said. "I really am. But this is necessary."

"I never did anything to you. God, don't. Take what you want and let me—"

Dietrich shot him twice in the heart, the silenced gun going *phut*, *phut*, putting the bullets so close together that he could have covered both holes with a single silver dollar.

The newsman toppled back in the dirt, his mouth making a wide, silent "O" beneath startled eyes. The uncapped whiskey bottle, nestled in the crook of his arm, rolled back with him, gurgling Bourbon across his breached chest. His left leg jerked off the ground and twitched twice, then settled until his heel drummed the dirt in a timpani of afterdeath.

Dietrich watched from the car seat until the brief symphony of twitches ended, then crawled out and stood over the body. Poor slob. If only it had been possible to explain it first. It might have made it easier to die if the man had known how important it was. But surely the easiest way was to get it over quickly, before the mind had time to dwell on it.

He picked up the nearly empty whiskey bottle and hurled it into the darkness. He could hear it slash through leaves and tumble into the bushes some distance away. Then he hooked the body under the arms and dragged it into the underbrush, beneath one of the tulip trees. He fetched a sack of lye from the trunk of the car, another of his afternoon purchases, and carried it to the body. He squatted and removed the newsman's wallet and the little sheet of paper in his breast pocket which told him when to report for his White House card, then ripped the lye sack open and sprinkled it liberally along the length of the body to keep the odor down.

He stood above the body for a few moments, examining the isolation, assuring himself that the area was sufficiently secluded to keep the body hidden for a long time. No one was likely to wander through here. It was satisfactory.

He separated the wallet and the folded note and started to put them in his pocket. Then he noticed that the note was sticky with Bourbon and blood, and he cursed quietly. He should have shot for the head. It would have been less messy.

THE FOURTEENTH DAY

Friday—June 26, 1942

I

There was a nameplate on the desk which identified the man as Albert C. Chesser. Dietrich stood in front of him cautiously and smiled. "Good morning," he said. "Do you have my White House card ready? Robert Sheppard. I was told to be here at eleven."

The man looked up and hoisted an eyebrow. "Sheppard?" he said. "Have you identification?"

"Certainly," Dietrich said. He opened Robert Sheppard's wallet and produced the newsman's Colorado driver's license and the Denver press pass. He handed them over, trying to appear nonchalant, and watched while the man examined them.

Finally the man smiled back and returned the cards. "You know, Mr. Sheppard, for a moment there I didn't recognize you. There was such a crowd in here yesterday."

"Yes, you were very busy," Dietrich said. "We're all working too hard these days."

"Yes, I suppose so, what with the war effort and everything."

"Anyway, I'm glad you remembered me," Dietrich said. "I'd hate to go through that telephoning business again. I'm certainly glad I don't have to pay your long-distance telephone bills."

"We have to be careful," the man said. He reached into a drawer and removed an envelope from which he extracted a small white card, embossed in blue. He handed it to Dietrich and said, "Here you are, Mr. Sheppard. This is your accreditation as a White House correspondent. Your name should be on the gate list by now, but if it isn't, just have them call me."

"Thank you," Dietrich said.

"Be sure and take good care of that card. Even with your name on the list, they won't let you through the gate without it, no matter how well they get to know you. Security is very tight these days."

"I'm glad to hear that," Dietrich said. "One can't be too cautious in times like these."

2

Special Agent Emerson Carter paced across his small cubicle in the Justice Building. Damn it, no matter what Grover and the others said, it would still be a hell of a lot easier just to talk to the captain and ask him why he suspected the presence of a spy in Washington. After all, Bureau people had been on Haupt's tail in Chicago for five days now, and still no sign of the eighth man.

He paused at the corner of his desk and stared at the telephone, sitting upright on its slender pole, speaker turned upward like an alert sentinel, earpiece dangling from the hook like a malformed arm. Yes, sir, it seemed to say. At your service, sir. Well, to hell with it. Pick it up and place the call. If this White House captain could give him a good lead, maybe he could locate the eighth man himself and be a hero. The Director liked heroes.

The White House switchboard passed him to some sergeant and Carter asked to speak to the captain. When he got him, he cleared his throat and said, "Captain Blaszek, you don't know me, but, er, I think we ought to get together for a talk."

"Who's this?" the captain said.

"My name is Carter. I'm with the FBI."

"I was expecting a call from the Director," the captain said.

"Yes, well, I'm not sure you're going to get it, Captain. There seems to be some, er, question over here about your theory. I've been assigned to check it out."

The captain seemed to sigh. "Okay. You want to come over here? Or shall I come over there?"

"Well, neither, actually," Carter said. "The Director is out of town at the moment, but he left instructions that we were to conduct the investigation without actually, er, talking to you." He heard the captain mutter something. "I'm sorry, Captain. I didn't quite get that. What did you say?"

"It was an old-fashioned four-letter word," the captain said. "It pretty well sums up the way I feel about the FBI."

"Oh, I see," Carter said, though he didn't. "Well, the truth of the matter is, I thought it might be better if we met elsewhere. Someone might see us if we met here and, er, mention it to the Director when he returns from New York."

"You're doing this without the Director's permission?"

Carter swallowed. "Yes. You might say that."

"I understand. All right. Where shall we meet?"

Carter cleared his throat again. "Well, we might meet in some ordinary place." He glanced around the office, wondering where to suggest. His eye lit on the erect pole of his desk telephone, towering black and straight above an open package of gum. He said, "How about the Washington Monument? Inside, about a third of the way up the steps. Okay? Say about four o'clock this afternoon?"

"I'll be there," the captain said.

"Good," Carter said. "Four o'clock, Captain. And, er, don't mention this to anyone, will you?"

He hung up and closed his eyes. God, why had he sounded so nervous? He was merely doing his conscientious best to do his job. The Director would be as pleased as anyone else if he managed to break this case and catch the missing spy. And yet . . . And yet, if work got back to Grover or the Director that he had made a move like this on his own initiative, he would be up the old scatological creek without a paddle. Like Grover was always telling him, there are old agents. And there are bold agents. But there are no old, bold agents.

He looked down at his shirt and was surprised to see that he was sweating profusely. He got up quickly and opened his office window. He stood in the warm breeze and held his arms out like wings, offering his underarms to the gush of air. Dry, damn it, and dry cleanly. God, if someone saw him with sweat rings . . .

3

The West Wing of the White House was built in 1902 by President Theodore Roosevelt in an effort to expand the living space of the first family by separating the public offices from the private living quarters.

It was a broad, white building, larger than it looked from the street, and it sat at the end of a long, low-windowed gallery which connected it to the main mansion. Called the "working White House" by most of the regulars, the West Wing contained the executive offices of the President: the famous Oval Office in which the President himself conducted business, the Cabinet Room in which he met his top-level advisers, the Fish Room, the Reception Lobby, and a whole array of administrative offices for the President's major and minor appointees, assistants, secretaries and a few military liaison men. It also contained a bright, cheery area in the northwest corner, a room with tall windows lining the two outside walls, a room cluttered with typewriters, desks, telephones and a coterie of bored newspaper reporters sitting around waiting for something exciting to happen—the White House press room.

Dietrich edged away from the credentials desk at the entrance and headed for the press room with his nerves clawing at his stomach. They had stopped him twice for a look at his credentials, once at the outer gate and again when he reached the double doors that led into the West Wing. The White House card seemed to be working, but Dietrich still couldn't get his nerves to settle down. The stakes were too high. The perils too awesome. Already, in his brief three-minute walk from the outer gate to the wing itself, he had been assaulted by a flood of alert, suspicious looks.

And the uniforms. Everywhere, uniforms. The blue and white of the White House security police force. The tailored mufti of prowling Secret Service agents. The nerve-shattering number of khaki military uniforms. Young enlisted men scattered about the grounds, standing sentry duty. Young officers with silver bars and brass buttons and holstered .45 automatics, bustling from sentry post to sentry post. All of them, lingering around the building, watching, watching.

Both credential and name checks had been thorough, but the second one had been the most numbing. Two White House policemen and a Secret Service man in a gray suit, standing guard like a three-headed Gorgon just inside the entrance to the wing, had looked him over and studied his card and consulted some kind of master list, presumably looking for his name and particulars, before they grudgingly admitted him.

But he had made it. He had breeched the White House grounds, run the gauntlet of watchful suspicion, bluffed his way past two checkpoints, and now found himself striding toward the press room, alone and unattended, as free to come and go, with some limitations, as any of the legitimate White House newsmen who labored or loafed daily in the room ahead of him. Maybe it would work. Maybe it really would work.

He stepped through the door and paused, surveying the press room, orienting himself to his new environment as a working member of the White House press corps. This was to be his base of operations. This large, bright room. A massive table in the center for coats and hats, surrounded by empty desks and covered typewriters. Along the south wall, the inner wall, a wire machine under a stuffed ox head positioned so low that the taller newsmen undoubtedly had to duck when they checked to see what was coming in.

Most of the twenty or thirty men in the room seemed totally uninterested in anything that happened around them. Reporters and photographers, lounging around the walls in stuffed chairs, killing time, reading, napping, staring into space. Others in shirtsleeves with ties loosened, playing cards at one of the desks. In a way, the lazy scene reminded Dietrich of the card rooms at the National Press Club, the same bored, indifferent expressions on the same deadpan faces. Men so inured by daily exposure to cataclysmic events that they found it difficult to arouse any enthusiasm for minor events. Not one of them bothered to give Dietrich a second look.

He slipped his hat off and laid it on the central table amid the piles of hats and coats, then did a circuit of the room, trying to look and feel casual, checking out the desks and telephones and the physical setup of the working area. Most of the desks and typewriters appeared to be communal in nature, to be shared by whomever happened to be on duty at any given time. But a few of the choicer desks near the bright windows were stacked high with reference books and personal notes and spiked carbons of news stories, obviously reserved for the older hands with seniority, probably the veteran wire-service men and leading lights from some of the nation's more prestigious newspapers.

He made up his mind to go easy at first, to learn the ropes and the pecking order before sitting at any of the desks and running the risk of offending tradition or any of the highly placed correspondents. He needed anonymity, at least until he figured out the best way to take advantage of his new entree. Once he had all the bugs worked out, and had set the roles for his backup men, he would make his final contact with the two submarine teams and start the clock ticking.

He paused by one of the reserved desks, a battered relic near one of the tall north windows, and eyed the stack of story carbons impaled on the spike. Later today, when he was certain the action would go unobserved, he would steal some of these carbons. Sarah had a little portable at her apartment. He could retype them the way Robert Sheppard prepared copy and file them to Denver under Sheppard's name. Something to keep Sheppard's newspaper off balance for an extra day or two. That's all the time he needed, actually. Just a few days' grace.

Satisfied with his preliminary survey of the news room, he headed cautiously back toward the doorway and out into the large central reception lobby, a high-ceilinged public room filled with green leather furniture and heavy wooden tables. This was apparently the room where the normal flow of presidential visitors and favor-seekers gathered to wait for an audience.

Dietrich knew it wouldn't be easy to learn everything he needed to know, not in so short a time. There were bound to be areas forbidden to newsmen without an express invitation, closed doors that would open only if he could manufacture an extremely plausible-sounding excuse. He knew the basic floor plan of the building. He knew, for example, that one of the doors to his left led out of the big reception lobby into the Fish Room, a largish auditorium where conferences and occasional press briefings were held. He knew that beyond the Fish Room, not visible from the lobby, would be the long, rectangular Cabinet Room, with its windows facing the rose garden. And in the southeast corner of the Executive Wing, the far opposite corner from the press room, behind the closed doors and the blank walls, beyond uncertain and unseen barriers, was his eventual objective. The Oval Office.

He would have to see it somehow. He had to get beyond the closed doors and into the working area. Otherwise he would be working blind. And he couldn't afford to work blind. He had to know every door, every turning, every danger if he was to get out alive.

He wandered toward the rear of the lobby, closer to the hidden area which interested him, feeling his breath come faster as he neared that egg-shaped seat of power. A man, apparently some kind of appointment secretary, looked up from a desk which guarded a set of closed doors. Dietrich nodded politely at him, looking beyond him, eyeing the doors.

Where exactly was the President's office? Directly behind the doors? No, more likely off to the side. Perhaps cordoned off by anterooms and alcoves? Guarded by platoons of Secret Service men? Could he, if he had his gun right now, manage to break his way past the guards, storm through the inner corridors, reach the man in the wheelchair, shoot him down, kill him? Could he snuff the man out impetuously before anyone could stop him? The prospect provoked him, brought an emotional pounding to his throat and temples. He would never try it. It was far too risky, the chances of failure, of unexpected obstacles, were too high. But the pure idea, the physical possibility, sent tremors racing through his body. He played the scene through his mind. He would burst through the doors, gun down anyone who obstructed him and . . .

"Hey, you. Where do you think you're going?"

The voice, gruff and demanding, startled him. He forced himself to turn slowly and calmly. One of the blue-shirted White House police officers, a burly man in his fifties, gray and sour-looking, came striding toward him. A name tag on his shirt pocket said "Greer."

"Who are you?" the policeman said. "What are you doing back here?" He braced himself in front of Dietrich, a suspicious look on his craggy face.

"I'm one of the White House correspondents," Dietrich said casually. "I was just taking a look around."

The policeman cocked his head. "I've never seen you before. What paper do you represent?"

"The *Denver Chronicle*," Dietrich said. "I'm new."

"Let me see your identification."

"Yes, sir," Dietrich said. He lifted his wallet from his hip pocket and fingered out his new White House card. "I'm sorry, officer. Was I wrong to come back here? No one said anything about it being off limits."

The policeman studied the card carefully, then shook his head, mollified. "No, sir. It isn't off limits. It's just that we have to keep our eyes and ears open. You're a new face, see, and we can't be too careful." He returned Dietrich's card.

"Would you rather I stay in the press room?" Dietrich asked. "I don't want to create problems."

"No, that isn't necessary. Just don't be surprised if you get tapped for your ID every once in a while. At least until we get used to you. Lots of new people around these days. It's hard for us to keep the faces straight."

Dietrich put his White House card back in his wallet and said, "Thank you, officer. I'll try not to be a bother." He smiled weakly and moved off toward the front end of the reception lobby, back toward the press room. For now, at least, he was better off staying

out of sight and in the safety of the press area. He wasn't sure his
nerves could take another brush with authority.

But later today, when he felt more at home, more at ease, he
could come out again. He would spread his horizons, probe the
accesses and corners of the Executive Wing, learn the layout of his
battleground.

When it was time, he would be ready.

4

Andy left his own White House office a little before four that afternoon for the short walk down to the Mall, wondering why the
FBI agent had found it necessary to meet him without the Director's sanction. Surely the Director was willing to consider the possibility that one of the German spies was loose in Washington. It
didn't make sense to ignore it.

At the grassy knoll in the center of the Mall, just south of the
White House and the Ellipse, he reared his head back and looked up
at the monument. He didn't really like the Washington Monument.
He never had. It seemed too crude a joke somehow, to honor a man
known as the Father of his Country by erecting a 555-foot phallic
symbol. He had remarked on it once to Gay, referring to it as a
white marble penis. Her reply had shocked and embarrassed him.
Now he couldn't look at it without blushing.

Up about a third of the way, the FBI man had suggested. God,
there were some nine hundred steps in this towering obelisk. That
meant he had to fight his way up three hundred of them before he
could even locate the man. Why hadn't they settled for the top?
That way they could have ridden the elevator.

He started climbing, trudging up the steps inside the dingy stone
structure, ignoring the tribute blocks set in the walls, the stones
from all over the world, bearing rich, flowery prose from the nine-
teenth century. Some people said it rained in here during the
summers. Every time there was a sudden hot spell, this damned
structure supposedly manufactured its own indoor rain. That's all
he needed, to be caught in an indoor rainstorm on the 300-step level
of the Washington Monument.

His breath was coming heavy and hard by the time he counted
off the required number of steps and sagged against the wall, con-
templating giving up smoking. He celebrated the thought by flipping an Old Gold out of his pack and firing up. Hardy tourists
marched past him, continuing upward.

He was halfway through his cigarette when a young man approached him from below, puffing with each step, sweat streaming from his face, and said with a phony smile, "Captain Blaszek?"

"Yes," Andy said. He looked the man over. Typical FBI, he decided. All FBI people seemed to look alike. Perfect physiques, heroic chins, clear eyes, carefully combed hair. It was as though they were selected as much for their photogenic qualities as for brains. Perhaps more.

"I'm Emerson Carter," the man said. "I called you earlier today." His voice was ragged, probably because of the climb. His chest heaved as he leaned against the wall for support. In a moment he recovered enough to produce an identification card and asked nicely enough that Andy do the same.

Andy took pleasure in the fact that he had arrived first, allowing his own breathing to settle down. He said, "What would you like to talk about, Mr. Carter? Would you like to hear my story, or has the Director already made up his mind?"

Carter flashed a smile, exposing perfect FBI teeth, and said, "Now, Captain, don't be bitter. You have to realize that there is always some resistance to outside interference. We get a great many calls in the course of our varied investigations, most of them from people who, er, people, er . . ."

"Crackpots."

"Yes, well, anyway, I thought it wouldn't hurt to listen. If you're willing to talk to me, that is."

"Hell yes, I am. You're the first FBI person who's shown any interest. Frankly, this thing is too big for me. I'm not equipped to handle it."

"Then you really think one of the spies is here? You're serious?"

"Of course I am. I'm more convinced every minute. Things keep adding up. Look, a woman was killed in a boardinghouse last week. And the man who killed her didn't move in until after the submarine landing in New York. Point. The police searched the man's room after he ran away and found all new clothing, purchased after he moved in. I saw the sales slips. Point. And he killed her on Thursday, the day that informer of yours came to Washington from New York. I think there might be a connection."

Carter shook his head. "You can forget that last one. I'm on one of the interrogation teams. I've talked to the informer myself, a number of times. We don't think he had any connection with a spy in Washington."

Andy's face fell. "Are you sure?"

"Well, that's what the guy says. I tend to believe him."

"Then, why did he come down here? Why didn't he just give himself up in New York?"

"You have to know the guy to understand. He's role-playing. He thinks of himself as a patriot, rather than a spy. We think he came here because he thought he was going to be dealing with the Director himself."

Andy grimaced. "Fat chance," he said. "I'm willing to bet he never got within ten miles of the Director. You guys protect that old bastard like he was stuffed with crown jewels."

"Now, now, Captain," Carter said nervously. "It isn't necessary to characterize the Director that way. He's really a very remarkable man. He's seldom wrong, you know."

"Did the informer get to see him?"

"Well, no, but . . ."

"That's what I figured. Anyway, this time I think he's wrong. Maybe the killing didn't have anything to do with the arrival of the informer, but there are other things. This guy who killed the woman was carrying a gun. He took a shot at one of the boardinghouse people before he ran. And there's more. The police found twenty thousand dollars hidden in the kitchen. They think it might have belonged to the man. It was watersoaked, as though someone might have carried it through surf."

"Watersoaked?" Carter suddenly looked interested. "That's odd. As you may know, Captain, we confiscated over eighty thousand dollars from Dasch, our informer. Some of it was watersoaked, too."

"See?" Andy said. "That's what really got me interested, the money. I saw it day before yesterday. I went down to the police station to check it out, and they showed me all sorts of things, things they took out of this guy's room at the boardinghouse. Now here comes the scary part. I saw a handful of railroad timetables, with little scribbled notations in the margins. I don't know all that much about railroad schedules, but I know enough to tell you he was timing trains on a stretch of track that carried the presidential train only two days after he killed the woman."

Carter's smile was gone. "You think he was after the train?"

"I'm not sure yet. I turned the figures over to a guy who works at Union Station. He's going to try to pinpoint the exact area and give me a call this weekend. I'll tell you this, though. I think this man was setting up something before he killed the woman and was forced to run. If it *was* the train, I think he was probably waiting for help from those spies who landed in New York, and you guys fouled him up by arresting them."

Carter nodded reluctantly. "There could conceivably be something to it. Our informer told us they'd been taught to handle all sorts of explosives and sabotage. One of the prime interests was in railroad sabotage. But it's at variance with our information. The informer swears that both of the remaining spies are in Chicago. We have no reason to disbelieve him. How would you explain that?"

"Yeah, well, it's so obvious it could bite you," Andy said. "Suppose there was another spy. A ninth man."

Carter shook his head. "No. No way. There are only eight. I've questioned the informer on that point myself. Four men on each team. He should know. They trained together for several months."

"Are you sure?"

"Reasonably certain," Carter said.

"No, are you *sure*. Absolutely, certainly, positively sure?"

"Damn it, no one can ever be absolutely sure about anything," Carter said, suddenly irritated. "But I can grant you this. The picture we've pieced together doesn't necessarily cancel your Washington theory. We're still missing one of the eight. We've been looking for him almost a week now, with no luck. If he's in Washington, that would explain a lot of things." He sighed. "Captain, maybe you ought to tell the President about this. Warn him to stay off trains for a while. At least until we locate the last man."

"The President doesn't exactly ask my advice on such matters."

A sympathetic little smile flickered briefly at the corners of Carter's mouth. "Well, do what you can. The important thing, of course, is for us to locate the missing man. Fast. Most of our people are still looking for him in Chicago. Why don't you approach the District police and see if you can get them to look for him here?"

"The police?" Andy was incredulous. "What about the FBI? Couldn't you guys do it better?"

"It might be better if we limit it to the police for the moment," Carter said. "You don't have to tell them exactly what they're looking for. Just say the White House has a special interest in the man who killed the woman at the boardinghouse. That way they won't call the FBI for verification and foul us up."

"I thought you believed me?"

"Oh, I do, Captain. I'll help all I can. Not openly, of course. Not just yet, anyway."

"But why? What's wrong with helping me openly?"

Carter looked away. "I'm not even supposed to be talking to you," he said. "How would I explain it?"

"But Jesus, if the man was trying for the President's train . . ."

Carter looked at the wall, at the stairs, at space, everywhere but at Andy's eyes. "You don't understand," he said. "I can't go against the Director's wishes without convincing him first. I've got to talk to him, persuade him. Gently."

"But when he hears about this, surely . . ."

"It's the *way* he hears about it," Carter said. "I've got to go out and develop this material on my own, so it looks as though I did it without your help. I'll go to the police station and ask questions. I'll get them to show me the money and things. I know this may sound chickenshit to you, Captain, but that's the way it has to be. If I just walk in and tell him I talked to you, it could wreck my career. I like my job. I need it."

"All right, all right," Andy said. "But do it right away, will you? God knows how much time we've got. Talk to the police. Get your evidence worked up. Then go see your boss and talk to him. The eighth man is here, in Washington. I'm sure of it. And if we don't get the FBI to switch its search here right away, something is going to happen and none of us will be able to stop it. Right away, you hear?"

Carter swallowed. "Right away? Yeah. Well, okay. When he gets back from New York. I'll, er, think about it."

THE FIFTEENTH DAY

Saturday—June 27, 1942

1

Special Agent Emerson Carter never had a chance to divert the FBI search for the eighth spy from Chicago to Washington. The very next morning, Saturday, June 27, 1942, Herbert Hans Haupt brought the Chicago search to a close when he parked his recently purchased red Pontiac convertible in front of a Chicago hotel and went in to ask for a man whom he called Henry Nicholas.

Federal agents from the Chicago Bureau, who had been following Haupt since Monday, deployed through the lobby and waited for the man to appear. To their immense relief, the man who came to the lobby to meet Haupt matched perfectly the informant's description of the missing German saboteur, Otto Neubauer, right down to the scar on the left cheek. The agents moved in quickly to apprehend them both.

Haupt, horrified, insisted that he was a loyal American citizen and tried to convince them that he had come to the hotel only to deliver a message for his uncle, whom he wildly claimed was a confirmed Bundist. But he was placed under arrest anyway.

The long search had ended.

2

"Mr. President?" the Director of the Federal Bureau of Investigation purred into the telephone. "I have some excellent news for you. We've broken the Nazi spy case. We just arrested the last two men in Chicago. We've got them all, sir. Every one of them."

He listened to the President's response, nodding, and beamed happily at the FBI men surrounding the conference table at which he sat, sharing his pleasure with them. "Yes, sir," he said, "in a mere two weeks. My men have outdone themselves, sir. It was a splendid example of teamwork. We may have stubbed our toes a time or two, but we got them, sir."

One of the older agents scribbled a note and handed it to him. He scanned it, then said, "Mr. President, one of my senior agents has suggested that we release this news to the press. Immediately. Perhaps if word gets back to Germany, it will discourage any such future attempts. What's that, sir? Yes, sir, names, backgrounds, everything we've managed to put together. With, ah, one exception, of course. I thought perhaps we shouldn't mention the informer. It might be a more effective deterrent if the Germans simply believe the FBI is too strong for them."

He listened, then knitted his brow, looking perplexed. "Ah, about that Coast Guard youngster, Mr. President. I'm not sure I agree with you. Of course we don't really care about things like public credit here at the Bureau, but wouldn't it appear more hazardous to the Germans if we didn't make a particularly big thing of the accidental nature of their early discovery? I mean, actually, I should think they would be less likely to try it again if they simply thought it was the thoroughness and the efficiency of the FBI which lay behind the capture of their men."

He nodded again and said, "Yes, sir, I'm glad you see my point. Very well, I'll notify newspaper and radio offices this evening, in time for the Sunday morning deadlines. Just as soon as my people can put together some press kits. What's that? Yes, I'll be back in Washington tomorrow, just as soon as I get this press conference out of the way. You're welcome, Mr. President."

He hung up and smiled around the room. "The President is delighted," he said. "Gentlemen, you have my congratulations."

3

At nine that evening, representatives of all major New York City wire services and newspapers, alerted only a half hour earlier, gathered at the FBI office in the Federal Building at Foley Square.

The newsmen were puzzled. They had no idea why they had been summoned. The official notification to city desks and wire services and radio networks had been both blunt and vague: the Director of the Federal Bureau of Investigation would make a statement to the press at nine o'clock. There was no hint of what he was to say, no suggestion of the magnitude of the upcoming disclosure.

Their mystification increased when they were ushered into a darkened room which had been set aside for the press conference.

Empty chairs faced a brightly lit table, atop which, amid fact sheets and stacks of photographs, were several enigmatic items—small brick-shaped bundles wrapped in paper, a few dark lumps which looked like fragments of coal, a board containing small button-sized devices not unlike dynamite caps, a gray-green military cap with a German insignia on the peak.

Two muscular young FBI agents flanked the table, hands clasped behind their backs, keeping the newsmen from straying too close to the display. The reporters were led wordlessly to the chairs and left to wait while the tension mounted. No one spoke to them. No one offered any explanations.

Then, with exquisite timing, just as the tension trembled near the precipice of commotion, a door opened to the rear of the lighted table, and the short, familiar figure of FBI Director J. Edgar Hoover came marching into the circle of light, looking very somber and businesslike. He took a position behind the table and flattened his palms on the surface, gazing out into the darkened audience of faces. With theatrical gravity, he said:

"Gentlemen of the press. I have a very important announcement to make. I want you to listen carefully. This is serious business . . ."

THREE

THE NINTH MAN

THE SIXTEENTH DAY

Sunday—June 28, 1942

I

Dietrich awoke as he always did, immediately and fully, and raised up on one elbow. He listened for a moment, then, as quickly, he relaxed. Outside the open window, sparrows were chattering in a forsythia hedge, and in the kitchen he could hear Sarah tapping a spoon as she measured coffee. Nothing in those sounds to be alarmed about. He yawned at the ceiling, unwilling to look at the small, untidy bedroom. Sarah obviously preferred to spend her money on bird feed and her appearance rather than her surroundings. But there would be coffee in bed. It was one of the touches she had adopted as a regular thing, and it was hard not to like it. One could even get used to a life like this.

He ran his palm over his chin, feeling the bristles, listening again as the front door opened and closed, then footsteps padded back toward the bedroom. The morning newspaper. He caught a glimpse of bare leg and quickly closed his eyes, feigning sleep.

She said, "Wake up, sleepyhead."

He smiled with his eyes closed, then went through a stretch-and-yawn routine. "What kind of a day is it?" he said.

"It's a gorgeous day. Wake up. Coffee will be ready in a minute. I brought you the paper."

She was standing over him, holding out the Sunday Washington *Star*, wearing only panties and bra. He had quickly kidded her out of the modestly buttoned pink cotton robe she had appeared in the first morning, and had a little more slowly kidded her into a realization that there was really nothing so abhorrent about a little bare flesh, but now he found himself staring at her panties, which sagged unattractively about her firm hips. The elastic had apparently given way. He wondered if he could next think of a tactful way to suggest that, barring total nudity, she buy some new underwear. Why have a good body and make it unappetizing in sagging underwear? It looked careless. And cheap.

She bounded across him, plopping into bed, and snuggled up to his bare side. She seemed to be gaining a new taste for skin. "Let me have the funnies," she said. "I want to see what Flyin' Jenny is doing today."

"Funnies," he said, not sure whether he was serious or only joking. "A world in flames and she wants to see the funnies. Don't you even want to peek at the front page?"

"I hate the war," she said. "I wish everyone were like me, and then there wouldn't *be* any wars." She stripped the comic section from his newspaper and scrooched up her knees, spreading the funnies across them.

A little piously, Dietrich raised the newspaper for a look at the headlines. The lead story hit him right in the midsection. A four-column head across the upper left said:

FBI CAPTURE OF 8, LANDED BY SUBS,
THWARTS SPECTACULAR NAZI PLOT
TO SABOTAGE VITAL U.S. WAR PLANTS

He bolted upright, his mind tumbling, his brain stunned by the shock his eyes had transmitted.

Sarah looked up in concern. "What is it?" she said. "Sweetheart, what's wrong?"

"What?" he said. "Oh, nothing. Just a bit of a muscular twinge."

"Shall I rub it? Would that help?"

"No. No, I'll be all right."

"I'll get the Ben-Gay," she said. "Oh sweetheart, does it hurt bad?"

"No. I'll just sit like this for a moment."

Unconvinced, she reached out worriedly and touched him. "Ray, are you sure it's just a muscle spasm? You look terribly upset. Is there anything I can do?"

"Damn it!" he gasped. "Leave me alone! Can't you see I don't want to talk?"

Her eyes blinked wide and she drew back, stung by the force of his outburst. She stared at him for a moment, then her chin began to quiver and she bounced out of bed, jiggling nudely toward the bathroom. The door slammed behind her. Moments later, piteous sobs rose from the bathroom and echoed through the apartment.

She obviously made sure they were loud enough to be heard, even through the closed door.

He ignored her, scanning the page quickly. There, bounded by photographs of George Dasch and Edward Kerling and a shot of the crates and their contents, was a lengthy story, datelined New York. The lead block said:

> Special Dispatch to the Star
>
> NEW YORK, June 27—Landed on the Atlantic Coast by Nazi submarines, eight Berlin-trained German sabotage school experts, equipped with $150,000 in cash and explosives for a two-year "terror campaign" against vital American war plants, have been captured, Director J. Edgar Hoover of the Federal Bureau of Investigation disclosed tonight.
>
> The eight men under arrest are all former United States residents, several are former German-American Bund members, and two are United States citizens, Mr. Hoover said, while one is a former member of the Michigan National Guard.
>
> One crew of four was landed on Long Island the night of June 12, Mr. Hoover said, and the other four landed at a beach near Jacksonville, Fla., three nights later.
>
> None of the spectacular missions assigned to the Nazi saboteurs was carried out, and all eight men are in custody, Mr. Hoover emphasized, the last having been captured today in Chicago.

His hands began to shake, and he lowered the newspaper, his face ashen. Sarah was still crying loudly in the bathroom. Dietrich plunged his face into his palms and squeezed his eyes shut, trying to close out Sarah, the newspaper, everything. He had to clear his mind, to think. God! All of them! Caught!

He sat still, face in palms, for several long minutes, until Sarah's wailing began to soften. Soon he would have to apologize to her, think up some minor excuse for his rudeness. Soon he would pet her, placate her, bed her, wipe the momentary madness from her memory. Because he still needed her. Now, more than ever, he needed her.

Because now he was alone.

2

"Yes, he was some kind of an artist, I think. I saw him a week ago last Thursday. He was out here most of the day. Can't for the life of me imagine why. There's nothing to draw out here but trees and weeds. He was over there, on that hill above the railroad bridge."

Andy followed the farmer's pointing finger to a knoll in the distance, overlooking a span of bridge. "Was there anyone with him, Mr. Hanlon?"

"Not that I saw. He was by himself when I passed, sketching in a big pad. I was on the road below, taking my tractor over to Ed McMasters' place. My two older boys used to do all the repairs, but they're both in the service now. Navy." He regarded Andy's plaid slacks and blue pullover shirt. "You said you were an Army man, didn't you?"

"That's right," Andy said. "Did you get a good look at the man?"

"Not really. My eyes aren't what they used to be. Oh, I stared at him as I drove by. We don't see many young people out here any more, not with everyone in the service. He was kind of dark and sturdy-looking. About your age, I'd say. He parked his car down at the foot of the hill, near the road."

"Did you see the license number?"

"I'm afraid not. They were D.C. plates, though. I remember thinking it was a long way to come, just to draw a few pictures. A waste of gasoline and rubber, if you ask me."

"What kind of car was it?"

"A nice little gray coupe. A Lincoln. Maybe a '38, maybe a '39. I'm not too good at models. My boys would have known immediately. They used to be pretty car crazy. I have one younger boy still at home, but with him it's airplanes. That's the war for you. He can't tell a Ford from a Chevrolet, but you point at a plane that's no more than a tiny speck in the sky, and he can tell you instantly whether it's a P-40E or a P-40F." The farmer leaned against a fence post and said, "I don't mean to be forward, but may I ask why you aren't wearing a uniform?"

"It's my day off," Andy said.

"Day off, huh?" The farmer grinned and shook his head. "You Army people have it pretty good. Both my boys are on destroyers.

God, I don't know why they picked the Navy." He looked beyond
Andy to the car, where Gay and Gaylynn were waiting. "You and
the family plan to have a picnic breakfast?"

"If it's all right with you," Andy said. "I'd like to go over and
take a closer look at that knoll above the bridge."

"Sure. Suit yourself. Anything for our boys in service."

"Thank you," Andy said. "Mr. Hanlon, I may want to get in
touch with you again about this man. Would you mind if I called,
or sent someone up later this week? We won't bother you unless it
becomes necessary."

"I'll do anything I can to help. What is he, a draft dodger?"

"Something like that," Andy said. He thanked the farmer again
and trotted back out to the car.

As he put it in gear and pulled away, Gay said, "That makes the
fifth farmhouse in a row, Andy. This was supposed to be an outing,
not a working session. Are we going to keep it up all morning?"

"No, that's the last one. I think I found what I was looking for."

"Good," she said. "I know you're just being conscientious, lover,
but Gaylynn is beginning to get a bit restless. We promised her a
morning in the country, you know, not a morning in the car."

"I'm not restless," Gaylynn said restlessly from the back seat.

"Just a few minutes more," Andy said. "I want to take a look at
that bridge over there."

Gay opened her mouth, then closed it. Andy glanced at her, feeling guilty. They had planned the picnic the day before, right after
he got the report from the railroad expert, narrowing the area of
the timetable notations to a few miles of track in upper Maryland. It
had sounded an enjoyable way to mix business with pleasure. But
Gay had seen the FBI spy-arrest story in the paper that morning
and had called his attention to it, apparently expecting him to realize that the trip was now, in all probability, a complete waste of
time. Andy had refused to accept it. He read it over, brooding, then
insisted unrealistically that it was some kind of an FBI trick, a
coverup to hide the fact that they couldn't locate the eighth man.
He even called around until he located Emerson Carter's home
number, then got the FBI man on the line and questioned him about
it. Carter said it was real. The last man had been picked up in
Chicago. Then, by God, the FBI had miscounted, Andy insisted.
Someone was still loose. There must be a ninth man. Carter hadn't
succeeded in discouraging him, nor had Gay when he hung up.

He drove down to the railroad bridge and parked on the road

below the grassy knoll. "This will only take a few minutes," he said. "Wait for me, huh?"

Gay touched his arm. "Andy? Are you all right?"

"Yeah, I'm fine."

She patted his biceps and smiled. "Sure you are. Look, why don't we get out with you? We can picnic on the hill."

"I thought you might prefer something a little farther down. Maybe I can find us some trees."

"Gaylynn will like this," Gay said. "It's high. We'll have a view. Then you can look around all you want."

He nodded gratefully and they all climbed out of the car. Gaylynn insisted on helping Andy with the picnic basket, walking along beside him with a hand on the handle as they climbed up the hill. Gay brought the coffee thermos and the blanket. As soon as Gay and Gaylynn picked a site and began to unpack, Andy excused himself and headed back down the hill, angling toward the railroad bridge for a closer look. He could feel Gay's eyes on his back as he walked.

He prowled around the bridge for several minutes, then climbed up on the tracks and looked south, toward Washington. A fly buzzed his face and he brushed it away. He sat down on a rail, shoulders hunched.

It was the same bridge. He was sure of it. He recognized it from the drawing in the sketch pad. The same spans and arches. The same hills and depressions surrounding it. And this was the track which had carried the presidential train. His railroad expert had verified that.

So how could he explain the story in the paper that morning? The FBI had caught them all. The last of them in Chicago, just as the FBI had predicted. Had he been wrong all the time? Had he made an ass of himself over a collection of simple coincidences?

"Andy?"

He looked up, startled to hear her voice. Gay was standing over him, her pretty face concerned. He started to get up, but she waved him back and sat on the rail beside him. She said, "You still think he's out there, don't you?"

He nodded. "Yes. For all the good it'll do. I'll never get anyone to listen to me now."

"Are you sure you want people to listen to you?"

"Hell, honey, if I'm right, the sonofabitch is after the President. I can't pull in my horns now."

She brushed back her hair in silence, as though forming what she wanted to say next. Her voice, when she spoke, was soft and sympathetic. "Andy, I know I encouraged you in this. But that was before we knew the facts. Now that they've all been caught, we have to be reasonable, both of us. It must have been a mistake. Maybe we just jumped off the deep end because it sounded exciting and possible. You can see that, can't you?"

"It wasn't a mistake. Nothing has changed, except that the FBI caught a man in Chicago. That doesn't mean he was our man."

"Sure, baby, but maybe there never was another man. At least as far as the Germans were concerned. Don't you see? There's probably a reasonable explanation for everything he did, every single thing, without tying him to the spies."

"He was here, Gay. Right here on the hill, checking the tracks. Just two days before the presidential train crossed this bridge."

"You can't be certain."

"I'm certain. The farmer saw him. And I saw a sketch of the bridge in his book. Why, Gay? Why would he come out here if he wasn't after the President?"

"Andy, be reasonable."

He sighed. "Honey, I'd like to do as you say. I'd like to stick my brain under a faucet and rinse it out, get rid of this whole thing. But I can't. It's like an old bird dog I used to have. Did I ever tell you about Pudge?" She shook her head. "Old Pudge wasn't much of a dog," he said. "Too fat for hunting. But he was mine and I loved him. He'd do anything I told him to. One day we were up in the mountains, back of Trinidad. Pudge smelled something in a willow thicket and tried to go in after it, but I wouldn't let him. I made him heel. We hadn't gone more than fifty feet before a big brown bear reared up out of the thicket and ran like hell. Pudge gave me the most reproachful look I've ever seen from a dog. I don't much blame him."

"What's that supposed to mean?"

"Nothing, really. I'm just trying to make a point. I don't think Pudge ever forgave me for not letting him tear in after the bear. It was his big moment, and I made him blow it."

"Did you have a gun?"

"I don't remember. I don't think so. Why?"

"Did it ever occur to you that you and Pudge would have both been in serious trouble if you had allowed him to rush into the thicket? That bear might have torn you both to pieces."

"Maybe. But there are times when I think it might have been worth it, for the dog anyway. Old Pudge had a pretty dull life. I guess that was mainly my fault. I was always making him heel."

She stared at him silently for a moment, then said, "Are you suggesting that I've been treating you like a pet dog?"

"All I can say, hon, is that there's a bear in that Washington thicket. Please don't ask me to heel."

She held his eyes for a few moments longer, then said, "You bastard. You never had a dog named Pudge, and you know it."

He shrugged. "Maybe not, but if I had, I'd have learned my lesson that day."

She nodded, only half smiling, then picked up a stick and waved it at him. "All right, tiger. It's your bear. Fetch." And she tossed the stick southward, along the shining tracks.

3

Special Agent Emerson Carter sat in the waiting room outside the Director's Washington office, clutching a pile of interrogation reports which he thought might give some credence to Captain Andrew Blaszek's Washington spy theory. He was wearing his best suit, a gray gabardine from Kann's, with a red-striped gray silk tie, and his hair, drenched in Vitalis, was carefully parted.

Carter had requested the audience with the Director, as Blaszek had urged, and now he was waiting to see if it would be granted. The door opened and closed several times while he waited, and FBI personnel hurried back and forth to do the Director's bidding. At one point, Carter's immediate supervisor, Special Agent Grover, hurried in with a manila folder, pausing only long enough to shake his head sadly at Carter, then vanished into the Director's inner sanctum.

Carter squeezed his pile of reports and swallowed. Perhaps Sunday wasn't the best day to approach the Director on the Washington spy theory. Even if Blaszek thought time was short, one more day couldn't have hurt. Particularly since the case had apparently been wrapped up yesterday. Eight men had now been caught. Unless there was a ninth man, the case was closed. And the Director seemed awfully busy. Maybe Carter should withdraw his request for an audience and take the day off. He still had time to pick up his mother and take her to church, if he hurried. The Director liked agents who went to church.

He was still trying to decide whether or not he could gracefully disengage himself when the inner door opened and Grover leaned out to beckon him.

"Me?" Carter said hoarsely.

Grover nodded. Carter gathered up his bundle of reports and walked uncertainly toward the door. He hesitated a few steps short of it and whispered, "Has someone already told him I want to see him?"

Grover sighed. "Yes. That's why he sent for your file."

"My file? He sent for my file?"

Grover nodded again, regretfully Carter thought, and gestured at the door. Carter took a deep breath and strode through it.

The Director was sitting at his desk, his palms and arms out-spread, holding the edges, as though trying to keep the desk from becoming airborne. He watched Carter expectantly. Scattered on the desk top before him were the front sections of several newspapers, all bearing headlines about the captured Nazis.

Carter came to a nervous halt and cleared his throat. The last time he was in here, with all the agents for that briefing, the office had looked smaller, crowded. Now it seemed larger somehow, more awesome with only the stubby figure of the Director ensconced in that large leather chair.

"Special Agent Carter, isn't it?" the Director said pleasantly, as though he remembered. But Carter could see the edge of his personnel file peeking from beneath the *Washington Post*, and he knew there was a photograph attached.

"Yes, sir," he mumbled. Don't mumble, he told himself. The Director hates mumbling.

"I understand you want to talk to me," the Director said.

"Sir, perhaps this isn't the best time," Carter said. "I know you're busy. I could come back. It's almost time for church services, and I–"

"This is an excellent time," the Director said. "I'm always prepared to talk to our bright young people. Remember, the Bureau is a family. A happy, co-operative family. I'd like to keep it that way."

"Yes, sir, only–"

"Have you read the morning papers?" the Director said. His hand fluttered lovingly among the front pages. "Americans across the country are reading these today. It's about time, too. There hasn't been much good news lately. Stories like these, stories of success in the face of adversity, stories of honorable and dutiful men standing shoulder to shoulder to do their best in awkward times—these stories help to renew faith in government when it's most needed. Faith, young man. That's a wonderful commodity in times of stress. And none of it would have been possible without the cleaving together, the family feeling, the love and respect of Bureau agents, one for another. I admire men who work together, who pull . . . *as a team.*"

"Yes, sir."

"There are some who might wish to wreck that faith," the Director said. "Outsiders who meddle in Bureau business. I understand there was such a movement afoot last week. Some rank amateur at the White House, a certain Army officer, who insisted that there was a spy in Washington. It has been brought to my attention that this meddling Army officer may even have gone so far as to arrange a meeting with one of our people at a certain local memorial, in order to intrude himself in our affairs and try to convince us that we were making a mistake. Can you believe, Special Agent Carter, that he would actually try to pervert the loyalties of one of our own people?"

"Well, er, what if he has a point, sir? What if there's a ninth man?"

"There is no ninth man," the Director said. He tapped the front pages again. "These newspapers all report—and quite accurately, I might add—that *all* of the spies have been caught. And do you know why they report that? Because I told them so at a press conference last night. At the express orders of the President of the United States. Loyal citizens everywhere will sleep better tonight, secure in the knowledge that the Bureau has caught and jailed these war criminals. Would this Army captain have me call the editors and tell them that I was wrong? That a minor military officer with a dubious record has now reached the conclusion that the Director of the Federal Bureau of Investigation and the President of the United States are idiots? Do you suppose that's what this White House captain wants?"

"Sir? Oh, no, sir. Surely not, sir."

"Very well. I trust I have made myself understood. I want you to feel free to come in again anytime for a little chat. This has been very pleasant and I've enjoyed hearing your views. Good-bye, Special Agent Carter."

"Yes, sir. Thank you, sir."

When he got back out to the waiting room, he sank down in one of the chairs, all the starch gone from his legs. "Jesus Christ," he said to Grover. "How the hell did he know?"

Grover sighed. "You're an ass, Carter. You called the man through our own switchboard. Good God, the Washington Monument. How trite."

THE SEVENTEENTH DAY

Monday—June 29, 1942

I

Sarah zipped her dress, a crisp, cream-colored chambray that almost matched the color of her lightly tanned skin, and turned to the dressing-table mirror for some last-minute touches to her hair. But her eyes were on Dietrich's reflection, leaning back in bed and watching her, trying to keep an impatient expression off his face. She said, "Ray, are you still mad at me?"

He smiled briefly. "No, of course not. I never was."

"You've been acting funny since yesterday morning. Honest, if I've done anything or said anything, I'm sorry."

"No, you haven't done anything."

"Then, what is it?" She combed the short bangs down over her eye. "Aren't you feeling well? Look, I can take the day off if you want me to. I can fetch things for you and take your temperature and, you know, kind of watch over you. Mr. Cooper wouldn't mind."

"No, I feel fine," he said quickly. He shifted to his elbow and reached for a cigarette. "You go on to work. I've got some things to do."

"Okay, Ray, if you say so." She picked up her lipstick and applied artful lines, then blotted away the excess. She appeared to admire herself briefly in the mirror, then said, "Are you sure? You don't want me to stay?"

"I'm sure," he said. "I've got a job interview at Sears, Roebuck. I can't afford to miss it."

"Silly," she said. "I've told you not to worry about a job. I make plenty for both of us." She reached for her purse and came over to the bed to lean over him. "Kiss me good-bye," she said. "And be sure to feed the birds."

He gave her a peck and stayed in bed, smoking, until he heard the apartment door close after her, then swung quickly to the floor. Since yesterday he'd counted the minutes, waiting until she would finally leave, but now he found himself walking swiftly through the cramped little apartment and could find no destination. He forced himself to halt his nervous animal-like pacing and went into the kitchen for another cup of coffee.

She wanted to know if something was wrong. God. Eight good men sacrificed for nothing. And now he would have to accomplish the rest of it alone.

He lit the burner under the coffee pot and sat down at the breakfast table, and from the depths of his mind, unbidden, floated an alluring question—what would happen if he just chucked it? What would happen if he just got out now, while he still had his own skin? It would be easy to vanish back into the American system. He could use his false identities to fade out of sight. He would be safe. He could settle in with Sarah, get a job of some kind, and just disappear. He could even make his own cautious way back to the bright blue bowl of Texas sky, but there was no need to go to that extreme. Life with Sarah wouldn't be so bad. She had a certain appeal. A lot like Gerta, in many ways. Young. Pretty. Naïve about sex, but she was learning to please. It would be easy. A quiet existence. Sundays in the park. Lum and Abner on the radio. Making love in the evenings. An occasional Saturday movie. Ignore the war. Become an observer for the duration. Take a step back from reality and stand on the outside once more, looking in. Dasch and Kerling could talk their heads off to the FBI and he'd still be safe. Neither of them knew enough about him to make any trouble.

After all, was it really so important that he kill a President? Would it really make a difference? Would anyone really care? Even Oberstleutnant Grützner, who had set the mission for him, who had filled his head with glittering generalities about how important the mission was, how the whole of Germany depended on him, on his success. Would Grützner care? Was Grützner sitting in his Abwehr office at this very moment, waiting nervously for word, watching Allied newspapers, analyzing radio reports, living for the moment when Dietrich's hand struck the American President down? Or, more likely, had he already dismissed Dietrich from his mind to turn to other equally glittering important missions, like arranging a small bribe for some Liverpool butcher whose cousin had access to Allied shipping information? No, no one would care. Not even Grützner. Insiders had their own lives to lead, their own problems to surmount, their own successes to achieve. That's what made them insiders. If Dietrich slavishly followed his instructions and the President died, the insiders might take time off to celebrate for an hour or two, perhaps even a full day. Grützner would go to the officer's club and buy drinks for the house and brag cryptically about his part in the success. Then they would forget about it and go on with their lives. On the other hand, if Dietrich did nothing, if he faded from view and let the President live, the insiders could continue their lives uninterrupted. What difference would it make to them if a man they didn't know failed to execute a mission they never heard of?

But no, if he were to be honest with himself, he knew he wouldn't fail. Whether or not the mission was important to others, it was vital to him. If he were to drop out now, if he were to back away from the danger, to consign himself to the outside, here, after his attempts in Germany to become a full-fledged member of Somewhere, he knew he would never find his way back in. He would commit himself to being a permanent outsider, drifting from window to window for the rest of his life. No. Perhaps for the lucky ones, belonging was something they were born to, but not for the unlucky ones like him. The unlucky ones had to pay a membership fee.

Nor could he ignore his eight comrades. That was part of being on the inside, compassion for others. Wasn't it? Now eight good men had been picked off, trying to help him. Already the American public and the American press had begun to scream for their blood. In yesterday's Washington *Star*, only hours after the FBI announcement, someone had already editorialized about the fate of the eight, complaining that a loophole in U.S. law might allow them to escape with a two-year sentence. If the men were allowed to claim that they were only saboteurs, the *Star* said, then they were uncovered by law. The most they could get would be two years under the conspiracy statute. But Dietrich knew the American public would never stand for that. If the newspapers screamed long enough and loud enough, someone in authority would come up with a bit of extra-legal hanky-panky which would allow longer sentences. His eight comrades would rot in jail. If his comrades were sacrificed, could he expect any less for himself?

And that was easily what it might come down to. Earlier there had been a better-than-average chance for survival. But now?

Working alone? No diversionary tactics from the two submarine teams, no help with the escape route? Even if he planned carefully, even if everything worked, what about the return submarine? What good would it do to head for the rendezvous point? The FBI knew where both submarines had landed, had named the locations in the newspaper story. That meant local citizens would be more alert, more likely to see the sub when it surfaced and waited for him to make his way out to it.

The coffee began to boil. He turned it off and simultaneously turned off the unacceptable thoughts. He must survive. He must improvise. Plan an alternate escape route. He knew now how he would reach the President, but he must be clever if he was to come out of it afterward. And he must make his move soon. Before someone realized what he was up to and put the President on his guard. When? How long would it take him to prepare? Set a deadline. Thursday. He could be ready by Thursday.

But first, today, back to the White House. Search. Probe. Look for weaknesses. Then, tonight, seek the tools. Locate a source to replace the explosives lost when the two teams were arrested.

He left the coffee pot untouched, cooling on the stove, and headed back to the bedroom to get dressed.

An hour later, he lingered in the big West Wing reception lobby, waiting for the burly, gray-haired White House policeman who had stopped him and asked for his credentials that first day. It was not a long wait.

The policeman, when he appeared, wandered through the dark wood-and-leather room, taking his time, checking doors, turning off unnecessary lights, picking up loose magazines from the green leather couches and stacking them neatly on end tables. Dietrich waited until he was closer, then stepped out and cut across his path, intercepting him as though by accident.

"Oh, hello," Dietrich said. "Officer Greer, isn't it?"

The officer's craggy face turned on him. There was no sign of recognition.

"I'm Sheppard," Dietrich said. "One of the newspaper people. You gave me my first lesson in security a few days ago."

"Oh, yeah," the policeman said. "How's it going? Guards beginning to leave you alone yet?"

"Yes, everyone has been very kind."

"Good. Most of us try. It isn't always easy to remember the new faces."

"I'm amazed that you do so well," Dietrich said. "You know, someone ought to do a feature on you and the rest of the White House police force. I've been giving it some thought myself. A kind of in-depth study of the men who guard the corridors of power."

The policeman's eyebrows went up a fraction of an inch. "Good idea," he said. "Most people don't know a whole lot about the White House police. The Secret Service gets most of the attention around here."

"So I've noticed," Dietrich said. "Maybe I *will* write that story. At least it'd be a fresh angle. Do you suppose you or one of your colleagues could take me around, kind of show me the security drill?"

"We're pretty busy," the policeman said.

"It wouldn't take long. Just a quick tour to give me the feeling. You know, a stroll through the back corridors. Touch the walls. Look out the windows at the grounds. Kind of like seeing the White House world through a security man's eyes."

The policeman frowned. "They don't like unauthorized people in the back of the building," he said. "You'd have to check through Mr. Early's office for permission."

"Sure, I could do that," Dietrich said, "but if I go through channels, they'll probably want to pick the man who shows me around. The way I see the story, it should be from the viewpoint of one officer, one dedicated officer, set against a background of dignity and respect for duty. If I let them pick the guy for me, I might end up with someone who's too young and inexperienced. Not much meat there."

"You want an older man?" the policeman said. He looked interested.

"Yes, definitely. Someone who knows the ins and outs of the White House. What about that officer up by the front door? The one with glasses. Do you think he's what you might call dedicated?"

Officer Greer flicked his eyes toward the front, then cleared his throat and said, "You wouldn't want him. He hasn't been with us long enough. If you want one of the old-timers, you'd be better off with someone like me. I wouldn't expect you to do the story just on me, either. Of course, if you're determined to write your story about just one man and his experiences, I guess I know the ins and outs about as well as anyone."

"Hey, terrific," Dietrich said. "Actually, you were my first choice, but I was afraid you'd be too busy. I know how it is. The more responsibility they load on a guy, the less time he has."

"Well, we're supposed to help out all we can," Officer Greer said. "When would you want to do it?"

"How about now?" Dietrich said. "If I get an early jump on this, I may be able to arrange a syndication to some of the other newspapers, too."

"Syndication, eh?" Greer glanced at the front again. "Well, why not? I guess I can take a few minutes. Come on. But don't expect too much. There really isn't much to see except for a few offices."

They crossed the reception lobby, the policeman leading the way, and paused at the desk by the rear doors. The policeman murmured something to the appointment secretary, then led Dietrich through the forbidden doors to a bright, clean corridor on the south side of the Executive Wing.

The policeman looked up the corridor to the east, then turned and said, "Don't look now. That's the Oval Office behind me, but we can't go up there. The President is in it. You can always tell by those guys standing outside the door. They're Secret Service men. There's a little study through the door behind them, where visitors sometimes wait. Maybe we can sneak a look at it later when it's empty."

Dietrich let his eyes roam briefly across the officer's shoulder, taking in the two neatly tailored men outside the closed door. Their double-breasted suit coats hung open, offering them easy access to shoulder holsters, and they were watching Dietrich and his White House police escort.

"They look very alert," Dietrich whispered.

"Yeah, you bet," the officer said. "If I wasn't with you, they'd probably have you down on the floor by now with their guns stuck in your ears." He chuckled.

"Are there more Secret Service men in the Oval Office with the President?"

"Probably. He's got three or four with him, no matter where he goes. For protection, mainly, but that's not all. They have to push his wheelchair, too." He nodded along the corridor in the opposite direction. "Now, down here we've got offices on the south and west walls. These two big offices belong to the Chief of Staff and the President's personal secretary. Then up there, around the corner, the hall hits the elevator and the stairwell to the basement. Come on, I'll show you."

Dietrich looked back at the Oval Office briefly. A tingle of excitement teased the hairs at the back of his neck. So close. So damned close. He tightened his mouth and followed the policeman.

"The Vice-President has an office down here," Officer Greer said. "He doesn't use it much, though. Lots of other offices back here, too, as you can see. The place is bigger than it looks."

"Yes, it is," Dietrich said. He scanned the offices as they walked, noting the windows, trying to estimate the thickness of the walls. He wondered vaguely what chance a man would have if he broke through one of the windows and tried to race across the grounds to the fence. Not much, probably.

"I was born in Kansas," the policeman said. "Little town called Phillipsburg. My father was a constable, so it kind of runs in the family. Good morning, Captain Blaszek. How are you today?"

An Army captain, tall and raw-boned, nodded in response and entered one of the offices on the south side of the corridor, looking preoccupied.

Greer lowered his voice and said, "That's another of the security people. He runs the military end. You know, all those fuzzy-cheeked kids marching around on the grounds, playing tin soldier. Temporary, because of the war. We never used to have to worry about soldiers. They just get in the way, most of the time."

They rounded the corner and Greer stopped in front of an elevator. "This leads to the basement. There's another whole floor of offices and things. Our locker room is down there. The swimming pool is down there, too."

"Swimming pool?" Dietrich said.

"Yeah, sure. You really *are* new, aren't you? Some newspaper publisher in New York took up a public subscription to help build it for the President. That's how he gets his exercise. They say swimming is good for people with that infantile paralysis. Keeps the muscles from going to ruin. There's a private passage to the Executive Office Building next door, too. Kind of an underground tunnel."

Dietrich looked up quickly. A tunnel? A way out of the building? He said, "Is it all right for us to take a look at the basement?"

"Not much to see," the officer said. "Just more of the same."

"I'd . . . I'd like a look at the swimming pool," Dietrich said. "It sounds pretty unusual."

The policeman shrugged. "It's just a big room with a swimming pool in it. Here, we better take the stairs. They don't like us to use the elevator. Never know when the President might need it."

He led Dietrich down the steps, heels clicking noisily in the empty stairwell. "My wife is from Iowa. But I guess you wouldn't want anything like that in your story, would you?"

"I might," Dietrich said. "A touch of family life might make the story more human. Perhaps I can arrange to meet her one of these days for an interview, and get the real inside story of what it's like to be married to a man who holds the President's life in his hands."

Greer flushed in pleasure at Dietrich's words. "I guess I do kind of help take care of the President," he said. "We don't all get to work in the West Wing, you know. Only the guys with seniority. Most of our people ride herd on the tourists over in the mansion and watch out for the antiques. You'd be surprised how many thieves there are nowadays. Nicest-looking people you ever saw, but you turn your back for a minute and every piece of china in the China Room would disappear. That's the pool room down there. Come on, I'll show you."

As they walked toward it, Dietrich said, "This passageway you mentioned. What's it for?"

"The passage to the EOB? Oh, lots of things. The President has another office over there. He doesn't use it much because of his affliction, but when we have healthier Presidents, they like to have a place to get away. Nowadays, we use the passage mainly for secret visitors." He grinned. "When you reporters get troublesome and the President wants to see someone without you knowing about it, we bring them in through the EOB. But don't quote me on that, because I'll deny it."

They entered a large, tiled room in which refracted chips of light from the surface of the pool danced on the walls and ceiling and Dietrich, impressed, said, "This is very nice." His voice echoed across the humid, chlorine-scented room.

"The President swims like a sonofabitch," Greer said. "Meaning no disrespect, of course. It's just that you wouldn't think a man stove up with infantile paralysis like that, a man who can't even get across the street or climb into a car without help, could do so well once he gets into water. But he's got powerful arms. You ever look close at his arms? I'd hate to arm-wrestle him, I'll tell you that."

They edged out of the room and started down the hall. Dietrich glanced about him, trying to locate the passage to the neighboring Executive Office Building. Officer Greer kept talking. "As long as we're down here, I might as well show you our locker room," he said. "I can dig out some papers and stuff for you while we're there, and you can make some notes."

"Sure, terrific," Dietrich said. He wanted desperately to make notes, but not on the policeman. His mind was on a series of images already seen and catalogued—the inner doorways and offices, the outlets on the upper floor to windows and other possible escape routes, the Oval Office with its Secret Service guards, the basement passage about which the officer had spoken. He implanted them in his memory, along with mental estimates of distances and difficulties, trying hard to ignore the personal chatter of his uniformed escort, hoping he could retain everything with complete accuracy until later, when there would be time to record it all.

2

As soon as Andy turned into his White House office, he picked up the telephone and called the Washington Police Department to ask for Lieutenant Savage, the detective who had helped him earlier. Sergeant Huffman raised his head long enough to overhear who Andy was calling, then rolled his eyes and went back to his typing.

Savage came on the line, snuffling, and Andy identified himself. "Yes, Captain," the detective said. "What can I do for you?" He snuffled again and blew his nose.

"I'm calling about that guy who killed the landlady," Andy said. "Have you had any luck finding him?"

"Nope, not yet," Savage said. "We're trying, Captain. But you've got to realize what we're up against. The odds are in his favor. It would take an army to scour the city, and I've only got a couple of men to spare. If you people are really so interested, why don't you get me some help?"

"I wish I could," Andy said. "Are you still checking hotels and room rentals?"

"We've done some spot checks," the policeman said. "Frankly, Captain, I think it's a waste of time. The guy may not even be in town any more. He could have skipped by now."

"He's in town," Andy said. "Look, what about his car? If you find the car, you'll find him, won't you?"

"Possibly. But we wouldn't even know where to start. I told you, none of our witnesses recalls seeing it."

"It's a Lincoln," Andy said. "A gray Lincoln. Probably a '38 or '39 coupe. With D.C. plates."

The sergeant stopped typing and looked up again.

"How do you know that?" Savage asked.

"I talked to someone yesterday who saw it. A farmer in upper Maryland. I can send you his name and particulars if you want to check it out."

Sergeant Huffman sighed and dropped his head across his arms.

Savage blew his nose into the phone again and said, "Did he get a license number?"

"No, but he was sure they were D.C. plates. Doesn't that help?"

"Not much. There are a hell of a lot of Lincolns in Washington."

"Well, at least it tells us he bought the car locally. And if this guy is the one we think he is, he had to buy it sometime after June 13. That ought to narrow it down a little."

"Unless he stole it," Savage said.

Andy hesitated, considering the possibility, then said, "No, I think he bought it. You could check the hot sheets to make sure, but I think our man is too smart to drive around in a hot car. If we could find the dealer who sold it to him, we could find a license number to go with it, right? And once we have a license number, we should be able to locate the car. All we have to do is check the car dealers."

"That's all?" the detective snuffled. "Captain, do you have any idea how many car dealers there are in the District and environs? And how many Lincolns they're likely to have sold in the last two weeks? That's a lot of checking, particularly for a few overworked cops with other bacon to fry."

"What about the money?" Andy said. "He must have paid for the car with some of that watersoaked money. Have your men ask about that. Surely someone will remember it."

"Maybe," the detective said grudgingly. "Okay, Captain. I'll put some heat on. But it would be a hell of a lot easier if you could throw your weight around and get us some help."

"I'm working on that," Andy said. "Give me a call if you come up with anything, okay?"

He hung up and lit a cigarette. The sergeant was staring at him again, but he ignored it. He blew impatient smoke in the air, then picked up the phone and called the FBI offices. He asked for Special Agent Emerson Carter.

Carter came on the line and asked timorously, "Yes? Who's calling?"

"Hi," Andy said. "This is Blaszek. Listen, I—"

"How dare you!" Carter exploded. "I thought I made it clear last Friday that I didn't want to talk to you again. You can't go around trying to pervert FBI loyalties and get away with it. If you call again, I shall have to report you." He slammed the phone down.

Andy blinked and stared at the telephone. He cradled the earpiece slowly, shaking his head in confusion. What the hell was that all about?

3

Officer Greer opened the door to the reception lobby and held it for Dietrich. "I'm sorry about the Oval Office," he said. "I'd like to show it to you, but it looks like we're out of luck today. Maybe this Thursday when you shoot those pictures you were talking about."

"Thursday will be fine," Dietrich said. "You sure they won't mind if I bring a camera in?"

"Nah, guys do it all the time," Greer said. He closed the door and pointed across the familiar lobby. "The Cabinet Room is over there, beyond that wall. I could probably get you in for a quick look if you want to give me a few minutes to set it up with the Secret Service."

"No, that's all right," Dietrich said. "We can wait until Thursday, when we do the Oval Office. I don't want to be a bother to the Secret Service men."

The appointment secretary's secretary looked up as they passed and said, "Excuse me. Is your name Sheppard?"

Dietrich stopped, the ridge of hairs rising again across his neck. "Yes. Why do you ask?"

"There's a phone call for you," the secretary said. "In the press room. One of the newsmen was just out here looking for you."

"A phone call?" Dietrich said.

"You want me to wait for you?" Greer asked him.

Dietrich shook his head. "Thanks, but I guess I'd better tend to business for a while."

"Okay," Greer said. "Look, about those pictures Thursday. You want me to wear anything special? Our tunics look good, but they're winter issue."

"No, just your regular uniform," Dietrich said. He smiled and waved good-bye and headed for the press room, his nerves jumping. A telephone call? From whom? Sarah? No, not Sarah. She had no inkling that he was playing the part of a reporter. The man at the credentials office? Had they discovered a discrepancy in his story? Oh, God.

He hurried into the press room and asked a reporter where he could take an incoming call and was directed to a bank of phones along the west wall. A bald man at a typewriter near the phones looked up as he approached and said, "Sheppard?"

Dietrich nodded.

The man hooked his thumb at an open phone and said, "When you're expecting calls, don't go wandering off. Some of us are on deadline. We don't have time to go traipsing all over the place looking for you." He went back to his typing.

Dietrich raised the receiver to his ear. He took a deep breath and said tentatively, "Hello?"

"Bob?" a woman's voice said. "Bob, is that you?"

Dietrich looked around at the typing newsman and said, "Who's calling?"

"Bob?" the voice said again. "Excuse me, is this Robert Sheppard? I was calling Robert Sheppard."

"This is he," Dietrich said.

There was a momentary silence, then the voice said, "No it isn't. I know my husband's voice."

A flush of heat spread across Dietrich's forehead. "Mrs. Sheppard?" he said.

"Yes. Who is this? Where's my husband?"

"This, uh, this is a friend," Dietrich said.

"Where's my husband? Why didn't he come to the phone?"

"He, uh, asked me to cover for him," Dietrich said. "He's on an assignment. Where are you, Mrs. Sheppard? In Washington?"

"No, I'm calling from Denver. What kind of an assignment? He didn't tell me anything about an assignment."

Dietrich breathed a little easier. At least she wasn't in town where she could gum things up completely. "I'm afraid it's classified," Dietrich said. "I'm not supposed to talk about it."

"Somebody had better talk about it," she said. "He was supposed to call me this weekend. I stayed at home all day Saturday and Sunday, but he didn't call."

"He isn't allowed to contact anyone while he's on this assignment," Dietrich said.

"I don't believe that. I called his hotel last night to see what was wrong. They told me he hasn't been back to his room for four days. And all his clothes are still there. I want to know what's happening."

Dietrich grimaced. "He's . . . perhaps I can explain it this way. You see, here at the White House we sometimes have to work out of a pool. Sometimes there is limited space for reporters, so we draw lots to see who will cover an assignment for all of us. We had one like that last Thursday. Your husband was the lucky man. Believe me, I would have traded places with him in a minute if I'd had the chance. It's a top-notch assignment."

She hesitated, then said, "That still doesn't explain why he didn't call. What kind of an assignment is it?"

"Well, that's the point," Dietrich said. "It's classified. You see, Mrs. Sheppard, one of the prerequisites of the assignment is that the reporter simply drop out of sight until it's over. If word got to the enemy, they might—"

"Enemy?" she said. "Is it dangerous? Bob promised me he wouldn't do anything dangerous. He has a heart murmur, you know."

"It isn't dangerous," Dietrich said. "Actually, I'm not supposed to say anything, but you're his wife, so I guess I could give you a hint. If you've been reading the newspapers, then you know there was a very important visitor in Washington last week. From England. Well, that important visitor had to go home last Thursday. He took an American diplomat with him and three White House newsmen. So you see, secrecy was very important. If the enemy had known when he was leaving, they could have arranged a fleet of fighter planes to try and shoot him down."

"My husband is with him?"

"I can't tell you that," Dietrich said. "All I can tell you is that in a week or two, when everything is finished, you'll be hearing from him. So will the whole world. You'll be very proud of him, Mrs. Sheppard."

"He could at least have dropped me a post card, so I wouldn't worry," she said.

Dietrich sighed heavily into the phone. "No, he couldn't. From the moment he was selected to go, he was placed under quarantine. Believe me, Mrs. Sheppard, I've probably told you too much already. If you say anything to anyone, even the most trusted of friends, you could be putting your husband's life on the line."

"I won't say anything," she assured him.

"Good. You could do him a favor, too, while you're at it. He was worried the day he left, afraid his newspaper might wonder why they hadn't heard from him. I've been sending them a few of my stories under his by-line to keep them from worrying, but it occurs to me that you could handle it better. Why don't you call them and tell them you just talked to your husband and that he's sick or something. Say he has the flu and won't be able to stir for a few days. That way they won't worry."

"I don't know," she said. "It might make them mad later, when they find out I lied to them."

"It's the only way we can be sure he stays safe," Dietrich said. "Besides, they won't mind. When he comes back in a week or two, they'll understand why it was necessary. They'll be happy to forgive him. He may even win a Pulitzer Prize."

"Yes, all right. I'll call them right away."

"That's excellent," Dietrich said. "Remember, not a word about this to anyone. Not until Bob comes home."

"I'll remember. Thank you very much."

Dietrich hung up and let his breath flutter from his lungs. He looked at his hand. It was shaking. He glanced at the typing newsman quickly to make sure he hadn't noticed, then stuck his hands in his pockets and walked away from the phones.

Had it gone well? Possibly. Had she believed him? Probably. Would it hold for long? Not too likely. Eventually she would think about it. Question it. Perhaps even pursue it.

That made the Thursday move even more imperative. He must get on with his assignment and get out. Immediately. While there was still time.

4

The White House telephone lines stayed busy that morning. The next call was, in effect, a return call to Andy. It was from Special Agent Emerson Carter.

He said, "Captain, this is Carter. I'm in a phone booth on D Street. Listen, don't call me at the Bureau any more. Someone's been listening in on our conversations."

"What difference does that make?" Andy asked.

"What difference? Jesus, you should have been there yesterday. The Director reamed me out all the way up to the throat. You don't know how pissed he is at you."

"I take it you didn't manage to convince him."

"I never had a chance. He jumped on me before I even got my

mouth open. I tried. God, I argued with him for almost an hour. But he says the case is closed, and that's the way it's going to stay. You know, he could be right. We really didn't have that much to go on. Just a few coincidences."

"I've got a couple more for you," Andy said grimly. "I found the place in Maryland where he made those timetable notations. There's a railway bridge there, the one he drew in his notebook. He was there on Thursday, just two days before the presidential train passed."

"That could be another coincidence."

"Maybe. But they keep piling up. We've got a lead on the car now. A gray Lincoln coupe with D.C. plates. The D.C. police have agreed to check out car dealers. But we need help. You've got to see the Director again. You've got to convince him."

Carter gasped audibly over the phone. "I can't."

"You have to," Andy insisted. "Go see him this afternoon."

"Listen, no, I don't think so. I think maybe we should wait a few days. Give him time to cool off. Maybe by then you'll have something more substantial to offer him."

"We can't wait," Andy said. "See him today."

"I'll, er, I'll try," Carter said unconvincingly. He cleared his throat. "I've got to get back to my office before someone misses me. Remember, don't call me at the Bureau any more."

5

That night Dietrich drove across the Anacostia River and headed down into the southeast sliver of Washington where the sprawling grounds of both the Naval Station and Bolling Army Air Field cozied up to the Potomac. He motored slowly through the darkened streets, surveying the chain-link fence which separated the military reservations from civilian residential property.

The citizens of Washington had thoughtfully provided him with a black night. Since early in the war, local patriots had started turning off their lights at dusk to show their commitment to the hardships of the war effort. The Capitol dome had set the pattern. Two days after Pearl Harbor, officials had ordered the dome floodlight extinguished for the duration as a precaution against air raids, and most of the city's patriotic citizens had quickly followed the official precedent by dimming their own unnecessary lights. It was an exercise in frivolity, of course. Dietrich knew that none of the Axis powers had aircraft capable of reaching the American capital, and most Americans knew it, too. But air-raid precautions apparently made the war seem more real to them, like rationing sugar and gasoline and rubber bands and metal-tipped shoelaces. They needed the illusion of hardship to bring the war home to them. Even the khaki-clad machine-gun crews mounted atop many of the federal buildings and presidential memorials, pointing their futile guns at the empty sky, seemed to buoy up the local morale.

He spotted the building he was seeking, a low rambling warehouse far below the fence, down at the bottom of a mild slope. A munitions armory, according to the library research he had done that afternoon. He drove off the main road and pulled under some trees. Sudden silence rushed in as he killed the motor, and after a moment he could hear the call of tree toads and, somewhere in the distance, an insomnious mockingbird running monotonously through its repertoire.

He sat quietly for a few minutes, examining the terrain. There was a wide expanse of flat ground, perhaps a couple of hundred yards, between fence and armory. No brush or trees. Only dim moonlit darkness. He could cross it easily. Just scale the fence and make his way across the darkened ground. Of course there would be guards. There always were. Helmets and leggings and unsheathed bayonets. But they wouldn't be very alert. Not in the safety of their own national capital. They would only go through the motions, doing their rounds, calling out signs and countersigns. They might challenge an occasional night sound. But they wouldn't expect the sounds to reply.

He gathered his flashlight, his gun and a wad of tow-sacking and climbed out of the car, but a new night sound off near the river made him pause and stand listening with unwilling eagerness. It was an explosive bird cry, repeated over and over, three notes to the second with the stress on the last note. A whippoorwill, they would call it here, but its real name, the one he learned in his boyhood, was *el perdido*.

El perdido, the lost one. Night and the smell of mesquite smoke and some Mexican family's three calves so near dead with the scours that they came for the vet. Then the three-note cry down by the stock tank, and while his father worked on the calves, a soft, Spanish-accented voice telling the vet's little boy the story of the bird, so rarely seen, always just a cry in the night. *Per-di-do. Per-di-do. Per-di-do.* I am lost. I am lost. I am lost.

Listening, Dietrich couldn't remember the full story he'd been

told, but the bird apparently did something and the other birds
made him an outcast and ever since the bird had been alone in the
night, crying out his hopeless cry of the lost.

Perdido. Unable to block out the sound, Dietrich blocked out the
thought, and headed silently for the fence and the long, slow
traverse of open ground that lay between him and the dangerous
sanctuary that was the darker shadows of the building.

He didn't use the flashlight until he had neared the loading dock
doors, and then he flicked it on only briefly for one quick look. He
worked on the lock in the darkness. Not until he was inside and the
door was closed behind him did he relax and flick the flashlight on
again.

From that point on it was easy. He roamed quietly and efficiently
through the long pitch-black aisles of the munitions armory, checking the contents as though he were a supermarket shopper, playing
his flashlight beam across shelves laden with the massed provender
of destruction. Here you are, ladies and gentlemen. Row two,
household items—a hundred yards of rifles, carbines, machine guns,
mortars. Row three, fruits and vegetables—crates of hand grenades
stacked from floor to ceiling, cases of ammunition, flares, land
mines. Rows four, five and six, the meat and potatoes of war—shelf
after shelf of neatly piled high-explosive artillery shells, fuses and
propelling charges.

In a pinch, he could always turn a fragmentation shell into a
workable demolition device. All he had to do was separate the
projectile from its case and hook it up to a makeshift detonator.
But it wasn't the most effective explosive weapon in the world on a
pound-for-pound basis. The steel jacket on a standard 105mm how-
itzer shell would weigh over thirty pounds and contain less than
five pounds of high explosive. He wanted something more compact,
something more devastating.

He moved on, continuing to prowl the aisles, searching for the
basic staples, the condiments of annihilation. A gourmet demolitions
man would never settle for prepackaged meals when he could con-
struct his own. He found what he was looking for on row nine.
Great shadowy chemical barrels with stenciled labels like cordite,
melanite, potassium nitrate, guncotton, sodium chlorate, nitramine.

He moved softly to the barrels. This was more like it. Mix to
taste. Sodium chlorate, for example. Combine with sugar, three
parts to two. Pack in lead pipe. No detonator needed. Just fuse and

serve. A little timing mechanism to allow him to get away, and he could give a party guaranteed to raise the roof.

No, not sodium chlorate. A good base for an excellent explosive, but not these days. Where the hell would one get the sugar? Without ration cards or a flourishing black market, sodium chlorate was useless. Ridiculous. A bomb that wouldn't go, just because someone had decided to ration sugar.

What then? Potassium nitrate? That would require only charcoal and a bit of sulphur. He could get sulphur from any drugstore, or a match manufacturer, if he didn't try to buy too much in any one place. Maybe even from a garden supply shop. Yes, potassium nitrate. That would be better.

He balanced his flashlight on a crossbeam and pried one of the cardboard barrels open. The powder was packaged in tightly wedged paper bags, forty or fifty to the barrel. He wrenched one of the bags out and hefted it. About ten pounds per bag. One would be enough, but he decided to take two, just in case. That would give him about twenty-five pounds of high explosive by the time he mixed in the other ingredients. He transferred two of the powder bags down into his tow-sacking and tied up the corners, making a bundle which he could hook over his arm.

Now he needed some kind of timing device. Something to give him the margin of safety he would need to make good his escape. Surely there would be an adequate timer somewhere in this vast store of weaponry. He anchored the tow-sack bundle on his left arm and moved cautiously back toward the front of the warehouse, creeping through the black canyons of stacked destruction, touching the towering palisades with the beam of his flashlight, seeking, searching.

As he turned once again into row four, he heard a sound which froze him. A dog barked. A deep-throated woof, somewhere out in front of the armory loading dock. He flicked off his flashlight and shrank back in the darkness, listening. A voice, muffled by distance, said, "Quiet, Ajax. Quiet. What is it, boy?"

Dietrich reached for his Mauser. Dogs. That could complicate matters. Human guards were one thing. Dogs quite another. Dogs were seldom as careless as their human masters. He held his breath, waiting.

Footsteps, man and animal, echoed across the loading dock, coming toward the string of shed doors which serviced military trucks during daylight hours. One of the doors rattled as the man tried the lock. Dietrich involuntarily held his breath. If man and dog kept coming, they would surely find the door he had forced.

He had to hide. There was a dark gap in the middle of the row, just a few feet down, a cul-de-sac where some of the munitions had been removed, presumably to be shipped elsewhere or relocated in the warehouse. Dietrich moved softly to it and slipped into the black gully, pressing back out of sight.

Another door rattled. Then another. Then one slid open noisily and the dog growled.

"Good boy," the voice said. "Easy now."

Shadows and light played dimly through the rafters as someone swung an electric torch back and forth near the front of the warehouse. Footsteps moved through the aisles, touching the floor warily. Dietrich laid his bundle on the floor and released the thumb safety on his Mauser.

The dog whined. The voice said, "Where is he, boy?" There was a metallic click, a hook being unsnapped from a collar, and the voice said, "Good boy. Go. Find him."

Dietrich squeezed into the far corner of his cul-de-sac, holding his pistol in one hand and his unlit flashlight in the other. Ticking noises, like toenails on tile, pattered quickly in and out of the aisles as the dog searched. The man's light bobbed closer, sticking to the main aisle at the head of the storage rows.

The dog sounds passed, grew fainter. Why? Following Dietrich's earlier trail to the back of the warehouse? Confused by the heavy smell of gun oil and cosmoline? Dietrich waited, his breath shallow and quiet, then edged forward briefly to peer out of his shallow hiding place. The electric torch moved into view at the head of the row and Dietrich saw the man, a Marine guard, walking in a crouch with a rifle extended in front of him. Dietrich ducked back. Where was the damned dog? Why couldn't he hear it?

The light moved on, scouring the shadows. Maybe he should make a break for it. They were both behind him now, off toward the rear of the building. If he hurried, he might . . .

Then he heard the low growl. His nerves shrieked and he jerked his eyes up. It was there, poised on the crates above his cul-de-sac, teeth bared. God, how . . .

He tried to raise the Mauser, but the black, muscular body sprang at him. He spun aside, flailing his flashlight like a club. The dog thumped into him, driving him back, and went for his arm, rending, tearing. Dietrich stifled a cry of pain and swung his arm, slinging the dog against the crates. Above the noise of the scuffle, he heard the Marine guard cry, "Ajax, where are you? Hold him, boy."

Dietrich slammed the dog against the crates again and again, his arm dead with pain, until finally the dog let go and skittered across the floor, scrabbling to stay erect. Then, teeth flashing in two lines of jagged fury, it attacked again.

Dietrich lurched back and squeezed the trigger. The silenced pistol made a soft sound and the dog yelped, flipping over backwards. It whimpered and tried to regain its feet, then collapsed.

Dietrich whirled away, doubled over in pain, his arm throbbing. He could hear the dog's master, coming on the run, GI boots thudding against the floor. He scooped up his tow-sack bundle and slung it over his injured arm. Then he stepped into the open and started up the aisle.

But he was too late. The Marine guard skidded into view at the head of the aisle and swung his electric torch down into the shadows, pinning Dietrich against the crates. "Halt," the Marine yelled. The light bobbed as he whipped up his rifle and tried to aim it one-handed.

Dietrich shot him twice. The torch flew out of the man's hand as he fell backward, and the rifle discharged, blamming away at the ceiling, echoing through the cavernous warehouse. Dietrich gritted his teeth and waited for the racketing sound to die away. Damn it to hell. That would bring everyone.

He flung himself toward the open end of the aisle and leaped over the Marine's body. He raced to the front of the warehouse, the heavy bundle flapping painfully from his aching arm. As he rushed through the dockside doorway into the night, he could already hear shouts and shrilling whistles from other guards across the military compound, reacting to the unexpected gunshot from the Marine's rifle.

Dietrich wasted no time. He sailed off the end of the dock and headed up the mild incline toward the road, running openly, racing across the broad field which separated him from the chain-link fence.

When he was halfway to the fence, he heard the other dogs, ranging free in the darkness behind him. Fear rose to his chest and throat, giving him extra speed. The new dogs had picked up his scent now, wailing in the background, and were coming at a dead run. Far below, perhaps a hundred yards behind the dogs, he could see several guards swinging their lights across the open terrain.

He hit the fence and flung his bundle across the top of it, then scrambled up and over. The dogs came bursting out of the darkness after him, glancing off the fence and ricocheting to the dirt. Three of them. Two Dobermans and a German shepherd. They crouched and barked furiously at him through the fence.

He paused and touched the muscle of his left arm, feeling the ache and the damage. His sleeve was mangled where the first dog had ripped at him, and his arm seemed to be bleeding, though it was hard to tell how badly in the darkness. God, how it hurt. The bastards. The dirty bastards.

He scowled in the darkness and fired his Mauser through the fence. Three times. One for each dog. Then, when the growling stopped, he picked up his bundle and headed for his car. The whippoorwill called. *Perdido. Perdido.*

As soon as he opened the apartment door, he heard her voice. "Ray? Is that you?"

He closed the door softly and said, "Yeah. Hi, sweetheart."

Sarah hurried out of the bedroom, her face red and swollen with recent tears. "Oh, Ray. Where have you been? I've been home for hours. I thought . . . I thought you had . . ." She plunged into his arms, new tears, this time of relief, running like raindrops.

He flinched as her body pressed against his left arm. "Hey, take it easy," he said. "What's all the fuss?"

"I was so worried," she said. "I thought you were gone. After the way you acted yesterday, I thought you were gone for good. I was afraid it was something I did."

He pushed her away as gently as he could. "Hell, sweetheart. I've just been out looking for a job, that's all. Found one, too. It's a warehouse thing. I'm, uh, off-loading merchandise at Sears, Roebuck. Dollar and a half an hour."

"You should have called," she said. Her face softened. "You poor man. You look so beat. Here, sit down. Let me get you a drink."

"Bring it to the bathroom, will you, Sarah? I'm pretty dirty. I'd like to crawl into the tub and relax a bit."

He waited until he was in the bathroom to peel off his jacket, sliding the left sleeve away from the arm gingerly. He tossed the jacket on the floor and rolled his mangled shirtsleeve back so he could see the arm. Blood and dirt had congealed across the torn muscle. Damn dog. It hurt like hell. He held his forearm under the sink tap and ran water, carefully washing the dirt and blood away, trying not to think of the ridiculous and remote possibility that he'd get safely back to Germany only to come down with rabies.

He heard Sarah coming down the hall and started to roll his sleeve back down. Then he stopped. What good would it do? She was bound to see it sooner or later, if not now, then later when they went to bed, thanks to his having taught her to make love with the lights on. He sighed and turned on the tub spigots, running his bath water.

She came through the door smiling, apparently determined to keep her best face forward, in spite of the fears she had earlier entertained. He turned his back to her briefly, slipping out of his trousers. But as he unbuttoned his shirt and pulled it off, he turned so she could see the arm. She gasped.

"Ray, my God, what happened to you?"

He looked at her blankly, as though he had no idea what she meant, then let a flicker of recognition move across his face. "Oh, the arm?" he said. "I'd already forgotten about it." He glanced at it casually. "It's nothing. I got hung up in a load of baling wire. I guess I must have cut it."

"They should have dressed it for you," she said. She inspected the damage. "Good Lord, that's terrible. What's wrong with those Sears, Roebuck people, anyway? Don't they take care of their employees?"

"I guess they would have if I'd mentioned it. But I was afraid to say anything. I was afraid they might lay me off if they knew about the cut. I need the job."

"It's more than just a cut," she said. "It looks as though you stuck your arm in a lion cage."

"Don't worry about it," he said.

"Here, let me fix it for you. Sit down."

She took a bottle of Mercurochrome and a roll of gauze from the medicine cabinet. As he sat on the edge of the tub and contentedly sipped his drink, she cleaned the wound. The Mercurochrome stung like the devil when she applied it, but he gritted his teeth and kept quiet. When she was done and his forearm was neatly bandaged, she said, "You can take your bath now. But don't get your arm wet."

"That isn't as easy as it sounds," he said.

She hesitated, looking suddenly timid, then seemed to collect her courage and said, "I'll wash you. Get in the tub."

He shucked his shorts and slipped into the water. It felt good.

Very relaxing. He leaned back and allowed himself to groan a little in contentment. Sarah gathered the washcloth and soap, then hesitated again, as if uncertain about where a girl began when bathing a man. Funny Sarah, sometimes bold, sometimes shy, and he liked both characteristics in her. Sweet Sarah, so worried that he had left her, and in three days he would have to. She would wait, he knew, like the bold, shy, hungry little sparrows that gathered on her telephone wires to wait for her every morning and evening. "They depend on you," she'd said that first afternoon in the park. "You start feeding them, they get to expecting it. What happens if you go away?"

She wouldn't wait long. He told himself that. He tried to stop thinking of it, but he couldn't, and he felt worse and worse as she perched on the edge of the tub and began to lather his chest. It didn't help when she soon began to smile.

THE EIGHTEENTH DAY

Tuesday—June 30, 1942

I

Sergeant Huffman was waiting at the office door when Andy came in the next morning. The sergeant had a serious expression on his face and an open newspaper in his hand. He said, "Captain, I think you ought to see this."

Andy set his briefcase on his desk and took the newspaper. The sergeant pointed a stubby finger at a story on page three. A two-column head over about six inches of copy. Andy scanned it and his face went white.

"Get me the FBI," he said. "Ask for Emerson Carter."

While the sergeant placed the call, Andy ran his eyes over the newspaper story again. An armory break-in, last night, with a Marine guard killed. Theft of unspecified materials. Thought to be the work of a single assailant, working alone. Police co-operating with military authorities.

Huffman handed him the phone. Carter's voice said, "Hello? Hello?"

Andy hesitated. He had been asked not to call Carter at his office again, but this seemed important. He said, "Emerson, this is your old buddy. You called me yesterday."

"What?" Carter said. Then, "Oh. Er. I thought we decided it would be better if we didn't, er . . ."

"This is an emergency," Andy said. "Did you talk to the Director yesterday?"

"Well, not exactly. He was pretty busy, and I . . ."

Andy clamped his back teeth together. "All right. We'll have to tackle it from a different direction. I need to see you. Can you get out?"

"Not very easily," Carter said. "I have to, er . . ."

"Think up an excuse," Andy said. "Someone broke into the naval armory last night. There's a story in the morning paper. Give me thirty minutes to do some checking, then meet me somewhere. The Capitol building. In Statuary Hall. Okay?"

He hung up before Carter could answer and looked at the story again, shaking his head. He said, "Sergeant, call the armory for me, will you? Find out what was stolen. If it has anything to do with explosives, let me know. I'll want to talk to the officer in charge."

"Yes, sir."

"And when you finish that, see if you can set up a meeting with one of the President's personal advisers. Watson, or McIntyre, maybe. The highest level possible. Tell them Mr. Carter of the FBI will be with me. Stress that it's urgent."

"Right away, sir."

Andy cocked an eyebrow at the sergeant. "We're being awfully proper, aren't we?"

The sergeant shrugged. "Until I saw that story, I thought you were nuts."

"And now?"

"I still hope you're nuts, but I'm not so sure any more."

"It could be another coincidence," Andy said.

"Yes, sir, it could."

"Okay. Make the calls."

2

Dietrich knew something unusual was about to happen the moment he walked into the White House press room that Tuesday morning. The usual poker game had been abandoned. Several of the photographers were digging expectantly through their gadget bags, arranging film plates and flashbulbs. Reporters stood in hushed clots, going over their notes, exchanging occasional comments. Even more astonishing, they had straightened their ties and buttoned their collars.

He stood at the door for a moment, nursing his left arm. Then he spotted a man he recognized as one of the habitual card players and strolled over to him. "Hi," he said. "What's up?"

"Press conference," the man said.

"Press conference? Where?"

"The Oval Office. Prexy sent word about ten minutes ago."

Dietrich went rigid. "Are we all invited?"

The newsman laughed. "It isn't exactly an invitation kind of thing. More like a command performance. Prexy likes to see the press every once in a while. When he calls, we jump."

"But the Oval Office? Isn't that unusual?"

"Nah, it happens all the time. He doesn't get around too well in that rubber-tired buggy. So we go to him."

"I've never been in the Oval Office," Dietrich said. "What do I do?"

"Nothing," the man said. "Just remember protocol. The old hands get the front rows. Hang back in the rear and take whatever space is available. If you haven't got a sharp question worked out, keep your mouth shut and let others do the asking."

"What about . . ."

"Uh-oh, look lively," the newsman said. "There's Steve Early. Prexy must be ready."

Dietrich jerked around to see the President's plump press secretary smiling through the open press-room door, gesturing for the reporters and photographers to follow him.

"I've got to go," the newsman told Dietrich. "I'm one of the privileged front-rowers. Just follow the herd. You'll be all right." He hurried into the van of the news group and squeezed through the door, following the press secretary.

Dietrich grabbed up several sheets of copy paper and folded them in half as he had seen other newsmen do, then fell in with the tail-enders, following them through the big reception lobby and into the Fish Room. His heart was pounding. The newsmen, some forty strong, passed through the Fish Room into an alcove, then past a couple of Secret Service men flanking a doorway, and into a big airy office with sweeping curved walls. Flags on standards, frail gilt chairs, bright morning light streaming through tall windows and glass doors to flay a thick scarlet presidential carpet. And there, in a wheelchair, behind a cluttered desk covered with personal knickknacks and small ceramic figures, sat the President of the United States, eyes flashing, teeth exposed in a set smile, great trunk looming massively above withered legs.

The crowd of shuffling newsmen gravitated to the desk, blocking Dietrich's view. He tried to find a spot in the rear where he could see, but as the reporters and photographers drifted to their accustomed stations, it became progressively more difficult to find a clean line of sight.

He moved in on the rear of the crowd, trying to press forward, but one of the newsmen, irritated, gave him a subtle elbow. It caught Dietrich on the left arm and he sucked in his breath sharply. He took the hint and drew back. The murmur of sound began to settle to silence.

The President began to speak. He joked with a few of the veteran wire men first, then chattered about the success of the Churchill visit, then launched into the announcement which was ostensibly his reason for calling the conference. The rubber drive had been on for two weeks, the President told them, but the results were far below expectations. Rubber was extremely important, the President said, since the Japanese had cut off 92 per cent of the normal supply. He was therefore extending the rubber drive to a total of ninety days.

Dietrich closed his eyes as the man talked. How easy it would be. The bomb, if it were ready. A small packet of high explosive with a quick fuse, perhaps hidden under the lip of a table. Or tucked into one of the wastebaskets. Then step out of the room. And in moments the room would rip apart in a fiery explosion, obliterating the satin and damask, cutting down everyone. What havoc. Chaos. Confusion. It happened vividly behind his closed eyelids.

Then suddenly his eyes were open again. The President had stopped talking about rubber and was discussing the recent surprise announcement from the FBI, regarding the eight Nazi agents who had been arrested. From the tone of his voice it was obvious that this was the real reason he wanted to talk to newsmen. He sounded terribly pleased.

After suitable praise for the quick efforts of the FBI, the President entertained questions. One of the newsmen asked him about the public response. According to a wire story from Pennsylvania, members of an American Legion Post there had volunteered their services as a firing squad for the captured Nazis, but if they were to be tried in a civil court, the newsman suggested, there was no guarantee that the death penalty would be assessed. The President replied that Attorney General Francis Biddle was presently conferring with War Department officials on the feasibility of a military trial. But the men were arrested as civilians, another newsman said. Didn't that mean, under the law, that they must be tried in a civilian court? There was a precedent, the President said, for trying them in a military court. The civilians charged with conspiring with John Wilkes Booth in the assassination of President Lincoln had been tried and sentenced by a military court. Was the President, then, strongly considering the possibility of surrendering the eight to military jurisdiction? It was being considered, the President said. He would make his decision in a few days. He sounded jovial.

Dietrich stiffened. Assignment to a military court was tantamount to an automatic death penalty for all eight prisoners. He shifted to his left and strained, on tiptoe, trying to catch a glimpse of this man who could speak so lightly on the subject of life and death. But the crush of newsmen around the desk blocked his view completely.

3

Andy hurried past rows of big trees, each bearing a neat little tag proclaiming its species, and scampered up the long, long flight of stairs that led to the Capitol Rotunda. He was late. He rushed through the Rotunda and into one of the south corridors, not sparing a glance for the ornate Brumidi panels on the walls, and headed for Statuary Hall. The Capitol passages, dark and shabbily magnificent, were filled with tourists and he was forced to be rude more than once in breaking through the groups.

In the semi-circular statuary chamber he spotted Emerson Carter standing amid the silent rings of marble and bronze figures, waiting impatiently. "Carter," he called out. "Over here." He continued walking, angling toward the short corridor which connected Statuary Hall to the House wing. A trio of tourists, offended by the loud sound of Andy's voice, interrupted their inspection of a statue of Nathanael Greene and stared at him disapprovingly.

Carter joined him in the corridor. A tall, bronze statue of Will Rogers, crowded out of the main chamber by too many earlier donations from each state, smiled down on them wryly as they came together.

"Did you read the story?" Andy asked.

Carter nodded glumly.

"Well, what do you think?"

Carter looked uncomfortable. "It could have been anyone."

"Maybe," Andy said. "But I talked to a man in Navy security right after I called you. The thief got away with enough explosive material to start his own war."

"And you think it's our man?"

"It figures. He needs explosives. He lost what he had when your people picked up the crates from the submarines Now he has to start over."

"That's conjectural," Carter said. "We need something a hell of a lot more solid than that."

"We may get it," Andy said. "I asked the police to run a ballistics test on the bullet they took out of the Marine. If it matches the one they dug out of that boardinghouse wall, then we've really got something."

Carter's eyebrows lifted. "How soon will they know?"

"Sometime today. A detective who's been helping me said he'd get to the military as soon as he can. He said not to be too optimistic, though. That bullet from the boardinghouse was pretty chewed up. In the meantime, I've requested an appointment with one of the President's advisers. Someone will probably agree to see us as soon as they can find an open spot in the schedule."

"Us?" Carter said.

"Yes. I want you to go with me. You can answer a number of procedural questions that I can't handle. And we'll need all the credibility we can get if we're going to convince anyone that this is serious."

Carter was aghast. "I can't do it. Word would filter back to the Bureau in nothing flat. I'd be out on my ass in no time."

Andy frowned impatiently. "How the devil can you worry about your job at a time like this? If I'm right about this guy, who the hell do you think he's after?"

"Yeah, yeah, I know," Carter said. "The President. But you could be wrong."

"Do you want to take that chance?"

Carter winced. He leaned against the pedestal supporting the smiling statue of Will Rogers. The tips of Will's bronze shoes were shiny where people had rubbed them, following tradition, for luck. "Yeah, okay," Carter said. "Okay, I'll go with you. But it isn't fair."

Andy smiled at him. "Cheer up," he said. "You may help save the President's life."

"Big deal," Carter said. "At least he isn't likely to lose his job."

As they started out of the corridor, Carter glanced at the statue's shiny shoetips again. He hesitated, then with Andy's eyes on him, he gave the nearest toe a quick rub with trembling fingers.

4

Dietrich untied his parcels and spread his afternoon purchases on Sarah's kitchen table—dry-cell batteries, an assortment of corks, brass screws, a jar of glue, a roll of wire, a package of dried peas, a set of glass test tubes, two boxes of ball bearings.

He turned on the radio for company and went to work. First he whittled a cork to fit inside one of the test tubes, small enough and loose enough to float freely. He attached a lead wire to it and ran the wire to a small electric bell. He selected another cork, a tighter cork with which he could stopper the test tube, and hooked it to the other lead wire. Then he constructed brass screw contacts for each cork, one top and one bottom, with the screw heads facing each other.

With the mechanical work completed, he funneled dried peas into the test tube, just over halfway to the top. He measured water into the test tube until it covered the peas and left a shallow layer on which the inner cork could float, brass contact upward. He capped the tube with the tigher cork, contact downward. The two screw tips were about a half inch apart. Then he sat back to wait.

Fifteen minutes passed. The dried peas slowly soaked up the water and began to grow, expanding gradually in the tight confines of the test tube, forcing the smaller cork upward. Thirty minutes. The corks got closer. Forty-five minutes. Closer still. Then, three minutes after the hour, the brass screw heads touched and the electric bell began to ring.

Good. An hour would give him time to set the device and get out of the building, past the guards at the gate and on his way. He emptied the test tube and started again. One more test to make sure he could rely on it.

Tomorrow he would arrange a receptacle that could be carried into the building without attracting too much attention.

By Thursday everything would be ready.

5

Emerson Carter's stomach gurgled noisily and nervously, and he looked up to see if either of them had noticed. Andy Blaszek, cool and crisp in his tailored uniform, was still talking, and the older man, sitting six feet away behind the desk, appeared to be completely caught up in what he was saying. Carter cleared his throat twice in an effort to disguise the sound of his jittery stomach rumbles.

Carter had been forced to wait in the captain's office for almost two hours before they were summoned. Two hours of silence in which he had only his thoughts to keep him entertained. Thoughts which repeatedly returned to his empty Bureau office and the possible retribution which awaited him when word leaked back to the

Director. God. His job. His career. Down the tube. Why hadn't he listened to Grover?

They had been kept waiting right through the lunch hour. Andy Blaszek had sent one of the young enlisted men out for sandwiches, but Carter's stomach was far too fluttery by the time they arrived for him even to consider eating. So he watched and sweated and grew queasy while the big affable Army captain wolfed down both sandwiches as though this whole episode had done nothing more than increase his appetite.

Then the curt summons had come by telephone and the captain had led him to this office, to face this skinny, sallow chain-smoker, Harry Hopkins, friend and confidant of the President.

"And that's about it," the captain concluded. "Except that the police called while we were waiting. I'm afraid the ballistics test won't do us any good. Lieutenant Savage says they can't get any conclusive results because of the damaged condition of the boardinghouse bullet. But the two slugs were the same caliber and approximate weight. They *could* have come from the same gun."

Hopkins leaned back in a leather chair and rocked slowly. "So you think this man may be in Washington to make a try for the President?"

"Yes, sir," the captain said. "I'm sure of it. Only I can't get the FBI to pay any attention to me."

"I can see why," Hopkins said. "It all sounds pretty circumstantial."

Captain Blaszek's face sagged. "Then you don't believe us either?"

"I didn't say that," the man said casually. "It doesn't really matter whether I do or not, does it? If there is a chance you might be right, no matter how remote, we'll have to take steps to prevent it."

"Yes, sir," the captain said. He stole a triumphant glance at Carter. Carter tried to respond with a pleased look.

"I assume you'll need help?" Hopkins asked.

"Yes, sir. I've been in contact with the police detective I mentioned, Lieutenant Savage, and he's been helping all he can, but he's pretty busy."

"Have you filled him in on everything?"

"No, sir. Not in detail. I've been leaning on my White House title."

"Good," Hopkins said. "Let's keep it that way. I'll call the Commissioner this afternoon and request continued co-operation, as a favor to the White House. But I'd rather keep it low key for the time being. No sense in setting off any false alarms until we know for certain whether or not there is a substantive threat."

"Anything will help, sir."

Hopkins looked at Carter. "I assume you've talked to the Director about this?"

Carter cleared his throat again. "Well, sir, I, er, talked around the edges about it. He didn't seem too responsive."

"I can understand that," Hopkins said. "It doesn't matter. We'll handle it as an in-house problem. I'll talk to John Calhoun, to get the Secret Service plugged in."

"Yes, sir," the captain said. "Uh, do you think you could ask Mr. Calhoun to lend us one of his men to handle some of the leg work? I'm thinking of Jerry Fenton. He's the only one I really know."

"I think that could be arranged."

"And Special Agent Carter here. Could you request his temporary reassignment from the FBI to the White House? He knows more about police procedure than I do, and I'm not sure I can get along without him."

Carter sat straighter and shook his head at the captain. But Hopkins only shrugged and said, "I'll put a request through channels as soon as we finish here."

"Mmmm, er," Carter said. Hopkins looked at him. "Sir," Carter said, "do you think you might make that a personal request? The Director might look more favorably on it if the request came from an upper-echelon office."

Hopkins nodded. "I'll call him myself," he said. "But I wouldn't count on his favorable reaction, if I were you. He isn't going to appreciate the interference, no matter what level it comes from." He smiled sympathetically. Carter felt his stomach churn toward a new burst of rumbles.

Captain Blaszek stood up. "We're grateful for your help, sir. We'll keep you advised."

"Is here anything else you need?" Hopkins asked. "A larger office? Clerical help?"

"Maybe a couple of clerks," the captain said. "Manpower is our biggest problem. I thought I'd ask Lieutenant Savage to forward copies of all the police crime reports from now on. Thefts, burglaries, muggings, major crimes. Anything unusual. It will take time and a lot of people to plow through them."

"That's a pretty tall order, Captain."

"Yes, sir, I know. But most of our leads so far have come from police reports. And we don't really have much else to work on. We're operating pretty much in the blind on this. We have no idea when or where he might try again."

"Whatever you think best," Hopkins said.

The captain nodded and glanced at Carter. He made a minor hand signal, apparently trying to indicate that it was time to leave, but Carter couldn't make his legs work.

Hopkins said, "Is there anything else, Captain?"

The captain looked at Carter again, then said, "Well, yes, sir. There's one more thing. We had hoped you might ask the President to stay out of sight for a while. At least until we find our man. If you could explain the danger, tell the President about the explosives and the drawing of the railroad bridge . . ."

Hopkins nodded. "Yes, I can do that. I'll talk to him this evening. I'll ask him to stay off trains for a few days. I'll convince him to stay here, in the White House, where he'll be safe."

6

"Oh, shit!"

Gay Cogswell, who had been lounging in bed lackadaisically doing leg-ups when Andy told her about the afternoon conference with Harry Hopkins, now sat up and stared at him, her long, loose hair spilling everywhere, her rich, luxuriant body faintly obscured by a pale-green peignoir. She shook her head slowly and added, "Tell me you're kidding, lover. Harry Hopkins? You talked to Harry Hopkins?"

Andy's hands drifted apart awkwardly and he shrugged. "It seemed a logical step."

"Oh, shit!" she said again. "Andy, how could you be so naïve? It's one thing to pursue a will-o'-the-wisp quietly, on your own. But to make a fool of yourself by going in to see someone like Harry Hopkins . . ."

"It isn't a will-o'-the-wisp," Andy said. "The guy exists. He's out there."

She impatiently brushed her hair off her face and said, "We've been over all this. The FBI says there is no ninth man. The Germans themselves say there is no ninth man. Andy, what does it take to convince you?"

"They're all wrong," he said stubbornly.

"And you're right? Good Lord, what a towering display of conceit."

"I thought you agreed with me," he said. "Sunday, up in Maryland, you said . . ."

"I was willing to go along with you as long as you kept it to yourself. What else could I say? You'd already made up your mind. But to spread it around like this, to go in and talk to someone like Harry Hopkins . . . My God, Andy. Do you realize what you've done?"

"I've tried to do my job," he said.

"By making a laughing stock of yourself? Because that's what will happen when this gets around, lover. They'll all be laughing at you. My God, why didn't you talk to me about it first?"

He found himself grinning placatingly, but he said, "Gay, you don't understand. It was a decision I had to make for myself."

"Well, you certainly made it," she said. She tumbled to her feet and paced the floor, then jerked her head around toward him. "That's the most selfish thing you've ever done, Andy. I'm very disappointed in you."

"Selfish?" he said. "I'm not sure I follow you."

"You knew how I felt about that White House job. I worked my tail off, getting you set up down there. I had plans for you. Now you blow it all with one simple dunderheaded wrong move."

"I happen to think I'm right," he said.

"Oh. Well, that makes all the difference, doesn't it?" She shook her head sharply. "No, Andy. You've bought yourself a one-way ticket to obscurity. You might as well kiss your future good-bye."

"It's *my* future."

"Is it?" she said. "And what about me? Don't I count?"

"Of course you do, honey. But Jesus, can't you show a little confidence? If I think it's worth the risk, why can't you . . ."

She rolled her eyes. "Don't be so dense, lover. I haven't spent the past six months working on your image just so you can go diving off the deep end. You think I want the town joke for a husband?"

"Husband?" He blinked. "You do skip around, don't you?"

"I don't consider it skipping around," she said evenly. "Why else should I give a damn what you do with your life? After all, that's what it's all about, isn't it? I've got my own position to consider."

"You make it sound pretty cut and dried."

She frowned at him. "Are you telling me you never considered marriage?"

"Sure I've considered it," he said. "I just thought it was a decision we might reach together, that's all."

"Don't be an ass, Andy. Of course we would have decided together. I'm hardly in a position to force you into marriage."

"Yeah, I understand that. But I'm getting the idea we would never have reached the decision unless I measured up to some set of standards you've laid out for me. Isn't that what you're saying?"

"Let's postpone this discussion, Andy. We'll only end up saying things we'll both be sorry for later."

"No, no. Let's talk about it now," he said. "A lot of things are coming very clear to me. That's why we did the bit with the weekend guests and the tennis and all the third degree, isn't it? A series of tests. What were you going to do? Pass out ballots?"

"They're my friends," she said. "Their opinions are important to me. That's why I wanted them to know you, to love you. Is that so devious?"

"And if they didn't like me? You haven't answered my question. Would that have ended it?"

A telephone rang somewhere downstairs. She shrugged and said, "We'll talk about it later. I have to answer the phone."

"Let Mattie get it," he insisted. "I want to know. What about it? Couldn't you take me with my rough edges?"

A touch of crimson flashed across her cheeks. "Don't be so childish, Andy. You can't blame me for wanting you to be better. I'm a mother, remember? I have obligations."

"Gaylynn and I get along just fine. We always have."

"Of course you do. You and I get along, too. At least we used to. But something is happening to us, Andy. Ever since you got mixed up in this spy business . . ."

"Don't blame it on that," he said. "Let's get back to basics. You were just telling me how I'm not good enough for you. Andy Blaszek, the Hungarian-American jerk. Just a nobody from Colorado, with no background and no family to speak of. Maybe you'd rather save it for some guy with a pedigree, like that rich tennis-playing bastard from Philadelphia."

"You sorry sonofabitch," she hissed. She tossed her head angrily and leveled a finger at him. "You could have made yourself a hell of a future in this town, but you seem determined to throw it all away. You think I give a damn about your family history, one way or the other? Well, I don't. But I do care about your future. I don't intend to stick Gaylynn with a father who's going nowhere."

His own face reddened. "Now it comes out. That's been a sticking point for us for a long time, hasn't it? That political crap. You don't want a husband. You want a lap dog that's been to obedience school. Well I can't hack it, Gay. If I'm going anywhere with my life, maybe I want to choose my own road map."

"So choose it and go," she said. "I'm not stopping you."

"Go? Gay, don't say that unless you mean it."

"I mean it."

He nodded, his face turning hard and grim. He started to pick up his uniform tunic, then paused. He swallowed hard, choking back the anger, and said, "Gay?"

"What?"

"Let's not do this. Anyway, not this way," he said.

"You're the one who wanted to talk it out."

"What if we . . . what if we backed off and started over. Maybe we could find a compromise."

Her voice softened slightly. "I suppose that's possible. Where would we start?"

He hesitated. While he waffled, trying to make up his mind, Mattie knocked on the bedroom door and said, "Captain? Telephone call for you."

Gay shook her head at him and raised her voice. "Tell them to call back, Mattie. The captain and I have a powerful lot of talking to do."

"Man says it's important," Mattie called. "It's a policeman. A Mister Savage. He says the captain should come to the phone right away."

Andy looked at Gay and said, "I better go down."

"I think that would be a mistake," she said. Her voice turned cool again.

He sighed. "The word was compromise, Gay. Not surrender. This will only take a minute."

He opened the bedroom door and stepped into the hallway. Mattie was standing off to the side. Her eyes were wide and fascinated. Apparently she had heard them shouting at each other on her way upstairs. He clenched his back teeth so hard it hurt and followed her down to the telephone.

Savage was excited. As soon as Andy picked up the telephone and identified himself, Savage sneezed and bubbled over. "The car dealer," he said excitedly. "We found the car dealer. Just a few minutes ago. He runs a place up on Vermont, just above T Street."

"He remembers the car?" Andy said.

"Yeah. The watersoaked bills did it, just like you said. The guy says a man came in over a week ago, bought a '39 Lincoln coupe and paid for it with watersoaked bills. He gave his name as Patterson. Raymond Patterson. The description fits."

"Great," Andy said. "Did you get a license number?"

"He's digging out the documents now. I was just about to drive out myself to talk to him. You want to meet me?"

"Yes, I'll be there," Andy said. "It'll take me a few minutes. I'm out across the Maryland line."

"I'll wait for you," Savage said happily. He blew his nose and said, "This does it, fella. I'll put the number on the hot sheets tonight. It may take two or three days, but if he's still in town, we've got him."

"Good," Andy said. "I'll see you in a few minutes."

He hung up and started to turn, then caught sight of Gay leaning over the upstairs banister. He shrugged and said, "You heard?"

"I heard," she said.

"It'll only take an hour or so. Then I'll be back. We can finish talking."

"Don't bother," she said. "I'm going to bed."

"Honey, we ought to talk this out."

"We already have, Andy. There's nothing more to say. You can send someone for your things tomorrow."

He frowned. "Don't say that, Gay."

"You'd better go," she said. "You'll be late."

He wavered for a moment, then ducked his head and headed for the front door.

THE NINETEENTH DAY

Wednesday—July 1, 1942

I

Sarah Miller didn't want to go to work the next morning.

She was dressed appropriately for the heat of the day, in a spun-rayon summer frock, rose with white vertical stripes, but her face was wan and her eyes slightly glazed. "Maybe I shouldn't go in," she told Dietrich. "I'm not really feeling very well."

Dietrich, who had work to do, smiled and took her in his arms, patting her gently on the back. "Come on, sweetheart, buck up. You'll feel a lot better if you don't give in to it. A little fresh air on the way down. That will perk you up."

"It sounds as though you're trying to get rid of me," she said. She tried to smile at him, but the exaggerated redness of her lipstick against the pallor of her cheeks only made her look gaunt and unappealing.

"Nonsense, sweetheart." He kept his arm around her and walked her to the hallway. "I'll tell you what I'll do. You try it, keep going through the day, and see if it doesn't make you feel a hundred per cent better. Be my brave little girl. Then I'll take you out to dinner and a movie when you get home. There's a Veronica Lake film on at the Capitol."

She looked tempted. Veronica Lake was one of her favorites. But she said, "I don't think I'm going to feel up to a movie, Ray. I have a scratchy throat and I feel kind of feverish. Darn, I hope I'm not catching a horrid old summer cold."

"We'll decide about tonight later," he said. "If I'm right, you'll come home full of energy." He opened the door for her. Morning sunlight streamed in and he could see her sparrows sitting, as always at this time of the morning, in a chattering crowd, waiting for her. He stepped outside and measured out the grain she sloppily kept in an old bread box on the front stoop, and handed it to her to scatter. The birds watched, as if agonized, waiting for the people to go away so they could eat. "Now listen, sweetheart, you be sure and have a good lunch," he said.

"All right, Ray."

"And don't work too hard. It's best not to give in to these little illnesses, but it's also foolish to overdo. Promise?"

She smiled again, bravely, breathlessly, and kissed him on the cheek.

He went inside to the kitchen and sighed. Role-playing again. She'd been acting weak and ailing since coming home last evening. Wouldn't cook. Tepid love-making. Fitful night's sleep. Come to think of it, her face had felt a little warm when he kissed him good-bye. Maybe she wasn't acting. Maybe she was really coming down with something. God, he didn't need a sick woman around the house. Not now. Not with so many things to do.

He took the dried-pea timer from beneath the kitchen sink where he had hidden it the afternoon before and set it on the kitchen table, thinking about her. She was probably just suffering from an emotional hangover. Some people were like that. Hot and eager to get in on a little solid sinning, but not mentally equipped to handle an aftermath of depression. Poor kid. It wasn't her fault that she'd apparently been brought up to feel guilty about a little perfectly normal sexuality. But it was a damned good thing she hadn't stayed home this morning. He still had the touchy part to go. The construction of the bomb itself. He could just see himself doing that between trips to the bedroom, toting cups of broth to her sickbed.

He fetched the tour guide he had purchased the previous week, a splashy four-color booklet on the White House, and thumbed through it, looking for the pages that had attracted him. Most of the photographs and copy were devoted to the main mansion—the Lincoln Room with its eight-foot bed, the Monroe Room with couches and crystal chandelier, the Green Room, the Red Room, the Queen's Room, and on and on, ad nauseum. But there was also a brief floor plan of the West Wing toward the back of the book, with lines and arrows showing, none too accurately, where the greats and near-greats did their work.

He propped the guide book open on the table and began to work out some figures. There was no scale on the page, but he knew the approximate dimensions of the press room and of the reception lobby. By translating that to the other rooms, rooms he hadn't had a chance to measure, he managed to estimate the size of the Oval Office. He used the estimate to work out a formula for the most efficient charge. When he was satisfied with his figures, he put his pencil in the book to mark his place and set it aside.

Next, he brought the bags of potassium nitrate, charcoal and sulphur to the table in order to mix his charge. A hefty one. It would probably be strong enough and destructive enough to do the job purely on its own blasting power. Nevertheless, he intended to coat it with the heavy ball bearings, to act as a kind of shrapnel, to make certain no one within reach survived. It would be bulky. Too bulky to carry in the building without notice. He would need a fairly large carrier for it, something that would appear perfectly natural. Something no one would give a second look. That's why he had set up the picture session tomorrow with Officer Greer. He would pick up his receptacle in a couple of hours, as soon as he finished here.

He took Sarah's measuring cups from the kitchen cupboard and began to measure potassium nitrate into a large mixing bowl. He grinned to himself at the image he presented. He must have looked quite domestic, stirring and ladling ingredients into Sarah's mixing bowl. Like Aunt Silke in the old days, whipping up a large cake.

2

Andy Blaszek almost felt triumphant the next morning. His office fairly hummed with activity. Emerson Carter off in one corner, talking on the telephone. Jerry Fenton, still a bit sour at having been dragged into the affair, sitting on the opposite side of Andy's desk, going over the most recent police reports. Sergeant Huffman and the two corporals chalking blackboards with "Frank Daniels" and "Raymond Patterson" headings, toting up all the known facts and descriptions. A couple of girls from the White House clerical pool breezing in and out, answering phones, transcribing notes, charting events by time and location as Fenton called them out.

But Andy couldn't keep his mind fully on his own personal war room. His thoughts kept going back to Gay and to the sudden sharp argument which had seemingly developed out of thin air, driving him out of her bed and back to his own apartment. He had played and replayed the words, trying to decide who was most at fault. His mind said he was in the clear, that he had reacted in a totally blameless manner, heaping the guilt where it belonged, squarely on her pretty, stubborn head. But his mind had competition from a dark coil of his gut, a maverick bit of matter that nagged it wasn't all that easy to parcel out the blame. Arguments are never one-sided, it told him. Person A snaps at Person B, and Person B snaps back at Person A, and before you know it, the brouhaha sluices are open and the ugly words gurgle through from both sides. It didn't matter who started an argument. It mattered only if no one stopped it.

Worse, what if she had been right? What if he was, as she delicately put it, making an ass of himself? Gay would laugh at him. Twice already this morning he had caught himself hoping against hope that he was right, just so he could prove himself to the others.

That was the most embarrassing aspect of all. To think that he could prefer to prove himself correct, even at the expense of the President's safety.

3

Two hours after Andy reported to his office and started helping Fenton sift through the police crime reports, another crime was on the verge of perpetration, one which would undoubtedly appear on the next day's police ledger, and one which would just as undoubtedly be ignored as unimportant when it crossed Andy's desk in the White House.

The current crime was only a case of theft, a newspaper photographer's fully equipped gadget bag, containing a battered 4×5 Speed Graphic, a spare ten-inch lens, a chrome flash gun, three cartons of flashbulbs and fifteen 4×5 film plates.

At that moment, it rested on the floor near the door of the game room in the National Press Club, high atop the Press Club Building in downtown Washington. Its owner was a pudgy, sallow man, staring at two red queens and a pair of fours, trying not to show his excitement as he gripped the stub of a cigar between crooked teeth. He was scheduled to be at the Naval Observatory in fifteen minutes to shoot pictures of a new star-gazing device, but he was down ten dollars in the poker game and this was the first good hand he had seen since being bluffed out of a low straight almost an hour earlier.

As the photographer worked to keep a straight face and pushed his bet into the middle of the table, Dietrich quietly picked up the camera bag and stepped into the hallway. He walked quickly toward the elevator, hoping to be out of the building before the betting was concluded and the hands exposed.

The photographer lost not only his camera bag and equipment, but his bet as well. When the showdown came, it was three deuces across the table which pulled in the pot. The only crime involved here, however, was that a reporter from Cleveland had folded in the middle of the betting with three sixes.

4

Sarah let herself into the apartment and called weakly, "Ray? Ray, sweetheart, are you here?" No answer.

Darn it, she felt terrible. So completely washed out. And headachy. There was no sense in staying down at the office when she felt this bad.

She passed through the living room and into the bedroom, looking for him. Gone. Was he supposed to work at that Sears, Roebuck job again today? She couldn't remember. Her brain simply wasn't working with this fever. Darn it, she should have stayed in bed. Ray could have stayed with her, helped her. A cool washcloth on the forehead every once in a while. That would have helped.

She took several deep breaths, feeling dizzy. Maybe an aspirin. At least get rid of the headachy feeling. Poor Ray. He tried so hard to be sweet, and she repaid him by getting sick, by moping, by worrying.

She slipped out of her dress and staggered sluggishly to the bathroom medicine cabinet for an aspirin, then carried it into the kitchen for a glass of water. As she turned on the tap, she saw her mixing bowl and the measuring cup, upside down in the dish drainer, drying. Bless his heart. He had to make his own breakfast. She hadn't even done that for him. At least he could cook. Stupid Ben couldn't cook at all. He wouldn't even try.

Why was she always thinking of Ben? Why Ben? Ray was good to her. Ray took care of her. Ben had no right to go away and leave her alone like this. Alone. It was Ben's fault. She couldn't help what had happened. It was Ben. It was the war.

She swallowed the aspirin and washed it down with water, then picked up the mixing bowl and the cup, intending to put them away. The cup went into the dish shelf easily enough, but when she opened the cabinet under the sink to put away the bowl, she saw something which stopped her.

What on earth was that? It hadn't been there yesterday. A kind of sticky package, about the size of a lumpy loaf of bread, covered with some sort of glue. A lot of little steel marbles embedded in it. And batteries. What was it for?

She set the bowl on the floor and eased the odd contraption out into the open. One of the marbles, not yet dry, broke loose and rolled across the floor. There was a little glass tube tied to the side of the package, filled with peas, and some loose wires. She put it on the kitchen table, confused, and stared at it.

5

While Sarah stared at the contraption on her kitchen table, a retired botanist climbed on his bicycle for an afternoon run with his dog. The botanist, who did occasional freelance consultation work with the Department of Agriculture, made a regular summer habit of bicycling through his neighborhood on his afternoon runs, forcing his dog to scramble to keep up. It served not only as an efficient method of exercise for the dog, but also as a pleasurable, body-toning experience for the man.

On this particular Wednesday afternoon, the man selected Rock Creek Park, with its rambling glades and hiking trails that passed behind his house, as the exercise arena. It was an unusually enjoyable experience for him, guiding his bicycle up and down the narrow flowering trails at this time of year, winding along a wooded portion of the twelve-mile-long park. His dog seemed to be enjoying it as well. He could hear the dog thrashing through the underbrush just off the trail, panting happily.

They were nearing Dumbarton Oaks when the man abruptly lost track of his dog. One moment the happy panting sounds had been there, the next, silence. The botanist braked his bicycle and straddled the crossbar, thankful for the momentary excuse to catch his breath. He waited in the wooded surroundings for perhaps two minutes, expecting the dog to catch up. When it did not, he called out to it, cheerfully at first, then with some irritation. He had to call three times before the dog finally bayed in response. But it didn't come.

Finally the man reversed his bicycle on the narrow trail and pedaled back down the hillside until he could see his dog, straining excitedly in a thick stand of trees, sniffing at something in the underbrush, tail wagging in jerky arcs of delight. The elderly botanist, miffed at his dog for not coming when summoned, leaned his bicycle against a tree at the edge of the path and trudged angrily into the bushes to see what was so fascinating.

Thus it was that a stiff, lye-covered body, with two bullet holes in the chest so close together that they could have been covered with a single silver dollar, first came to official light.

6

A little less than an hour later, Dietrich inserted the key and unlocked the apartment door, clutching the stolen camera bag, pleased with himself for pulling it off so easily. Of course he could have bought his own camera and camera bag, but this beat-up, obviously well-used case would look more natural. That poor dumb photographer would look all over the place before he . . .

Sarah was standing in the shadows by the kitchen door, staring at him. She was down to her half-slip and bra. Apparently home from work early. His muscles twitched and he quickly turned on a smile and set the camera bag on the floor, trying to think of a way to explain it if she asked. He said, "Hi, sweetheart. What's the matter? Are you feeling worse?"

She turned wordlessly and walked into the kitchen.

Dietrich kept the smile on his face as he followed her. "What's wrong, sweetheart? What are you doing home so early? Did . . ."

She was poised beside the kitchen table, watching him with cold eyes. On the table, piled in untidy heaps, were the bomb, the timer, the coil of unused wire, half a package of leftover peas, the White House guide book, the bundle of fake identity cards, including some from the dead newsman's wallet, his Mauser, damn near everything.

She said, "Ray, can you explain all this?" Her voice was frigid.

He let himself laugh lightly, fighting to control his nerves. "Looks like you've conducted a pretty thorough search, Sarah."

"I found some of it by accident," she said. "What is it, Ray? What's it all about? I want to know."

"Just a little experiment," he said. "I guess I haven't talked about it because people always joke so much about mad inventors, but I'm hoping to get a patent on a new gizmo for unclogging drill holes. I told you I used to do a little wildcatting. I guess why I really came to Washington was to be able to watchdog the thing through the rigamarole at the Patent Office."

"Patent?" she said. "And the gun? The different identifications? Don't lie to me, Ray. What are you up to?"

He smiled again, keeping it casual. Hell's bells. What kind of a careful operator was he? Everything going so well, yet he allowed this one dumb little girl to come home early and spoil everything. He should have hidden things better. That was twice he had been careless. First the landlady. Now Sarah. Both women. What was it with him? Did he have some kind of blind spot with women? Something that forced him to underestimate them? Do something, fella. Say something. Jolly her out of it.

"Don't get excited," he said. "Look, sweetheart, appearances can be deceiving. My ex-partner in San Antonio was trying to cop my idea. He's one mean bastard, too. I want to stay out of his way if I can, but if I can't I've got to be able to defend myself."

"Oh, Ray." Her eyes filled with tears and she jerked her chin away. The smooth muscles of her face, twisted with hurt and disappointment, had turned ugly. "You've been lying to me, Ray. All this time, you've been lying. Why?"

"I never lied to you," he said.

She shot an angry look at him. "You're lying to me now."

"No, sweetheart. I'm not. Honest."

"Liar. When I found all this, I called Sears, Roebuck and asked for you. But they said you didn't work there. They said they'd never even heard of you."

"Well, I can explain that. I—"

"Oh, stop it," she said. She looked away. "You said you loved me. You made me believe you. How could you do a thing like that?"

"Sarah, you've got to trust me. It's important. Damned important."

"You've been using me, using me and leading me on and lying to me." She shuddered. "God, I feel so dirty."

"Sarah . . ."

She shook her head and said, "Get out, Ray. Go away. I've had enough of your lies. I don't want you here any more."

"Sarah, you've got to listen to me."

"Get out!" she shouted.

"Just one more day, Sarah. I need one more day."

She came around the table toward him, shoving with both hands as she brushed past and headed for the living room. He rocked back, off balance, surprised at her strength, then righted himself and followed her slowly. He paused at the kitchen door and watched as she reached angrily for the hall telephone.

He sighed. "Don't do it, Sarah."

She glared at him and lifted the earpiece from the hook.

"Put it down," he said coldly. He started toward her.

When she saw him step forward, she whirled with the telephone and jumped quickly into the bathroom, pushing the door shut over the telephone cord. The bathroom lock clicked.

He moved to the door and said, "Sarah, open the door."

He heard her voice, murmuring behind the door, but not in response to him. She was talking into the telephone. He leaned over quickly and gripped the telephone cord and yanked it from the wall.

Then he stood back and kicked the door open.

She was sitting on the edge of the tub with the phone in her hands when the door splintered open. She looked up at him in terror. He snatched the phone from her and threw it into the hallway.

"That won't do you any good," she said. "I'll call again as soon as you're gone."

"I'm not going," he said quietly and steadily. He put his hands around her throat and pulled her off the bathtub. He pressed, cutting off her air.

"Ray, don't," she said in a choked, indignant voice. Her hands fluttered to his wrists and tried to pull them away. At first she looked merely angry, as though she thought his roughness outrageous. But as his hands continued to grip her throat, squeezing her windpipe, her eyes widened with fear. He kept on choking, forcing her down, down toward the floor.

She tried to scream, but no sound came. She kicked and thrashed her legs. A runner leapt up one hose-clad calf. Still he pressed downward. Her eyes rolled up under her lids and her body convulsed in terror. Her knees swept from side to side, knocking against the tub, as he pressed her head beneath the bathroom basin, throttling, pushing, choking. There was a tearing sound as her slip caught on a pipe beneath the sink and split open. Her knees trembled in one last rending convulsion, and at the last moment he cursed her. "Bitch!" he spat. "Whore!" And then she was still.

He held her for a moment, staring at her stringy hair, once pretty, now tangled and matted in her face. He looked at his fingers, white with tightness against her small neck. He heard the faucet drip. Finally he turned her loose and sagged back on his heels. Poor Sarah. Poor, pretty Sarah. He hadn't meant what he'd said. Why had he cursed her? He rocked on his heels, watching her. Then he backed away and sat down on the toilet lid, his hands folded in his lap.

He sat quietly for several minutes until something moist dropped to his folded hands and splattered against the skin. He looked down in surprise, then touched his cheek, feeling the unexpected trail of wetness.

THE LAST DAY

Thursday—July 2, 1942

I

Patrolman Harry Pribble and his partner, Max Turner, had been on duty since six in the morning, cruising the northwest section of the city in their 1940 Plymouth black-and-white, and by the time they turned off Calvert and nosed into the apartment area on Twenty-ninth Street, the city was awake and the first wave of government office workers was already beginning to rev up for the ride into the city.

Pribble and Turner envied the apartment dwellers their normal lives and normal hours, in bed by midnight, up by eight. In more peaceful times, Pribble and Turner might also have lucked into tidier work shifts, but because the D.C. Police Department was war-depleted and understaffed, their summer duty schedules were frequently stretched to ten hours a day, sometimes even to as much as twelve hours a day.

If Pribble had been given his way, the Department would have been short at least one more man. He had tried to enlist two days after Pearl Harbor, but a cleft palate he'd been born with rendered him unsuitable, according to the Army doctors. And yet they had taken a bunch of jackasses that same day, college kids who had never held a gun in their lives, would probably puke their guts out the first time a Jap or a German took a shot at them. It was no good trying to be patriotic when a bunch of jackass doctors paid more attention to some sorry little accident of Mother Nature's than to what a man had inside, where it counted. A man didn't march with his mouth, or shoot with it. He'd have made the best of soldiers if they'd given him half a chance. Now he was stuck with hassling whores and roughing up an occasional drunk serviceman and cruising endlessly with Turner, an old guy in his fifties with such lousy kidneys that he would never stop anywhere for coffee.

Pribble looked at Turner as his partner wheeled them off Twenty-ninth Street onto Cathedral. Him and his kidneys. He always claimed that if he started on the coffee, they'd be making pit stops at gasoline stations the rest of the morning. But he was a nice old guy. At least he didn't give a man a hard time about some little speech problem. Pribble was thankful for that. He'd had other partners who always spent the first week or two saying "huh?" every time he spoke.

Old Turner, chewing gum contentedly, swung them onto Twenty-seventh Street, toward Garfield, and Pribble yawned, thinking about one strong, steaming cup of coffee. Just one. He hated to get sleepy. It was going to be a hot day, and he always had trouble staying awake in the heat. Maybe if they didn't work him so hard, he could . . .

Suddenly alert, Pribble said, "Hey, hold it!" He sat forward and looked past Turner's nose at a line of cars parked outside a row of one-story apartments. Turner amiably eased the police car to a stop and sat with his arms locked over the steering wheel, chewing his gum, waiting until Pribble gave him the word to move on.

"That little Lincoln," Pribble said. "The gray one. Back up a few feet so I can get another look at the license plate."

Turner obediently eased the car backward until Pribble told him to stop, then watched while Pribble took a clipboard off the dash and flipped through the bulletins they had been handed before going on duty.

"There!" Pribble said jabbing his finger at a short memo sheet. "I knew it. It's a hot car, or something. We're supposed to put in a call for Lieutenant Savage if we spot it."

Turner nodded cheerfully. "You want me to get on the horn?"

"In a minute," Pribble said. "You wait here. I'm going to take a closer look at it."

2

Thirty minutes before the police car pulled up in the street outside, Dietrich had rinsed the lather from his shaving brush and looked down at the contorted tangle of arms and legs on the bathroom floor.

She was cold now, quite cold, and stiff. Her flesh, once so appealing, had taken on a pale, bluish hue in the slanting rays of sunlight. Her torn slip, hiked to her hips in the last thrashing moments of her life, exposed a patch of blue rayon panties, skinned with worn spots and abrasions, like the run in her stockings. He leaned over and gently tugged the hem of the slip down to her knees, covering the panties.

He hadn't been able to face the big bed without her last night, so after finishing off the explosive device and packing it into the body of the Speed Graphic with the bellows extended, he had sacked out on the living-room couch. Odd that she should matter to him. He hadn't really known her that well. He wasn't even sure he liked her. But he missed her.

Nor had he slept very well. Perhaps it was because his mind, triggered by the importance of what he would face today, had restlessly presented him with a series of frozen scenes, like candid snapshots, out of his past. Aunt Silke, pressing his bewildered face to her ample bosom. A Texas mortician, whose unsmiling face was as grim as the black business suit he wore. Brown legs and lederhosen, strutting at a Nazi youth camp. Gerta, joyous Gerta, with a trickle of sweat rolling off her down-covered belly into pubic hair that smelled of soap and hand cream. And, amid the scenes from the past, confusing scenes of the present which jolted him awake. A train, roaring overhead in the darkness on a bridge that remained untouched. Sarah, with her expectant brown eyes trained on a movie magazine. A Denver newsman, toppling out of the car with his mouth curled into a small "O" of surprise.

So he had awakened early and sat, smoking in the presunrise darkness, thinking, sorting out his thoughts of the future. With Sarah dead, he would soon lose the use of his car. Someone would miss her in a day or so and come looking for her. Once they found her, there would be questions, a police investigation. Someone was bound to remember the Lincoln parked on the street outside.

No matter. He only needed it a bit longer. After he was done today, after the bomb had been set and the timing device activated, he would leave the White House and use the car to head immediately south, using his hour's grace before the bomb exploded to get as far away from a Washington dragnet as possible. Forget the submarine. Too risky. He would simply drive the car southward until it ran out of gas, then abandon it. He could catch a bus or hitchhike from there, make his way to Texas, lose himself while the hue and cry arose and Americans went crazy trying to figure out who had killed their President. Unless they hushed it up. Could he be that lucky?

Once he was safely in Texas, it would be easy to make his way to the Mexican border. Getting back to Germany wouldn't be so easy though, not since Mexico had declared war on Germany in late May. But he would find a way. The pity was that he would be delayed. The celebration in Germany, and there would be a tremendous celebration, would inevitably be over before he could return to claim his part of it.

There would be a problem about money. He hadn't much left. He'd already gone through Sarah's purse, finding $27 and some change to add to his own $40 or so. It wouldn't last long. But once he reached Texas, once he got home . . .

Home? Good God, what made him think that? Thorny mesquite thickets and a bird calling *perdido* had never been home for him. Not really. And yet, facing the supreme test of his life, facing too the possibility of death if everything didn't run smoothly, his thoughts had instinctively turned southward. Even his escape route. Why Texas? Why not Canada?

Because he knew Texas. Hate it though he might, he could sink out of sight in Texas, drop from view, be swallowed up by the twangs and cotton twills and country informality of her insular citizenry. He would be just another face, another good-old-boy in the Stetson network. An outsider with an insider's accent. Not like his father, his poor father with the snicker-provoking Germanic speech rhythms. Even the Mexicans who lived around him, who brought their dogs and sick cows, used to . . .

He stiffened. Of course. Suddenly it came to him why he had cursed Sarah yesterday, cursed her as she died by his hands in the bathroom. The way his father used to kill. The dying dogs, too sick to save, too worthless to worry about. Dietrich's father used to take them out back of the barn and tie them to a post, murmuring quietly as he hitched them to the iron ring. Then he would pull out that mail-order .38 revolver with the cheap taped handle and point it at their heads. Always, just before firing, he would curse them, hating them, working up a righteous feeling before he pulled the trigger.

Dietrich hurriedly put the memory out of his mind. The escape route south was vital to him. He couldn't allow it to be spoiled by wayward thoughts. To keep his mind clear, he went into the living room and while the sparrows woke up and began to chatter outside he added the last touches to his day's preparations. He fetched his freshly cleaned and oiled Mauser and inserted a ten-shot clip in the magazine. He screwed the fat silencer tube on the end of the barrel, then wrapped the gun in a black focusing cloth and stuck it in the camera bag beside the bomb-rigged camera.

The readying of his workman's tools with cool efficiency steadied him, and he remained steady while he shaved, then went to Sarah's bedroom to get ready. He shucked his undershirt and shorts, and rummaged through his scanty belongings for clean undergarments. It was a ritual thing to Dietrich, like a matador donning his suit of lights. Like every other aunt who ever took over the rearing of a boy from every other mother, his Aunt Silke had told him over and over when he was growing up, always wear fresh underwear and socks when you go out. You never know when a truck might hit you and they have to undress you at the hospital. Be a good boy, a clean boy. Don't embarrass yourself in front of doctors and people on the street. Well, today his truck was a distinct possibility. He would be ready.

Strange that Sarah should be so careless about her underwear. A good, firm body. Flat stomach, good legs. Hair always brushed and perfect. Make-up meticulously applied. Yet she always wore those saggy panties with holes and worn elastic. Dietrich firmed his mouth and told himself to stop thinking about her. But it was sad that she had not been ready when her own truck came.

The resident manager was in the yard when Dietrich, the camera case on one shoulder and a small valise packed with his few possessions in his hand, let himself out of Sarah's apartment. The man, busily sweeping birdseed hulls and bird droppings from the sidewalk, paused long enough to look pointedly in Dietrich's direction. He would obviously have enjoyed complaining to Dietrich about the mess, but he was too timid, just as he had been too timid to mention Dietrich's recent residence in a young woman's apartment. Instead, the man nodded grudgingly and said, "Is Mrs. Miller feeling any better today?"

"Yes," Dietrich said. "She's much better." He hesitated, but for Sarah's sake he bent over the old bread box on the stoop and filled the coffee can with fresh birdseed, then sprinkled it for her waiting sparrows on the narrow sidewalk beside the forsythia hedge. The manager mumbled to himself and walked away. It was a pity to vex such an inoffensive little man, but at least the birds for which Sarah had come to feel an unwilling responsibility would not go hungry. Not yet.

Dietrich was uncomfortably aware that as soon as he started toward the street, the birds swooped in behind him hungrily to attack the feed. Their beaks clicked like a light patter of raindrops against the cement. He was almost to the curb before he took in the policeman leaning through the window of the Lincoln, as if looking for the driver's registration. Beyond the Lincoln, sitting in a black-and-white police car with its motor running, was another policeman staring idly at nothing.

Dietrich stopped instantly. His car? How could they be onto his car? Had the resident manager been complaining to the police? He glanced back at Sarah's walk, but the manager was gone. He started to pass on up the street, but the policeman by the Lincoln spotted him. "Hey, you," the policeman said.

The policeman glanced at the row of little one-story apartments from which Dietrich had come. He said, "Do you live in one of these buildings, fella?" His speech was nasal and hard to understand, as though he were mumbling while holding his nose.

"I beg your pardon?" Dietrich said.

For some reason, the policeman seemed to be irritated by Dietrich's inability to understand him. He said, "Don't get smart with me, fella." At least that's what Dietrich thought he said. "You just answer my question. Do you live around here?" He gestured at the apartments.

Dietrich followed his gesturing hand and said, "Yes. I'm staying with a friend."

"You know who belongs to this car?" The policeman jerked his thumb at the Lincoln.

Dietrich swallowed. "No. I've never seen it before."

The policeman gazed at the apartments. "Registration says his name is Raymond Patterson. You know him?"

"I'm new in town," Dietrich said. "I don't know anyone."

"What about the guy you're living with? Would he know this Patterson?"

Dietrich looked blank.

"Your friend, your friend," the policeman said. He pointed at Sarah's apartment again. "Would your friend know this Raymond Patterson?"

"I don't know. I don't think so."

"Suppose you take me back and introduce me. I'd like to ask for myself."

"Excuse me, officer. I have to go. If I'm late, I'll miss my bus."

The policeman hesitated. "Yeah, all right," he said. "Just tell me which apartment. I'll find it."

Dietrich tried to grin disarmingly. "I can't do that, officer. My friend is a girl. A married woman. You understand, don't you?"

The policeman looked disapproving rather than disarmed. He said, "What's your name, fella?"

"Pastor," Dietrich said. "Dave Pastor."

"You got any identification?"

Dietrich dropped his chin, cursing mentally. Yes, he had identification, but the wrong ones. He was a carrying a driver's license made out to Raymond Patterson for the car, and a wallet identifying himself as Robert Sheppard for entry to the White House, neither of which he could allow the policeman to see. The rest of his cards were tucked into his valise, and he couldn't very well sort through them and choose an appropriate one with the policeman looking on. He said, "I'm only a tourist, officer. I didn't think anyone would be asking me for papers."

"No identification?" the policeman said. "What about your draft card? Don't you know it's against the law to walk around without your draft card?"

"It's inside," Dietrich said. "If you'll wait here, I'll go get it."

"Just a minute," the policeman said. "Maybe I'd better go with you."

Dietrich hesitated. Apparently there was to be no easy way out. He set the valise down, then straightened up and unsnapped his camera bag.

"Hold it," the policeman said. He undid the flap of his leather holster. "What's in the bag?"

"I beg your pardon?"

"The bag, the bag. What's in it?"

"Just camera equipment. I told you, I'm a tourist."

"Hold it out where I can see," the policeman said.

Dietrich nodded and peeled the lid back and tilted the bag so the policeman could look inside.

"Yeah, okay," the policeman said. He relaxed a bit. "Now let's go inside and see about that identification."

Dietrich took a deep breath. He put his hand into the camera bag and touched the hard outline of the Mauser. "Are you sure you want this?" he asked the policeman.

"Stop fooling around," the policeman said. "Let's get going."

"All right," Dietrich said. He slipped his hand under the focus cloth and pulled at the Mauser.

The policeman seemed to realize what was happening even before the gun came into view. He flinched and jerked back, pawing at his own gun, but Dietrich shot him before he got it loose. The policeman spun against the side of the Lincoln and sat down hard in the gutter. He said, "Ow! Goddamn it!"

The feeding sparrows couldn't have heard the silenced shot, but the sound of the wounded policeman banging against the side of Dietrich's car alarmed them, and with a swoosh of wings like a great sigh they took flight. The commotion galvanized the other policeman. He flung his door open and started to pop out of the squad car, shouting, "What's this? What's this? What's this?"

Dietrich leveled the Mauser across the top of the Lincoln and squeezed off a shot, but the older policeman yanked back inside and slammed the car door, ducking out of sight.

Dietrich wasted no time. He whirled and ran across the yard, hurdling the scraggly forsythia hedge which separated the apartment grounds from a two-story stone house next door. The camera bag flapped against his hip as he hit ground. He kept running, between the two buildings toward the alley.

What could have gone wrong? How could they have gotten a line on his car? How? Damn it. Damn them. Damn everybody. But they wouldn't stop him. Not now. Nothing could stop him now.

He ran on, toward Connecticut Avenue. As always, the simplest way was best. He would catch a cab, and he hoped he could hail one quickly. His appointment would not wait.

3

"Take a look at this one," Andy Blaszek said. "A man in Rock Creek Park. Two bullets in the heart. A retired government worker found him yesterday."

"Any identification?" Jerry Fenton asked.

Andy shook his head. "Not yet. They're trying to check prints. You think we ought to look into it?"

"I doubt it," Fenton said. "Surely this spy of yours would be too careful to run around killing stray citizens indiscriminately."

"We could ask for a ballistics comparison," Andy said. "The cops could check these bullets off against those from the armory. If they aren't the same, then we could rule him out."

"That would take days," Fenton said. "Besides, it's just another homicide." He took the police report from Andy and tossed it on his discard pile. "Come on, Andy, let's rethink this. There's bound to be a better way. Why don't you let me and . . ."

Fenton paused. Officer Greer of the White House police was leaning through the door. The officer said, "Captain Blaszek, there's a D.C. policeman at the northwest gate asking to see you. He claims it's urgent. He won't talk to anyone else."

"Morning, Mr. Greer," Andy said. "What's the man's name?"

"Savage, sir. He's in an official car, but the guards won't let him through without an authorization. They phoned us. Didn't know how to reach your office."

"Jesus Christ," Andy said in disgust. "Yeah, okay. I'll vouch for him. Tell the meatheads to let him pass."

As the officer vanished, Fenton looked at the pile of unread police reports still to go and said, "Savage? Isn't that the police detective who's been siphoning all this stuff to you?"

"It sure is," Andy said. "What do you suppose he wants?"

Fenton grinned. "Maybe they're going to shut off your source of supply. There's a paper shortage, you know. I only hope they do it before I go blind reading this bilge. Look at this stuff—accident at Morgan and Kirby; drunk and disorderly on M Street; family disturbance on Wallach Place."

He was still droning three minutes later when one of the gate guards escorted a white-faced Detective Savage into the office. Savage was clutching a manila folder to his chest and he looked shaken. Andy jumped up and asked, "What's the trouble?" but Savage shook his head sharply and watched the gate guard withdraw.

The detective snuffled. He said, "They took my gun."

"Who took your gun?"

"The guards at the gate. They wouldn't let me or my driver come through until we handed over our guns."

"Oh, that," Andy said. "Don't let it bother you. It's standard procedure."

"Nobody ever took my gun before. I don't like it."

"You'll get it back," Andy said. He gestured at Fenton and Carter, and Carter started toward them, looking curious. "Here, I'd like for you to meet some people. Jerry Fenton, Emerson Carter, this is . . ."

But Savage waved the introductions away and said, "Can we talk?"

"Talk? Sure. Why not?"

Savage flicked his eyes at Fenton and Carter. "You sure it's okay? It's about that man you were hunting. Frank Daniels or Patterson or whatever his name is."

"They know all about him," Andy said. "Fenton's Secret Service and Carter's FBI."

Savage nodded and took a deep breath. "We found him. This morning."

"You what?" Andy said. "Where?"

"In an apartment area up on Twenty-seventh Street," Savage said. "A couple of my patrolmen had a run-in with him."

"Did they catch him?"

"No, I'm afraid not. It was that car tip you gave us. They spotted his car on the street. He came out a couple of minutes later. He must be crazy or something. He came out shooting. He wounded one of the patrolmen. About a half hour ago. Then he ran."

"Jesus. Why didn't you call?"

Savage gave him a peculiar look. "On the telephone? About something like this? Captain, I know a lot more about this business than I did before. You've been holding back on me about this guy."

Andy said uneasily, "What do you mean?"

"He's a spy or something," Savage said. "You didn't tell me that."

Fenton snapped like a trout taking a May fly. "How do you know he's a spy?" Carter nodded energetically.

"I've been out there," Savage said. "We got the manager to let us in his apartment. There's a dead girl there. Been dead maybe fifteen or sixteen hours. In the kitchen we found the makings of some kind of bomb. My lab man says it's potassium nitrate, the same stuff that was stolen from the armory the other night. If he used all the junk out of those empty bags, he's got a boomer big enough to flatten half a city block. Why didn't you tell me what we were mixed up in?"

"I . . . I couldn't," Andy said. "We didn't really have anything very solid to go on."

"You damned security types, you never figure you can tell anything," Savage said heavily. He didn't sound bitter. Just weary. He sniffled and rubbed a paw across his nose. "I guess I couldn't have done anything about it. I just wish you'd told me. He's after the President, isn't he?"

Fenton cocked his head at the big detective. "What makes you say that?"

"It figures," Savage said. "The train timetables. And the bomb makings. Now this." He unclenched the manila folder and extracted a small booklet. Andy took the booklet before Fenton or Carter could reach for it. It was a glossy little tourist guide with pictures and charts and columns of historical lore. On the White House.

"Where did you find this?" Andy said.

"In the kitchen," Savage said. "It was on the table with a lot of other junk. Turn to page twenty-six. There's some figures in the margins, next to a diagram of the Oval Office."

Andy riffled the pages and quickly studied the figures. He paled. He turned to Fenton. "Call Calhoun. Get him down here. Quick."

Fenton looked longingly at the guide book but he grabbed a telephone and jiggled the hook. Carter got the book instead, taking it bodily from Andy's hands. Savage watched them for a moment, then dug a badly wadded handkerchief from his hip pocket and blew his nose grimly and said, "Captain, I looked pretty stupid, not knowing what to do when I found that book. You didn't leave me much to do but hop in one of the squad cars and come down here as fast as I could."

Carter spoke before Andy could. "Are you sure this belonged to our man?"

Savage nodded. "We found it buried under a lot of stuff on the table. Wires and batteries and things like that. There was some camera equipment. A bunch of film holders and things. Some flashbulbs. He dropped a valise with some clothes and a little pile of phony identity cards. And this little book in the kitchen. Those figures in the margin, they're a lot like the figures in that sketch pad we found. Like maybe he was trying to decide how big a charge to set."

Fenton hung up. "Calhoun is on his way," he reported. Then, glancing eagerly over Carter's shoulder at the guide book, he said, "How? How could the guy sneak a bomb past the guards?"

"He was carrying another bag when he came out," Savage said. "Some kind of a leather thing on a shoulder strap. One of my officers talked to him before he started shooting, but it was the one he wounded, so we haven't had much chance to ask about it. My guess, based on the stuff he left behind, is that it's some kind of camera case. You know, the kind tourists carry."

Andy checked his watch. The tourist gate had already opened. He groaned. "How long ago did you say this happened?"

"About thirty minutes, give or take a few."

"Then he may already be out there," Andy said. "Jerry, we've got to shut down the tourist gate. And get all the tourists herded out of the building. You know his description. Alert the gate and pass it along. Tell them if they see anyone like that, pick him up and hold him."

There was a commotion in the hallway and John Bradley Calhoun came hustling through the door, flanked by two of his senior Secret Service men. "What's going on in here?" he demanded. "What's all this crap about an emergency?"

"We may have a bomber on our hands," Andy said. He jerked his thumb at Savage. "This is Detective Savage from the D.C. Police Department. He's just found evidence to indicate that our man may be on his way here, armed with a bomb. Fenton was just about to call the tourist gate, to get them to shut down."

"Take it easy," Calhoun said. "You're not shutting down any gates until I find out what this is all about."

"We don't have time for that," Andy said. "The guy could be waiting in line right now. Look, we'll fill you in. Everything we've got. But let Jerry get that gate closed."

Calhoun shot a look at Fenton, who ducked his chin in corroboration. "All right," he said. "Go ahead. Make the call." Then he glared at Andy. "Captain, I'll have a word with you later about just why you have failed to take me into your confidence about all this."

Jerry Fenton nodded. Emerson Carter nodded. Detective Savage nodded. Andy shook his head in despair, feeling like Chicken Little, who had rushed about trying to warn everyone that the sky had cracks in its seams. Now that the sky was really falling on their heads, they were blaming him for not mentioning it. Jesus.

"Yeah, yeah," he said impatiently. "I just hope we're in time to stop him."

4

But Dietrich was already in the White House. He had arrived prosaically by taxi well before Detective Savage and had passed through the northwest "working" gate with far less difficulty by showing his Robert Sheppard White House press credentials. The camera bag had received only a cursory look from gate guards, but it was enough to make Dietrich's mouth go dry. Then they had waved him on and he strolled down the curving tree-lined driveway to the West Wing, biting the inside of his still-dry mouth but keeping his steps moderate.

He had stashed the camera bag in the press room, knowing full well that it would never be noticed in the welter of camera bags belonging to regular White House press photographers. Then he permitted himself to hurry out into the West Wing reception lobby, looking for Officer Greer, the White House policeman.

Greer wasn't immediately apparent, so Dietrich sat tensely on one of the green leather couches and held a *Saturday Evening Post* in front of his eyes, waiting for the man. A story predicted that the Russians would be able to last through the summer and could be saved from the German drive by the Russian winter. Another cawed that the Japanese had embarrassed the Germans by their rapid advances in the Pacific. A serialized piece of fiction continued a tale by someone named Helen MacInnes. Dietrich tossed the magazine on the couch and drummed his fingers on the leather arm.

A good five minutes passed before the burly, gray-haired White House policeman appeared, coming into the lobby from the direction of the men's room. Dietrich grinned and popped to his feet. "Hi," he called. "I've been waiting for you."

Greer's face looked haggard. He tried to smile, but it came off weakly.

"What's the matter?" Dietrich said. "You don't look too good."

"I feel pretty lousy," the officer said gratefully, apparently pleased that someone had noticed his suffering. "Touch of the flu, I guess. It's worse than just a cold. I almost didn't make it in today."

Dietrich's grin froze for an instant. Almost didn't make it in? God. Over such little quirks of fate did monumental plans stumble. Thank God the man was the conscientious type. He said, "Well, I'm awfully glad you did. We're supposed to shoot pictures today, remember?"

It seemed to perk the officer up. "That's right. Damn. I almost forgot."

Dietrich kept his voice even by an effort. "I thought you might take me behind the scenes again. I'd like to get some shots of you protecting the Oval Office. That sort of thing."

"Sure," Greer said. "Why not? The President doesn't usually hit the office until about ten, after his morning swim." He winced suddenly and gingerly patted his stomach. "Damnation," he said. "It feels like I got knots in my middle. Terrible stuff, flu. It gives you the trots something fierce."

"Too bad," Dietrich said, trying to sound sympathetic. Then, "Well, how about it? Can we get started?"

"Yeah, I guess so," Greer said. "It isn't only the trots. Headaches, too. I get a shooting pain right through here." He indicated a broad stripe above his eyebrows. "And I can't smell or taste anything, and these damned stomach cramps are driving me crazy. I don't mind the headaches so much, but this damned diarrhea . . ."

Dietrich glanced at his watch, then toward the rear lobby door.

"You in a hurry?" Officer Greer said.

"A little," Dietrich said. "I thought I'd try to get the pictures done early so I can take the film out and have it processed before noon. That way I can have prints for you this afternoon."

"Prints? For me?"

"Of course," Dietrich said. "You've been very helpful. It's the least I can do."

"That's damned white of you," the officer said. "Maybe we can . . ." He winced again and said, "Damn it!"

"What's wrong?" Dietrich said.

"Ah, this damn bug. Look, you go ahead and get your camera loaded. I'll come by the press room for you in a few minutes." He gave Dietrich a half smile and hurried off toward the bathroom, clutching his stomach.

Dietrich closed his eyes and breathed deeply, cursing fate. Of all the times for his hand-picked policeman to come down sick. There was nothing to do but hole up in the press room and wait. And hope the officer didn't take too long.

As Dietrich started toward the northwest corner of the reception lobby, a door flew open behind him and two Secret Service men rushed through the room. One of them paused and spoke briefly to the men at the credentials desk, then hurried out into the sunlight and across the White House lawn. In moments the whole lobby became active. White House policemen and Secret Service agents streamed through, some headed out the front way, other passing through to the gallery which connected the West Wing to the main mansion. A couple of men even left the credentials desk to join the exodus.

By the time Dietrich reached the press room, word had apparently spread to the reporters and photographers. He saw them grabbing pencils and cameras, murmuring excitedly. A few ducked out of the room without waiting. Others quickly began to follow.

Dietrich angled over to a newsman who had just hung up a telephone and was grabbing several sheets of paper. "What is it?" Dietrich said. "Where is everyone headed?"

"Over to the east gate," the newsman said. "Bomb threat of some kind. They're flushing all the tourists out of the mansion."

"Bomb threat?" Dietrich said. His blood roared in his ears.

"Yeah. I hear they've already detained a bunch of tourists with cameras. Some kind of telephone tip. Excuse me, I gotta run. You better get there fast, too, if you want to cover it. They may seal off the wing to protect the President."

Dietrich let the man go. Feeling cold in spite of the oppressive summer heat, he stood back, frozen, as the press room emptied. He glanced at the corner of the room where he had stashed his camera bag. It was the only one left.

The dimensions of his situation flooded chaotically into his mind, and his thoughts took maddened flight. God above! How had they done it? First his car, with policemen waiting in front of the apartment building. Now this. His explosive-rigged camera, useless. A bomb scare, the man said. That meant the Secret Service would be swarming all over the place, searching. There was no way that he could place the bomb and expect it to last long enough to do any damage. Wasted. All that preparation. Lost.

Worse, with every second he was losing his own chance to get out. If they sealed the wing to make sure no one could get in, he, too, would be sealed inside, for surely no one could get through without an exhaustive check. Trapped inside with the President.

Dietrich grabbed at the thought and forced himself to concentrate on it. What about the President? Could he possibly hope to get to the President before someone spotted him? It was unlikely, he knew. All the other reporters had followed the exodus of Secret Service men. A lone civilian would be too noticeable. Unless he could somehow blend into the surroundings. Yes, that might do it. Protective coloration. An outer wrapping of the some kind of official authority. Then a direct frontal assault on the President.

But, God, with his bomb rendered useless, he had no way to buy time for his own escape, nor had he any plan. There was nothing left but hope.

If hope was all he had, he would have to use it. He ran to his camera bag and reached in for the black cloth that covered his

Mauser. He tucked the Mauser to his stomach, then hurried to the press-room door, pausing to peer out into the lobby. A few people here and there, not many, all looking confused and nervous. He ducked through the press-room door and into the corridor that led to the men's room.

The men's room was empty, except for the one stall which exposed a pair of hairy legs with uniform trousers bunched around the ankles. Dietrich slipped into the adjoining stall and stepped up quietly on the toilet seat. He peeled the black cloth from the Mauser and released the safety, then leaned over the partition.

Officer Greer looked up in surprise. A paperback detective novel spilled from his fingers. Seated as he was, in man's most defenseless position, save perhaps one, he just had time to focus his eyes before Dietrich shot him in the forehead.

Greer fell to the side, his head banging against the far wall. Dietrich quickly stretched his arm into the officer's stall and used the tip of the silencer tube to unhook the latch. Then he hurried around and pushed the door open. First he yanked the trousers from the dead policeman's ankles and laid them aside. Working quickly, he removed the policeman's shirt and tie. Then he stripped himself, fumbling with buttons, trying to switch into the dead policeman's clothing before someone strolled in on them by accident.

Greer's shirt was big, but it didn't look too bad. The pants were about the right length, but Greer's hefty girth made them far too expansive in the waist, so Dietrich hauled the heavy black uniform belt in an extra four notches. He checked himself in the mirror. The pants were bunched around his waist and they looked pretty baggy, but they would probably pass if no one looked too closely. He stuffed his Mauser into the waist, under the big shirt, and patted himself, checking the mirror image again. Good.

Before he left, he arranged his own pants around the policeman's ankles, then wadded up his shirt and jacket and wedged them behind the toilet. He closed the stall door and stood back for a brief appraisal. It looked quite normal, as though someone were in the john stall for natural purposes. They weren't likely to find him for a long time.

He took one last look at himself in the bathroom mirror, straightened his face, and headed for the corridor door.

As he let himself out, droplets of blood began to trickle down Greer's dangling arm and drip silently on the tile floor beneath the toilet seat. *Perdido. Perdido.*

5

Special Agent Emerson Carter trailed the delegation from Captain Blaszek's office out into the reception lobby, his adrenal glands pumping urgent command: act, put out the fire, slay the dragon, do something, do anything. But what?

John Calhoun, the Secret Service chief, hurried past the secretaries, and Carter could only hurry along after him as the big man collared that young Secret Service guy, Jerry Fenton, by the door.

"Any luck?" Calhoun snapped.

"Not yet," Fenton said nervously. He brushed a trickle of sweat from his temple and glanced at the crowd at Calhoun's heels. "We've shut off the east gate," he continued, "and we've got every available man out there looking through the crowd. But there's a hitch, sir. I'm afraid the reporters got wind of it somehow. Word's been passed to our people. Nobody is to answer any questions."

"What about the grounds?" Calhoun asked briskly. "Have our men started searching the grounds?"

"Yes, sir. We don't see how he could have slipped through, but we've got some men combing the foliage just in case."

"Someone ought to alert the President," Calhoun said. "Where is he?"

"Down in the swimming pool, sir. Shall I send someone?"

"I'd rather you go," Calhoun said. He glanced at the captain and said, "Captain, I'm reclaiming Fenton. Your job is done now and he'll be of more use with us. Any objections?"

"No, of course not," Captain Blaszek said. He appeared to be somewhat at a loss, and Carter felt a surge of common feeling with him. "What about the rest of us?" the captain said. He indicated Carter, Sergeant Huffman and the ill-at-ease police detective with the runny nose. "What can we do to help?"

"Nothing," Calhoun said. "This affair is out of your hands now. Just go back to your office and wait."

"Let me go to the gate with you," the captain said. "I've been over this guy's description so many times that I feel like I know him. Maybe I can spot something your people would miss."

Calhoun shook his head firmly. "I don't want you in the way. I don't want any of you in the way. This is a job for experts." He beckoned his two Secret Service escorts and hurried into the morning sunlight, leaving Fenton with the captain and the others.

Fenton shrugged and said, "Sorry, Andy."

Carter's adrenal glands were still juicing. He burst out, "He can't expect us to stand around and do nothing. Not after all the time we've put into this. Why don't we go on out there and do as we please?"

Fenton halted in midstride. "I wouldn't advise it," he said. "Calhoun has given orders to seal off the wing. Any of you stick your noses outside, you're likely to get them shot off. Most of our Secret Service people don't know any of you people well enough to recognize you, and they're pretty edgy."

As Fenton moved toward the rear doors, the captain sighed. "I only wanted to help," he said to no one in particular.

"They'll screw it up," Carter predicted bitterly.

"Damn right," the little sergeant from Blaszek's office chimed in. "What about that bomb-disposal unit we called in from Fort Myer, Captain? They'll be here any minute. And those Secret Service pricks probably won't even let them in."

"He's right," Carter said. "They wouldn't even let the detective here in, and that was before the Shinola hit the fan."

"Oh, Christ," the captain said.

Sergeant Huffman said. "You better go tell them, Captain. We can't have them turning the bomb guys away."

Captain Blaszek seemed to make up his mind. He turned abruptly and started for the front of the lobby, thudding into one of the White House policemen who had been standing nearby. The policeman stumbled back, stunned by the captain's unexpected move, and as the captain murmured a quick apology and rushed on out of the building, the policeman glanced at Carter and the others, then turned away quickly and hurried in the other direction, toward the rear of the lobby.

Carter, still keyed up, found himself unwillingly watching the White House policeman as he moved away. Funny. Hadn't the guy edged up during the conversation? Almost as though he were listening in. Even more peculiar was the way he was heading inward, toward the rear corridor. Most of the traffic flow had been outward since they reached the lobby, toward the front lawn and the eastern edge of the White House grounds. Fenton had headed inward, but that was only because Calhoun had sent him that way. Why the cop?

Sergeant Huffman said, "I guess we might as well wait in the office until the captain gets back. Some of our own men guarding the grounds might need help with the Secret Service creeps."

"In a minute," Carter said. He stared at the policeman's retreating back. Something about the uniform, too. It was a damned poor fit. The man looked at ease, as though he belonged, but his shirt and pants were a lousy fit. Far too big for him. Of course Carter hadn't really been around the White House all that much or all that long, but he seemed to recall that most of the White House policemen looked pretty natty. A little overweight, perhaps, but neatly tailored.

There were the shoes, too. The policeman's shoes were brown, like civilian shoes. But the others wore black, didn't they? He tried to remember when he had first noticed the policeman drawing up to them, eavesdropping on their chatter. It was shortly after Calhoun had headed for the door. He'd been several feet away at first, then closer, drifting closer, until he was close enough to get jolted by the captain. Listening to everything. Why?

The policeman put his hand on the rear door and turned the knob. Carter took a step toward him and called out, "Hey!" The policeman looked briefly over his shoulder, then quickly opened the door and stepped through, out of sight.

Sergeant Huffman and the sniffling detective looked around at Carter in surprise. "What's the matter?" Huffman said.

"I'm not sure," Carter said. "Did you see that cop?"

"What cop?"

Carter opened his jacket and pulled his .38 Special from the shoulder holster. He flipped the cylinder open and checked his load, then said, "You wait here. I want to check something."

"Check what?" Huffman said.

But Carter had already started toward the rear of the lobby. He let himself through the door and paused. He could hear footsteps pattering down a stairwell somewhere off to his right. A thin sheen of sweat dampened his upper lip. He hesitated, swaying on the balls of his feet, wondering if he should go back in the lobby for help or follow the policeman. He could be wrong, of course. In which case the others would probably ridicule him, poke fun at him for his display of nerves.

On the other hand, what if he was right? What if the cop was some kind of a ringer? Oh good Lord, wouldn't that be something? A superb way to get back in the Director's good graces. It would be an FBI man, a lonely, single FBI man, who settled the issue, in spite of the hordes of Secret Service men cluttering up the scene.

The Director would die laughing. He might even have a smile to spare for an alert special agent.

Carter chuckled nervously to himself and headed down the corridor, toward the stairway.

6

Dietrich stopped at the foot of the stairs and pulled the Mauser from beneath his shirt. The swimming pool. The President was in the swimming pool. Hurry. Before someone else tried to stop him. That man upstairs in the lobby. Why had he yelled? The baggy uniform? Was that it?

He primed the Mauser and stepped into the basement hallway with the gun dangling behind his back. He could see two Secret Service men down toward the end of the hall, standing outside the swimming-pool room. That was a good sign. The President was still there. He walked down the corridor toward the two presidential guards, forcing himself to keep his pace casual.

Because he was in a White House police uniform, neither of the Secret Service guards paid more than brief attention to him. He kept walking. When he was within twenty feet of them, he brought the Mauser out in the open and shot them both. *Phut, phut.* The first dropped instantly, like a puppet cut loose from his strings. The second spun along the wall, staggered a few steps, and tried to reach for his gun. Dietrich shot him again. *Phut.*

He could hear the echo of voices behind the closed door, bouncing against the moist cavernous walls of the swimming-pool room. At least two men talking. The soft sounds of his silenced gun had not penetrated their awareness. Good. He would have surprise on his side. But as he reached for the doorknob, he heard footsteps. Someone rushing down the stairwell, coming in his direction. He pressed back against the wall and waited.

Seconds later, Emerson Carter came trotting around the corner with a gun in his fist. He tried to stop when he saw Dietrich waiting for him, but he was too late. Dietrich held the Mauser in both hands and squeezed off a shot. Carter's feet skidded out from under him and he dropped to his seat, his eyes like marbles. He stared in disbelief at the blood pumping from his chest, then goggled at Dietrich. He tried to get up, but his hand slipped in a smear of his own blood and he rolled over on his side. He started to cough as blood filled his lungs. Dietrich took a few steps toward him and kicked him in the head, to stop the coughing.

By now the basement corridor was acrid and thick with gun-smoke, but Dietrich could still hear the buzz of conversation on the other side of the door. None of the furor from the hallway had touched them. He steeled himself and held the Mauser ready, then jerked the door open and thrust himself inside.

There were four of them. Two more Secret Service guards standing at the end of the swimming pool, beside an empty wheelchair. Jerry Fenton kneeling by the pool ladder, talking to the President. The President gripping the ladder, his big upper torso bobbing up and down in the water. All four of the room's occupants froze when the door burst open, like a tableau in a high school senior play.

Dietrich picked his targets instantly, but carefully. The first to react was one of the two Secret Service guards by the empty wheelchair, an older man with graying temples, so Dietrich shot him first, hitting him in the throat before his gun cleared his lapel. With a smooth, instant motion, Dietrich shifted the Mauser three inches and squeezed off a shot at the second Secret Service guard. Then he whirled to face Fenton. Fenton had fumbled his gun out and was trying to screen the President when Dietrich shot him. The gun spurted out of Fenton's fingers and onto the pool apron, and Fenton cried out in pain, clutching his stomach.

Fenton crumpled to his knees, staring at Dietrich, and began to crawl toward his gun. Dietrich wasted a moment in admiration, impressed by the man's determination, then stepped forward and nudged the gun over the lip of the pool. It went *plup*, and sank instantly to the bottom.

Fenton stopped crawling and sagged to his chest. He turned wide eyes up at Dietrich and cursed, a steady stream of obscenities, soft and low. Dietrich pointed the Mauser at his head and pulled the trigger.

Nothing happened.

Dietrich blinked. Ten shots already? It couldn't be. It seemed fewer. It had only taken seconds. He thought back quickly, running over the sequence, tracing each shot as though counting them would make it different. Eight. Only eight shots, including Officer Greer. No, wait. The two policemen outside Sarah's apartment building. Yes. That made ten.

No matter. Fenton's incongruous cursing had slowed to a foul-mouthed trickle and his eyes were already beginning to glaze. It was apparently all he could do to retain any degree of consciousness. His voice trailed to a whisper, then he jerked his head upright and the words spilled out again, halting, vile, shrill, fighting. Let him live, Dietrich decided. Let him watch if he could stay awake. He had earned it. He gave Fenton a respectful nod and went to the pool ladder.

The President, stunned by the speed and severity of the sudden carnage, clung helplessly to the second rung with shaking hands, withered legs trailing in the water. Unable to climb out, unable to defend himself, he watched in horror as Dietrich squatted in front of him and carefully laid the expended Mauser aside.

As Dietrich reached for him, the President lurched away in a panic, flailing his arms, churning the water. But Dietrich was too quick. He snatched a fistful of the President's graying hair and yanked him back to the ladder. The President wrenched and tried to thrash loose, but Dietrich held him tightly. Slowly, deliberately, he pushed down on the President's shoulders until the wide, staring face slipped under the water.

Perdido.

7

Andy Blaszek didn't get more than fifty feet from the West Wing before two Secret Service men leaped out into the open and stopped him. They demanded his identification, guns poised at his midsection, while he squirmed and watched the distant jumble of guards and tourists milling about the eastern fence, far across the White House lawn. No sign of the bomb squad yet.

"Come on, hurry," Andy told them. "I've got to see Calhoun."

"I'm afraid that's out of the question, Captain Blaszek," one of the Secret Service men said, reading the name off Andy's White House pass. He mispronounced it, making it sound like "Blaze-sick."

"I'm the military security liaison," Andy said. "One of my units will be here in a matter of minutes. I have to meet them."

"I don't care who you are," the Secret Service man said. "Our orders are to close off the wing. No one in, no one out, until this difficulty has been cleared up. You'll have to get back inside."

"Send for Calhoun," Andy demanded. "He'll vouch for me."

"Mr. Calhoun is busy," the Secret Service man said. "You go back inside, Captain. We'll meet your unit."

"But this is important," Andy said.

"Please don't argue with us, Captain. This is an emergency situation."

So Andy was forced to return to the West Wing within moments of his exit. He found Sergeant Huffman and Police Lieutenant Savage waiting inside the front door. Huffman looked surprised. "Already?" the little sergeant said. "That was quick. What happened?"

"Nothing," Andy muttered. "They wouldn't even let me explain. I guess we'll have to telephone the gate."

"Let me do it," the sergeant snarled happily. "I know all those guys. I'll get some action, by God." He whirled on his heel, leaving Andy and the police detective staring stupidly at one another.

"Uh, where's Carter?" Andy said.

"Who?"

"The man from the FBI."

"Oh. I don't know. He was standing here a moment ago, then he got itchy about something and took off that way." He pointed toward the back corridor.

"Itchy?" Andy said. "About what?"

"He didn't say. He just checked his pistol and took off like a shot. He was following that young Secret Service man, I think. He's only been gone a minute."

Andy hesitated. "Maybe I should see what's up." The detective neither agreed nor disagreed, and Andy hesitated a moment longer, then turned and trotted into the rear corridor and headed for the basement stairwell, wondering what could possibly have drawn the FBI agent this way. It wasn't as though Carter really knew his way around the building. Carter had been more of a satellite than a self-starter, ever since Andy had brought him into the White House, always hanging close to Andy or Jerry or even Sergeant Huffman, as though he was afraid he might commit some unpardonable social or protocol gaffe if left to his own devices. So what had prompted him suddenly to go flying off on his own like this?

Andy reached the bottom of the stairwell and trotted around the corner into the basement corridor. Then he saw. He jerked to a halt and gaped, too shocked to believe what his eyes were telling him. Three men lay sprawled in the corridor, strung out between him and the swimming-pool room. One of them was Emerson Carter, resting on his side in a red stain of his own blood. Andy's chest constricted, squeezing him until he could hardly breathe. Holy God.

He staggered forward, his heart thudding against his rib cage, his breath locked in his chest, half running, half stumbling, fighting an overpowering urge to vomit, and leaned through the open swim-

ming-pool door. More blood, more bodies sprawled across the
floor. One of the bodies moved. It was Jerry Fenton, bleeding on
the edge of the swimming pool. His head wobbled as he struggled
to raise it. Near him, by the pool ladder, a White House policeman
hunched over the water, fighting to keep something beneath the
surface.

"My God," Andy wailed.

Dietrich jerked his head around at the ragged sound of Andy's
voice, but he didn't stop what he was doing. He just kept pushing
down on whatever it was he held underwater, while his eyes, wide
and wild, searched Andy's face.

The two men gazed at each other, the Army captain at the door,
the White House policeman at the pool ladder, and an unspoken
dialogue crackled through the air between them. What are you
doing? None of your business. Stay out of it.

For a moment, Andy stood rooted to the damp floor, too astonished to react. Then abruptly, guided by an impetus which came
not from his shocked brain, but rather from laggard cells and muscles which responded blindly, instinctively, he yelled and broke into
a run. Dietrich released his grip and swung around, bracing himself
to meet the charge.

Andy bowled into him at top speed and hurled him backward
across the low poolside ladder. The President's head broke surface,
coughing and gasping, just inches from the side of the swimming
pool. Andy's numb brain barely had time to grasp the image and file
it away before he toppled into the water together with Dietrich,
plunging, tumbling, swirling end over end.

They touched bottom and grappled blindly, clawing at each
other. Dietrich, his baggy policeman's uniform blousing out in the
depths, managed to get his hands around Andy's throat. Their
bodies drifted and cartwheeled slowly upward as they scrabbled
and banged at each other, impeded by heavy shoes and waterlogged
clothing, Dietrich's tight grip closing on Andy's windpipe, Andy's
fists flailing back at him through the heavy water like slow-motion
sledgehammers.

Andy, lungs already aching for air, was overcome by a sudden,
frantic claustrophobia as Dietrich's fingernails continued to cut into
his neck. He kicked and lurched, trying to break free. Apparently
Dietrich was also short of breath, for he seemed perfectly willing to
let Andy go. They pushed away from each other and strained for

the surface. Their heads popped into the air, gasping for breath, almost simultaneously.

Dietrich whipped his head to the side, flinging water from dark, plastered hair, and backpedaled, cold eyes intent on Andy. Andy choked on a mouthful of water and swept his chin around, seeking some sign of the President. He saw him at the far end of the pool, clinging to the pool apron. Thank God, he appeared to be okay.

When Andy flicked his attention back to Dietrich, he saw, almost too late, what Dietrich was up to. Dietrich was bobbing hurriedly toward the shallow end of the pool, toward the spot where the two Secret Service guards lay like bloody bundles of clothing beside the empty wheelchair, toward their guns.

Andy winced and hurled himself into an all-out Australian crawl, swimming as hard as he could in his bulky clothing. He picked up some ground, but not nearly enough. Dietrich had already reached the pool steps and was scrambling to get his footing.

Andy frantically changed direction and plunged to the side of the pool, watching Dietrich from the corner of his eye, watching as Dietrich clambered out, drenching the cement floor. Andy grabbed the pool lip and hauled himself up to the edge, water streaming from his uniform. He pushed quickly to his feet. Dietrich had already reached one of the fallen Secret Service guards and was bent over him, digging for the man's weapon. Andy took three squishy steps and leaped at him.

Dietrich whirled with the gun just as Andy slammed into him and they both hit the floor with whoofs of lost breath and splatters of sodden clothing. The gun slipped away, spinning in lazy circles on the wet cement. They untangled from each other and went for the gun, crawling over each other, disengaging, jabbing, gouging, wrestling their way across the puddled floor.

And Andy won.

By inches, he outreached Dietrich and his hand closed awkwardly on the gun. He rolled over, kicking free, and scrambled to his knees, the gun outstretched in front of him. Dietrich froze. In the momentary silence that followed, Andy could hear the water droplets spilling and spattering from his uniform to the cement floor.

Dietrich looked wild-eyed from the gun to the gasping President, coughing and shivering in the water at the far end of the swimming pool. He looked at the body of the other Secret Service guard, with its gun half out of the holster. Then his eyes turned calm and he gazed at Andy almost serenely.

"Don't do it," Andy told him.

"You're going to have to shoot me," Dietrich said.

Andy blinked. Good God, the man wasn't even German. He couldn't be, not with that soft southwestern twang. Had he misread the signals? Had he made some terrible mistake?

Dietrich seemed to sense his confusion and coiled his legs, as though preparing to spring. Then an alien sound reached them both. Footsteps, hurrying this way. Lots of them. Dietrich's tongue touched his lips and he said, "This isn't your affair. Back away. Let me finish what I came for."

Andy blinked again. What? Not his affair? How could it not be his affair? He said, "You're crazy." Then he shouted, "In here! He's trying to get the President!"

Dietrich's face went blank and he slipped into a crouch once more, ready to spring. Andy wavered for a moment, then steadied the gun and gripped the trigger. As he pointed the gun at Dietrich, a team of four Secret Service men came spilling through the door. Andy thought, "Thank God!" and started to turn.

But the Secret Service men, guns ready and in a crouch of their own, had seen the sprawl of bodies out in the corridor and now saw more bodies in the pool room. Beyond the bodies, they could see only an Army captain and a White House policeman, both dripping wet. They had no time for niceties, no time to determine who was villain and who protector. All they knew for certain was that the Army captain had a gun in his hands and he was swinging it toward the President. They opened fire.

Andy felt the slugs tear into his side, his leg, his shoulder. He was knocked off his knees, buffeted by the force of the bullets. He landed on his back and the gun sailed away.

He saw vaguely, through the shock and the pain, the figure of Dietrich, hurtling above him, diving for the loose gun. He watched dimly as the men at the door shifted their weapons and blazed away at Dietrich. He saw Dietrich jerk and twitch as the shots hit him, still grasping for the gun. He saw more bullets plow into him, knocking him backward, saw him rise to his knees with the gun, saw him trying to aim it at the President, saw him cartwheeled off the edge of the pool by another salvo, saw him splash under, saw him float to the surface, face down.

Suddenly frightened beyond sanity, Andy thrust his hands up, begging for mercy. Then, mercifully, a film swam across his eyes and he blacked out.

THE AFTERMATH

Saturday—August 8, 1942

I

When tires crunched on gravel in the driveway out front, Gay Cogswell's little daughter stopped being Gene Autry and ran around the side of the house to see if it was Andy, back from the doctor. It was. One of those little no-nonsense Army cars, a Chevy, drab and severe in its official olive coat, rolled carefully around the circular drive and parked, and Gaylynn ran up to it, clutching her brown paper bag of dried apricots.

The process of being Gene Autry consisted, for some reason, of sitting on a sawhorse by the garage and eating the dried apricots Gaylynn had coaxed from Mattie. The sawhorse was an easy prop to figure out, but apricots? Provisions for a journey through the badlands, perhaps, Gay decided as she looked out a front window. She watched as Sergeant Huffman hopped out of the driver's seat and started around the car to help Andy, but Gaylynn offered the sergeant an apricot and he stopped and took one.

Gay smiled. The tough little sergeant looked so profoundly serious as he accepted the dried fruit from a Gene Autry dressed in crumpled white shorts and a little white halter that matched Gay's own unrumpled shorts and somewhat fuller halter. She didn't smile at the sight of Andy. Andy had been out of the hospital for almost two weeks now, and she was exasperated with him. She had only asked him back to the house so she could take care of him, oversee his recuperation. Some misguided sense of loyalty past, no doubt. And a decided mistake. It was bad enough that they wouldn't let her perform her acts of contrition immediately, wouldn't let her in to see him during the period of his hospitalization, wouldn't tell her anything, letting her think the worst. But then when he finally seemed to be mending and they turned him loose and she had picked him up and brought him home, trying to do the *right* thing, she had run head-on into his fits of depression. Depression, for God's sake. The man was a hero of sorts, yet he seemed to take no joy in it.

She had contended with the depression the first days, convincing herself that it was the expected human reaction to a great shock, particularly when he seemed to blame himself for dragging so many other people into it with him. She'd also made allowances for what she assumed would be his disappointment over the lid of secrecy they had clamped on everything after that terrible day in the White House more that a month ago. After all, the point in being a hero was decidedly blunted if no one was allowed to know anything about it. Gay was still sore about the secrecy. Andy should have demanded his due, instead of knuckling under to them. Just like the man, letting them walk all over him. Oh, Andy had tried to explain it to her, in that patient and polite manner which she found so irritating. Apparently the President, after counsel with his advisers, had decided against making public any of the events of that July morning in the White House, on the theory that the Germans must never know how close they had come. The Secret Service was apparently convinced they might try again if they knew what a near thing it had been. So newsmen were kept out of the West Wing until the mess had been cleared up and the wounded, Andy included, were taken to a military hospital. The whole episode had been passed off as a bomb threat which had not materialized, perhaps the work of some crank. And Andy's harebrained heroism had been locked away in a filing cabinet.

Andy had assured her, in that bleak spiritless way that attended him those first days out of the hospital, that the secrecy had nothing to do with his state of mind. But his depression had continued beyond the limits of her patience and she had to fight now to control herself, to keep her frustration and exasperation in check. He was simply no fun to be with any more.

Uh-huh, old sobersides wouldn't even accept an apricot from Gene Autry, just smiled a little and shook his head. Sergeant Huffman fetched Andy's cane and briefcase for him and started him toward the front door. Gay sighed and went out to meet them.

The sun dazzled her as she stepped onto the white gravel. Bright, high-noon sun. Deep black shadows under the elms ringing the driveway, harsh and stark. It had been a hot summer and she was ready for the fall to begin. As it would, one day soon. Already the sounds were different. The leaves of the big old trees had a brittle rustle as they dried out and whispered in the fevered wind. Mourning doves gasped and called, and in the tallest elm of all a cardinal whistled, dry and raspy.

Sergeant Huffman whistled appreciatively at Gay as she approached the car. Andy smiled politely, too.

"Hey, wow, you and Gaylynn are twins today," Huffman said to her. "Those shorts are really something." Gay touched Gaylynn's blond hair, limp in the heat, and smiled back. She and Huffman had become more friendly in the past couple of weeks, much as though an unspoken truce had been declared. She had wondered about it a few times, but had dismissed the question firmly after it occurred to her one day to wonder if the only reason the two of them had failed to get along earlier was that they were simply too much alike. Both manipulators, both busily trying to manipulate the same puppet. But their dumb puppet had managed to get his strings all tangled up, not to mention almost getting himself shot to pieces, and somehow the realization that he wasn't responding well any more had created a minor bond between them which overshadowed the barrier which had been there before.

"How is he today?" she asked Huffman.

"A lot better, Mrs. Cogswell. The doctor says another couple of weeks and he can start the exercises." He handed her the cane and Gaylynn the briefcase and said, "Shall I help you get him inside?"

"I'm okay," Andy said. "I don't need any help."

The sergeant nodded like an intelligent dog. "Then I guess I'd better get back to the office. You hurry up and mend, Captain. We sure need you down there."

"Sure you do," Andy said. There was an edge to his voice, but he softened it by smiling politely.

Gay ducked her shoulder under Andy's arm and helped steady him the last few steps through the gravel. Once inside, he had less trouble managing his cane.

"Did the doctor really say you were getting better?" she asked.

"Yeah, he says I'm fine." He grinned briefly. "We went by to see if Jerry Fenton could have visitors yet, but they said official callers only. Can you imagine? They wouldn't even let *me* in. God, this closed-mouth business is too much."

It was a good sign, Gay thought. He looked genuinely amused. It was the first thing that had tickled him in a long time, and she wondered if she should pursue it, laugh with him a little while, but his grin flickered away and the moment was lost.

Mattie was waiting for them inside. She immediately started fussing over Andy, complaining at the departed Sergeant Huffman for keeping him out in the heat too long, insisting that Andy remove his tunic before he came down with heat stroke. Gay watched wordlessly as he patiently unbuttoned the tunic. The look of patience and forebearing was a kiss of death to her. She'd seen it many times on his face. But she'd never realized it was an habitual response to bossing and mothering. She'd always thought it was something special, something just for her.

"Now you just get yourself into the morning room," Mattie told him. "This time of the day it's the coolest room in the house. Miz Cogswell, you make him sit and rest there while I fix his lunch. Gaylynn, you come with me. I got a little something for you to help me with."

Gay took Andy's hand. He gave it willingly enough, but there was nothing special in the touch and it disappointed her. She murmured that she'd run upstairs and get the little electric fan from her bedroom and left him, glad for the respite. But things were no better when she rejoined him. He was slumped back against the green-and-white chintz of a chair, staring out the east windows at the wide lawn that led down to the tennis courts, apparently not in the mood for conversation.

Gay tossed her hair out of her eyes. Damned if she was going to put up with that any longer. She plugged in the fan and said, in an effort to make him talk, "I hear the spies were convicted. There was an INS bulletin in the paper saying the President has approved the death penalty. Is it true?"

He turned blank-looking eyes to her. "I heard on the radio the President's still reviewing the case. I don't know any of the details."

"God, who does?" she said. She slid off her sandals and wiggled her toes, feeling hot. "I can understand the President not wanting to release anything about that man who got into the White House, but why all the secrecy crap over the trial?"

"I've given up trying to understand that kind of thing," Andy said. "The establishment makes the decisions. Slobs like me only follow them."

She looked at the sandals, wishing she could throw them. "God, Andy, are we going to have another of those afternoons?"

"What afternoons?" he said.

"You know what I mean."

He nodded slowly. "Yeah, I guess I do. I'm sorry. I've been thinking a lot these last few days. Gay, I think I'm going to ask for a transfer."

Gay's exasperation flamed into bewildered anger but she choked back the first half-dozen responses that occurred to her, all of them beginning, "Well, what do you expect me to do—cry?" As her silence lengthened, Andy added uneasily, "Of course I haven't decided, but I thought I'd ask for active service maybe. I think I'd like to get with an overseas unit."

"Good God. Why?"

"I don't know. It just seems the right thing to do."

Gaylynn came walking carefully into the room with a pair of gin fizzes in frosted glasses, Mattie close behind her. Mattie grinned. "A little surprise," she said. "You drink one of those, Captain. It'll perk up your appetite."

He smiled politely. "Thank you."

"The captain doesn't need any surprises," Gay said. "He's come up with one of his own."

"What?" piped Gaylynn. And Mattie simultaneously said, "What kind, Captain?"

"He's going to request overseas duty," Gay said. She had to struggle to keep the sarcasm from her voice.

Gaylynn came to lean on Andy's good knee. "Are you going away, Andy?" she said wonderingly.

Mattie answered for him. "Sure he is, honey. That's what all the men got to do, and we'll get this bad old war over and done with. I say good for you, Captain. I got two of my cousins overseas, fine boys. You're doing the right thing. A good, brave thing."

Andy looked away, embarrassed, and Mattie questioned Gay with raised eyebrows. Gay shrugged, but as soon as Mattie left the room, she said, "Brave, my ass. I know why you're doing this. You're doing it because you're afraid."

He looked up sharply, then the look changed to one of respect. "You always were ten times smarter than me, Gay. Maybe you're right. Maybe I am afraid."

Gaylynn was obviously finding the conversation hard to follow. "What are you afraid of, Andy?" she asked.

"I . . . I guess I don't really know. I guess I've had a long child-hood, honey. I guess I just wanted to take a crack at independ-ence."

"I know what independence is," she said, still sounding confused. "That's what's the Fourth of July."

Gay beckoned to Gaylynn and hugged the little girl. "No, baby," she said. "Andy's problem isn't that kind of independence. What it's about is, it's all about a bear. Andy thought there was a bear in the thicket and he went in after his bear and he killed it and he got mauled by it and he dragged a lot of people into the thicket with him. But now that he's been there, he's got to go find another thicket. Maybe he'd like not to, because it's scary as anything in a thicket, but if he turned back now he'd never be a real grown-up boy."

Gaylynn seemed to think that over, then said critically, in a very grown-up tone. "I'm not sure I understand that."

Andy grinned a little, a flicker of his old good-humored grin. "Then, you're in good company, Gaylynn," he said. "I'm not sure I understand it either."

Gay sipped her gin fizz. It was cold and a bit too tart. "When will you leave?" she said quietly. She watched as her little daugh-ter, apparently noticing her mother's bare feet, sat down and started taking off her own sandals.

"The doctor says it'll be a while, but I guess I could get the papers started. I'll talk to someone at the White House tomorrow. Maybe Harry Hopkins. I've got a feeling they'll be glad to see me go down there. Maybe they'll expedite matters."

Gay lifted her glass and leaned back, tasting again the bitter, tart gin fizz and the bitter, tart anticipation of Andy's leaving. It was finished, as she had known it would be. She felt a sadness at losing him, but at the same time she was glad.

She looked out across the grounds at the trees, dry and rustly, hanging limp in the heat. Well, what the hell. It would soon be fall. Spring and summer were marvelous annual miracles, but maybe fall was best of all.

2

That same day, a small crowd milled restlessly on the sidewalk out-side the District of Columbia jail, the site of the only electric chair within a hundred miles of Washington, waiting for word, any word, of what was going on inside. Reporters in the crowd, like the rest of the press, had heard rumors that the eight German agents from the submarine landings had been convicted and might receive the death penalty, but while some of their fellow newsmen accepted Franklin Roosevelt's assurance that no sentence would be carried out until he had reviewed the confidential trial transcript, and other of their peers had set up a death watch on the bridge leading to Fort Myer and a rumored firing squad, the impatient reporters by the jail put their faith in INS reporter Jack Vincent's tip that the Nazi agents were to be electrocuted today.

It was a frustrating assignment. The closest they had come so far to any substantial clue was when two Army ambulances drove up to the jail and soldiers in fatigues hurriedly carried six empty stretchers inside. The reporters immediately tried to question the soldiers, but a federal marshal shooed them away.

It was understandable that the die-hard reporters should linger now on the sun-baked sidewalk, hoping to glean even the slightest scrap of information. Thus far they had been blanked out entirely. The military trial of the eight Nazi agents had been conducted in total secrecy in Room 5235 on the fifth floor of the Justice Department Building. The press and its public had been excluded from the proceedings and given absolutely no information about the sixteen-day trial, an historic trial if only because it was the first time civilians had been tried by a military tribunal since the conspirators in the Lincoln assassination had faced a military commission some seventy-seven years before.

Like their predecessors in the Lincoln trial, all eight German agents were found guilty. The world was not to know until after the final execution took place, but on the morning of August 8, 1942, less than two months after they had landed from the submarines, six of the eight men were awakened early and served a breakfast of bacon and eggs, then visited in their cells by a prison barber who cut their hair short and shaved a patch on the left leg of each.

At noon, while the small crowd waited outside, the first of the prisoners, Edward Kerling, was taken to the execution chamber and strapped into the District of Columbia electric chair. A rubber mask with nose and mouth slots was pulled over his head. A metal plate containing a wet sponge was placed on the top of his head and another sponge was clipped to his shaved calf. When the two sponges were in place, the chamber was cleared and the switch thrown.

The executions took place one after the other, quickly, efficiently, with less than fifteen minutes allotted to each man. Six of the German agents died in less than an hour and a half.

Edward Kerling, the Florida team leader, died.

Herbert Hans Haupt, the young man from Chicago, died.

Heinrich Heinck, quick-tempered explosives expert, died.

Richard Quirin, big and dependable, died.

Werner Thiel, Kerling's New York partner, died.

Otto Neubauer, last to be located by the FBI, died.

At 1:23 P.M., a new rumor swept the crowd after the fact: the President's press secretary, Steve Early, had announced belatedly that the executions had begun at noon.

"Are they already dead?" asked an elderly mother with one son in the Army and another in the Navy.

"*I* dunno, lady," said a fat man in shirtsleeves, who had been joking good-naturedly for the past hour, but now looked suddenly queasy. "Jesus. Roosevelt sure didn't waste any time, did he?"

"I'm glad," the older woman said fiercely. "*They* wouldn't have waited so long over *there*."

Only two of the German agents survived. George John Dasch and Peter Burger were spared the death sentence for their assistance in breaking the German spy case and were given long prison terms which they began serving even as Radio Rome screamed, "Roosevelt's blood purge continues," and Radio Berlin commented grimly, "Our enemies have forfeited the right of protesting against the condemnation of saboteurs in the territory occupied by the German Army."

In 1948, three years after the end of the war, Dasch and Burger were abruptly released at the order of Roosevelt's successor, President Harry Truman, and deported to Germany. Dasch, for a time, was hounded by his countrymen as a traitor. Burger avoided public harassment by quickly dropping out of sight.

By then, the grave of their six comrades were long since overgrown with cat brier and wild hop in Washington's potter's field, a weed-choked cemetery where bluejays shrieked and brown thrashers courted near the Home for the Aged and Infirm. Their graves were marked by wooden slabs which bore no names—only the numbers 276 through 281.

A few feet away, in a similarly numbered grave, lay the remains

of the ninth man. Never formally identified, he was listed in the
Health Department grave register under an assumed name selected
at random from one of his many identity cards.

Though the wooden slab has long since rotted away, a whippoorwill in a nearby stand of woodpecker-ringed cedars still pierces the
night with his occasional cry. *Perdido.*